PROVOCATEUR

PROVOCATEUR

Images of Women and Minorities in Advertising

Second Edition

ANTHONY J. CORTESE

ROWMAN & LITTLEFIELD PUBLISHERS, INC.

Lanham • Boulder • New York • Toronto • Oxford

ROWMAN & LITTLEFIELD PUBLISHERS, INC.

Published in the United States of America
by Rowman & Littlefield Publishers, Inc.
A wholly owned subsidary of The Rowman & Littlefield Publishing Group, Inc.
4501 Forbes Boulevard, Suite 200, Lanham, MD 20706
www.rowmanlittlefield.com

P.O. Box 317, Oxford OX2 9RU, UK

British Library Cataloguing in Publication Information Available

Library of Congress Cataloging-in-Publication Data

Cortese, Anthony Joseph Paul.
  Provocateur : images of women and minorities in advertising / Anthony J. Cortese. — 2nd ed.
      p. cm.
  Includes bibliographical references and index.
  ISBN 0-7425-2497-3 (cloth : alk. paper) — ISBN 0-7425-2498-1 (pbk. : alk. paper)
    1. Advertising—Social aspects. 2. Minorities in advertising. 3. Women in advertising.
I. Title: Images of women and minorities in advertising. II. Title.
HF5823 .C5977 2004
659.1'042—dc22   2003024361

Printed in the United States of America

To Amber Richelle Cortese

May you grow in knowledge, discernment, compassion,
and love with each day.

In memory of my father

Joseph Cortese
November 19, 1922–December 13, 2003

Contents

Preface to the Second Edition ix

Preface to the First Edition xiii

1 Representations, Multiculturalism, and Mass Media 1

2 Visual Attraction, Body Display, and Advertising 23

3 Constructed Bodies, Deconstructing Ads: Sexism in Advertising 51

4 Symbolic Racism in Advertising 83

5 Ethnic Advertising 117

6 Speed and Fragmentation: Toward Postmodern Consciousness 137

Appendix: Advertising Evaluation 159

Glossary 161

References 163

Index 173

About the Author 181

Preface to the Second Edition

A lot of water has gone under the wheel since the original publication of *Provocateur* in 1999. The terrorist attacks in America on September 11, 2001, prompted Saudi Arabia to publish a full-page *institutional advertisement* (see chapter 1) in newspapers throughout the United States (see figure P.1). This ad, which features a white dove as a peace symbol, appeared in the *Dallas Morning News* on December 11, 2001. The copy is simple: "Two Nations. One Goal." Directly beneath it in close proximity lie the Saudi and American flags. Finally, at the bottom of the page is this simple statement: "The people of Saudi Arabia stand in friendship with the people of the United States."

The Saudi government was seeking to eliminate mistrust caused by these facts:

1. Fifteen of the nineteen terrorists who hijacked airplanes on September 11, 2001, were Saudi citizens, resulting in a one trillion dollar lawsuit by the families of the victims against the Saudi monarchy.

2. The Saudi government refused to allow American government officials to interview relatives of the hijackers.

3. The Saudi government has provided financial relief to the families of the hijackers.

4. The Saudi government opposes military use against Iraq and refuses to allow the U.S. military to use Saudi land as a base for attacks on Iraq.

At the one-year anniversary of the attack Saudi Arabia continued to publish institutional ads to counter claims of connections with the 9/11 hijackers. For example, the Justice Department is investigating whether the Saudi government funneled money to two students who assisted two of the hijackers. A draft report by a joint congressional committee is focusing on the possibility that two of the hijackers, Khalid Almidhar and Nawaf Alhazmi, both Saudis, were given Saudi money from two Saudi men they met in California in the year before the attacks. (Almidhar and Alhazmi were on the plane that crashed into the Pentagon.) The committee also accused the Saudi government of not fully cooperating with American investigators.

The two hijackers met with Omar al-Bayoumi and Osama Basnan, who were receiving financial support from the Saudi government. Financial records show payments to the families of al-Bayoumi and Basnan from a Washington bank account held in the name of Princess Haifa Al-Faisal, wife of the Saudi ambassador to the United States and daughter of the late King Faisal. The money filtered into the families' bank accounts in early 2000, just a few months after Almidhar and Alhazmi arrived in Los Angeles from an al-Qaida planning summit. Payments amounted to about $3,500 a month. The debate over a possible Saudi link raises a sensitive political issue for the Bush administration, as Saudi Arabia is our closest and most important ally in the Persian Gulf at a time when the administration is fighting terrorism and trying to stabilize Iraq.

The United States government has also done institutional advertising. See, for instance, the 9/11 commemorative postage stamp in figure P.2. The depiction of the bald eagle symbolizes patriotism and has been used previously in wartime. For example, figure P.3 illustrates a World War II poster by Dean Cornwell in 1945.

In the summer of 2002, Starbucks marketed its frozen summer beverages in a print ad featuring a large dragonfly nose-diving into one of two adjacent towering frozen drinks cups with straws emerging from their tops. The copy ("Collapse into Cool") and illustration reminded readers of the airplane attacks on the twin towers of the World Trade Center. An immediate and vigorous protest caused Starbucks to pull the ad after only one day of publication.

In another example of institutional advertising, AutoZone joins the post-9/11 "patriot" bandwagon by sponsoring the American Red Cross, a key player in post-9/11 recovery (figure P.4).

On April 20, 1999, Dylan Klebold and Eric Harris walked into Columbine High School in Littleton, Colorado, heavily armed with a semiautomatic rifle, a sawed-off shotgun, and hand grenades and opened fire on their classmates, killing twelve students and a teacher before turning the guns on themselves. The tragedy shocked the nation and raised the question of media violence as contributing to youth violence. Harris named his shotgun Arlene after a favorite character in the gory Doom video games and books that he liked so much.

Data from the 2000 Census indicate that Latinos have surpassed African Americans as the country's largest ethnic minority. Advertisers, recognizing their increasing buying power, are targeting Latinos with a wide spectrum of products and services (chapter 5). Unfortunately, advertisers sometimes unintentionally display cultural stereotypes. For

Fig. P.1

Fig. P.2

Fig. P.3

example, an AT&T ad represented two people of Mexican descent, communicating orally through large tin cans connected with string. This representation of Mexicans as technologically backward is an example of *symbolic racism* (see chapter 4). This edition examines more ads with Latino/a models that target a Latino audience.

On January 15, 2003, the police department in the small town of Hickory Creek, Texas, announced that it was replacing its five shabby police cruisers with five new ones provided by corporate sponsors. The department bought the new ones for $1 apiece. In exchange, the cruisers bear corporate logos and other advertising on their exterior. Other financially strapped police departments in Texas are expected to follow suit. Public reaction was mixed. Now police cruisers look like pizza delivery cars.

The cost of a thirty-second commercial during the 2003 Super Bowl was $2.2 million or $73,333 per second. Moreover, numerous corporations opine it is no

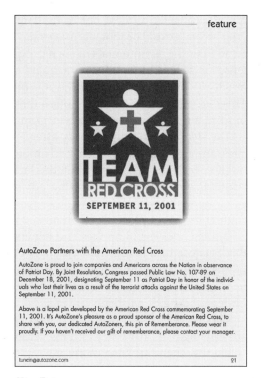

Fig. P.4

longer enough to simply market their wares and services on television's most watched event. People in more than 42.6 million homes watched the Super Bowl in 2002, according to Nielsen Media Research. A typical two-month pre–Super Bowl public-relations project can cost advertisers about $150,000 to $200,000, in addition to the cost of commercial airtime (Vranica and O'Connell 2003).

Provocateur transects media, cultural, gender, and ethnic studies and the sociology of advertising. This second edition signifies a tighter theoretical framework and expansion of the original model in the first edition. Most of the concepts used to critique images of women and minorities in advertising (e.g., ethnic assimilation, stereotyping, subvertising) are parsimoniously placed within the three major models (equal presentation, social reality, cultural attitudes). In other words, previously unrelated concepts are now arranged together.

This edition also explicates new pedagogical techniques for classroom use. The appendix provides an outline instructors may use to assign students written and/or oral analyses of advertising. This is based on the systematic methodology for a sociology of advertising (chapter 1).

This edition provides analyses of original case studies of eating disorders in young women (chapter 3). *Objectification* theory is used to answer the question: What are the consequences of being female in a society that sexually objectifies the female body (e.g., by gaze or "checking out")? The major assumption is that sexual objectification in our society pushes women and girls to internalize an observer's perspective of their physical selves, that is, to treat themselves as an object to be looked at and evaluated on the basis of appearance. This perspective is called *self-objectification.*

This volume also accommodates new preliminary evidence that sex and violence do not always sell—at least not in the United States. Watching a movie or TV program with strong sexual or violent images has been found to interfere with people's ability to remember the commercials in such programs. People watching shows packed with violence or sexual innuendo, performers with revealing clothes, or sexual scenes were much less likely to remember the ads, both immediately after the show and a day later. This cuts against the popular notion that more sex in shows equals more watchers and, in turn, a wider response to advertisements.

The steep declines in memory after the explicit shows were seen among adults of all ages, among men and women, and among those who liked the programs and those who did not. Perhaps more important, this lack of impact on memory was displayed in young adults (ages 18–25)—a group that advertisers covet as malleable consumers and that programmers try to attract with sexually alluring shows. Perhaps shows with sexual content cause people to think about sex instead of the products or services advertised.

Violent and sexual movies and television programs continue to be profitable despite this because of a sharp increase in global markets. Sexually explicit and violent programs allow programmers to sell films on the global market because sex and violence need no translations, no subtlety of plot and character development, and no deep understanding of a foreign culture.

This edition also introduces a new concept: *hybritising,* or combining two types of advertising (e.g., advocacy and institutional, ethnic assimilation and ethnic marketing).

Finally, there are also many new ads in this edition representing cultural changes since the original book's publication. I gratefully acknowledge Dallas artist R. Kevin Obregon for the use of figures 4.27–4.29.

Preface to the First Edition

There is nothing more difficult to take in hand, more perilous to conduct, or more uncertain in its success, than to take the lead in the introduction of a new order of things.

Niccolo Machiavelli, *The Prince*

The most significant series of events in postmodern times concerns the development of political democracy in Southern Europe, Latin America, Eastern Europe, the former Soviet Union, and, most recently, in much of Africa. Western politicians and scholars alike seemed to believe, naively but sincerely, that Western liberal democracy had, once and for all, conquered nationalism and totalitarianism and, moreover, that capitalism and its corresponding culture of advertising would readily be accommodated by formerly communist regimes.

Postcommunism, though, has led to new sets of global problems and escalating ethnic conflict. Regions have sometimes been broken into smaller, often hostile units. Examining global ethnic conflict, we have witnessed the Serbs' genocidal "ethnic cleansing" of their Croatian and Muslim neighbors in Kosovo and Bosnia-Herzegovina in the former republic of Yugoslavia, murderous tribal warfare in Rwanda and South Africa, persecution of gypsies in Romania, and oppression and near extermination of the Ainu, the native inhabitants of Hokkaido, Japan's northernmost major island. We are witnessing the annihilation of empathy in civil society across the globe. It is apparent that economic and social strains inherent in rapid postcommunistic social change have sometimes resulted in new surges of minority victimization and fanatical movements.

Ethnic cleansing is not a new phenomenon. What is new is the pervasive use of mass media to assist in shaping and intensifying one's cultural attitudes toward out-groups. "Hatred of the enemy, defined simply in ethnic or religious terms, is heightened through the use of television" (Ahmed 1997). Honor and ethnic nationalism are hailed, at the expense of much dissension and polarization.

Media violence encourages such hatred in real life. Ethnic cleansing of minorities is nothing more than the logical extension of ethnic pomp and self-righteousness. It is ideological rationalization out of control and the annihilation of empathy among members of a diverse community. Ethnic cleansing should be regarded within a global framework; what happens in one region of the world has a true and immediate impact on other regions around the globe (Ahmed 1997).

While acknowledging the necessity to stop the evil of death, rape, and torture prisons, we must also disdain and expose the more latent forms of ethnic cleansing, such as pervasive institutional discrimination, injustice in law enforcement and the court system, and racist immigration policies. In general, traumatic cultural, political, and economic strain is forced on ethnic minorities. Such processes and ideologies are the direct result of societies moving toward increasing specialization, fragmentation, and rationalization.

Social problems have become rampant not only in postcommunist countries but also within the United States and other westernized nations. Immigrants are arriving in near record numbers in the United States (Portes 1996). The migration of ethnic minorities into new communities greatly affects the economy (particularly employment opportunities) and social relations in general, including kinship and friendship networks and education. The increase in ethnic conflict with Asian Americans is also due, in part, to U.S.-Japanese tensions related to trade imbalances and environmental disputes (e.g., whale hunting).

The 1992 Los Angeles riots shattered a fragile social order in which new patterns of international migration provoked conventional racial stratification. The repercussions of the acquittal of four white police officers in the Rodney King case were felt all over the city as fifty-one people were killed, about five hundred arrested, hundreds more injured, and approximately two thousand troops collaborated with hundreds of city and state law officers.

More than one hundred Korean-owned grocery stores, liquor stores, cleaners, and other shops just west of downtown were robbed, burned, or looted, sometimes by people who had been their customers. Relations between Asian merchants and African Americans in Los Angeles have worsened in recent years. The association became even more strained in 1992 after a Korean American shopkeeper received probation for the fatal shooting of a fifteen-year-old African American girl. The store's video camera captured the shooting during a dispute over a bottle of orange juice. The riots occurred a week after a state appeals court upheld the probation.

The Los Angeles riots bore witness to the severity of racial problems. Polls taken immediately after the riots suggest that members of both majority and minority groups denounced the jury's decision in the Rodney King beating case and called for federal action against the law-enforcement officers involved (Morin 1993).

The Miami riots in the 1980s provide another example of how immigration and racial oppression spark conflict that often accelerates into violence. In Miami, periodic outbursts of racial violence during the 1980s seemed curiously out of step with the evolution of urbanization in the United States. Major riots engulfed predominantly black neighborhoods of the city during the decade, resulting in numerous deaths and hundreds of millions of dollars in property damage.

While black workers played an integral role in creating and staffing Miami's early tourist economy, they were subjected from the outset to strict southern segregationist norms. The riots solidified a widespread anger in black Miami over its failure to keep pace economically with other ethnic groups and its lack of political voice. (Black Miami is ethnically diverse, including non-Latino native-born African Americans and Caribbean immigrants, especially Cubans and Haitians.)

Ethnic conflict has become the biggest challenge confronting the international community. Tensions signal an urgent call for social justice. How do we justly address heightening ethnic conflict? Paralleling ethnic conflict and geographical fissures, cultural symbols and language meanings have also become balkanized.

Dialogue between cultures is at the core of postmodern international sociology. Such dialogue is beneficial when it aims to increase mutual understanding and facilitate the peaceful coexistence of diverse peoples. In a period of significant ethnic conflict at the global level, it is necessary to encourage dialogue between cultures in order to promote positive and liberating social change—humane change in a world where the denial of human rights and new forms of nationalism seem to be cropping up at an alarming pace. This dialogue is all the more important since it means an enlargement of the sphere in which the codes, values, and common features of language are spoken.

Ethnicity and conflict are themes embedded in the sociological tradition. Max Weber (1946), for example, notes that ethnic background is a key component of group membership. The notion of class conflict is clearly central to the writings of Karl Marx (1967). Emile Durkheim's (1961) moral theory highlights the necessity for society to go beyond conflict in order to achieve justice.

The study of ethnicity in sociology can be traced from the classical writings of Weber (1951) through the pioneering participant observation studies by faculty and graduate students in the then-hegemonic Chicago school of sociology (Cortese 1995; Tiryakian 1979) to the works of contemporary sociologists such as Stanford Lyman (1990), William Julius Wilson (1996), Peter Rose (1968), Pierre van den Berghe (1967), and Andrew Greeley (1974).

Over the years, critical scholars have noted the importance of the social construction of race, especially as an agent in racial supremacy movements, including the rise of Nazi Germany and Japan's nationalistic ideology based on notions of elitist racial dominance. Gunnar Myrdal's book *An American Dilemma* (1944) viewed the treatment of blacks as a direct contradiction to the American creed. Intellectuals around the globe condemned the system of apartheid in South Africa, fueling the worldwide anti-apartheid movement.

In the United States, ethnic conflict has taken many forms: expansionism and broken treaties between Native Americans and the federal government; slavery; the internal colonialization of the Southwest; discrepancies between Anglo and non-Anglo immigration policy and actual practices; patterns of assimilation and accommodation; miscegenation laws; an inability to control illegal migration, especially from Mexico; the internment of Japanese Americans during World War II (Kitano 1976); the civil rights movement, including the leadership of Martin Luther King Jr. and the Southern Christian Leadership Conference (SCLC), Malcolm X, Elijah Muhammad, Muhammad Ali, the Nation of Islam (Black Muslims), the Student Nonviolent Coordinating Committee (SNCC), the Council on Racial Equality (CORE), the Black Panthers, and the Brown Berets; and, more recently, the resurgence of white supremacy movements such as the Ku Klux Klan (KKK), the neo-Nazis, the American Nazi Party, the White Aryan Resistance (WAR), and skinhead groups that promote racial bigotry and violence; and a de facto system of medical apartheid resulting in the unequal distribution and quality of health care delivery (Cortese 1999).

It is urgent that social theorists and scientists examine the types of social questions that have begun to surface in postcommunistic postmodernity. Topics such as advertising should be inspected in a nonideological and scholarly fashion. This book attempts to take on this monumental duty by focusing on the role of the communications media (particularly advertising) in postmodern society. Is the United States still the planet's figurative master? If so, what exactly does this mean?

Baudrillard (1988, 76) essentially argues that (with the possible exception of Japan) the United States has become the world's center of the inauthentic. He describes America (or its culture or cities) as "illusionism" (59), "mirage" (63), "holographic" (66), "hyperreality" (28, 95), "special effect" (37), "synthetic" (66), "spontaneously fictional" (95), "an extraordinary piece of drama," and "the theatre of social relations" (85).

What is the relationship between culture in the United States and advertising, leisure, and fun? How does the unreal world of advertising resonate with the troubling plots that are unfolding across the globe today? Advertising "canonizes the way of [American] life through images, making the whole a genuinely integrated circuit" (Baudrillard 1988, 101–2).

This book incorporates interdisciplinary analyses—postmodernism, sociology, dramaturgy, feminist theory, ethnic studies, and the anthropology of visual communication.

In the 1950s and 1960s, "culture of poverty" explanations were in vogue. According to these explanations, minorities belong to a unique culture, passed on from generation to generation, that acclimates them so well to poverty that they do not even attempt to better themselves. Policymakers in the 1960s borrowed this stance to maintain that minorities need cultural enrichment to make proper use of jobs and higher incomes. Today the concept *underclass* is sometimes used to label minorities whose actions do not fit mainstream values—the "undeserving" minorities. I am sensitive to the biases and unexamined assumptions that too often find their way into "scientific" works (e.g., Herrnstein and Murray's 1994 book, *The Bell Curve*).

Cultural and gender images in advertising are intricately linked to social arrangements and the power structure. Social scientists should spend more time studying mass media and political institutions and processes and less time examining the behavior of ethnic minorities. I offer practical solutions to alleviate ethnic and gender inequality and conflict. A basic task of the project is to demonstrate how social structure and social processes affect individual attitudes and behavior.

C. Wright Mills (1959) astutely observed that personal troubles have social causes. Ethnic and gender inequality is a power struggle and a complex social process of blaming and labeling; often there are no clear-cut solutions to these problems. Attention is given to the mass media's construction of, and response to, these problems, especially the ideological position of media representations. This involves analyses of media control by persons or groups who represent particular ideological positions.

In conclusion, my rationale for writing this book is to critique postmodern social arrangements based on gender, race, and ethnicity. The ads chosen are those that are the hardest-hitting and most timely in contemporary society. The book ends with both a macro and a micro plan of attack against such social arrangements. This includes policy implications for advertising and a practical guide to combating symbolic racism at the individual level.

I would like to acknowledge the people who helped me with some of the ideas presented in *Provocateur*, as well as those who contributed to the production of many illustrations. The late Erving Goffman first steered me toward a dramaturgical analysis of advertising through his book *Gender Advertisements*. Dean Birkenkamp, vice president and executive editor, Rowman & Littlefield Publishers, Inc., discerned the possibility of a broad readership for my ideas and writings. Stjepan Mestrovic, Postmodernism and Social Futures series editor and professor of sociology at Texas A&M University, provided constructive criticism, encouragement, and ideas to develop some of the themes presented in the book. Joseph W. Scott, professor of sociology and American ethnic studies, University of Washington, contributed some of the early advertisements that display stratified race relations and racial stereotypes.

Cheryl Hoffman, Hoffman-Paulson Associates, was an unseen aid in this project. She subtly contributed much to the book's readability and diction. Julie Kirsch, managing editor, Rowman & Littlefield, offered encouragement and kept production on schedule. Rebecca Hoogs, assistant editor, Rowman & Littlefield, carefully helped with revisions, corrections, and rearrangements. Laura and Mike Foley assisted with computer graphics. Finally, many former students contributed ideas or advertisements found in this book.

I

Representations, Multiculturalism, and Mass Media

> Reality is never experienced directly but always through the cultural categories
> made available by a society.
>
> —Stuart Hall

The concept *representation* is one of the primary ideas in cultural studies. Much is at
stake in the discourse and skirmishes over ethnic and gender stereotyping in mass
media. The cultural sphere of meaning is a central part of human social life. It is also a
continuous course of confrontation and contention.

The primary objective of this book is to advance postmodern analysis by examining:

1. A semiotics of advertising as social life—deconstructing, decoding, and deci-
   phering that which is manifest or on the surface. *Ad deconstruction* is the analysis of advertising in such a way as to reinterpret implied meanings as symbolic
   rituals of postmodern societies. The present work centers on developing tools
   to understand, critique, and resolve the ubiquitous advertising images that
   bombard our everyday life. I attempt to provide theoretical analysis at the cutting edge of mass media and multiculturalism. In doing so, I hope to contribute to the production of critical and enlightened readers who engage
   knowledgeably and vigilantly with the representations of cultural life. Critical
   reflection on media representations deprives the industry of its undisputed
   power.

2. Major issues of postmodern sociological theory that seem to be crucial to the
   empirical investigation of commercial advertising and consumerism, specifically,
   gender, ethnicity, culture, and language. Like Erving Goffman (1976), I am interested in the appearance of events and of material and nonmaterial objects. This
   necessitates determining and positing underlying structures of social stratification or examining power relations. I prefer a hermeneutic, dramaturgical
   approach that is grounded in larger structural parameters.

3. Conceptual questions connected to the representation of marginalized groups
   in advertising (women, blacks, Latinos, Asians, Native Americans, and gays
   and lesbians). Representations of such marginalized groups may be contrasted
   with the dominant producers of mainstream culture—a set of white, male,

upper-middle- to upper-class, heterosexual ideologies. Target advertising correctly assumes that, despite their relative powerlessness, even these marginalized groups have a lot of money to spend. Moreover, they have developed the fastest-growing national rates of disposable income. (This is discussed further in chapter 5.)

4. Methodological approaches to a critical, hermeneutic analysis of advertising. I offer a systematic methodology for a *sociology of advertising:*

   a. Borrowing from the dramaturgy of Goffman (1976) and the human zoology (1986, 1996) and visual anthropology (1977; Morris et al. 1979) of Desmond Morris, deconstruct nonverbal behavior or body language, including a focus on facial expression, body posture, and both intended and unintentional gestures.

   b. Using marketing analysis, examine the placement and target audience of the advertisement in relation to the product or service.

   c. Render artistic composition analysis. *Art* includes "any graphics, photography, film, or video that offers visual information to a receiver" (O'Guinn, Allen, and Semenik 1998, 275). In postmodern image-oriented ads, the visual component is the main method for conveying meaning.

   d. Using a critical, structural interpretation, deconstruct the ad as a product of status display and consumer culture. Provide narrative or "tell the story" to which the advertisement alludes. This includes a chronological deconstruction of events leading up to and following the frame frozen in the print advertisement.

   e. Decode *copy*—"the verbal or written part of a message" (O'Guinn, Allen, and Semenik 1998, 275). Copy includes headlines, subheads, and all verbal or written descriptions intended to communicate a message to the consumer. In terms of linguistic analysis, evoke the implied or assumed message of the advertisement and distinguish it from its actual or literal meaning.

This model deciphers advertising in two different ways. First, of course, is the manifest function of advertising to persuade the consumer to purchase a particular brand of product or service. More important, the study of cultural objects, such as advertising, provides a pivotal and privileged entry to culture. Advertising is one of the most powerful mechanisms through which members of a society assimilate their cultural heritage and cultural ideologies of domination. Ideology refers to images, concepts, and premises that provide the frameworks through which we represent, interpret, understand, and try to understand some point of view of social life (Hall 1981). Ideologies synthesize ostensibly diverse elements into a distinctive set of meanings. For example, the depiction of ethnic relations to members of a society via advertising subtly colors understanding of status arrangements, social boundaries, and power. The transformation of cultural ideologies is a collective process, albeit often unconscious, not the result of individual consciousness or volition. Ideologies are often latent or unrecognized; they are taken for granted as real, commonsense, or natural. The structure of ethnic, gender, and class inequality is justified as being profoundly destined by nature.

Advertising

> Has there ever been an institution so reviled as modern advertising, so hectored, so blamed for the ills of society?
>
> Yet has there ever been an institution so responsible for conveying . . . the most alluring, the most sensitive, and the most filled with human yearning?
>
> —James B. Twitchell, *Adcult USA*

Advertising. It's not a bad word, but it has often been viewed as a bad thing. Here's a sampling of what some well-known writers have penned about advertising. Herman Wouk: "Advertising blasts everything that is good and beautiful in this land with a horrid spreading mildew." F. Scott Fitzgerald: "Advertising's contribution to humanity is exactly minus zero." And, finally, Sinclair Lewis: "Advertising is the cheapest way of selling goods, particularly if the goods are worthless."

Advertising has been credited with improving the quality of life for Americans, boosting the economy, and encouraging competition (Woods 1995). Yet it has also been blamed for subliminally urging people to purchase products and services that they do not need or even want, constructing false expectations, and adulterating language.

Advertising may be defined as "a paid, mass-mediated attempt to persuade" (O'Guinn, Allen, and Semenik 1998, 577). An *advertisement* is "a specific message that an organization has placed to persuade an audience" (577). Or more simply, an advertisement is *a message that has been called to the attention of a public audience, especially by paid announcement.*

The study of consumer behavior became recognized as a science in the late 1940s (Woods 1995). Since then, an impressive body of literature on target marketing, demographics, and social segmentation has emerged. The marketing research on ethnic subcultures is less impressive. Motivational research (i.e., the latent reasons why people buy particular brands of goods and services) developed in the 1950s, while greater indepth psychological research developed in the 1960s (Woods 1995).

During the early years of consumer research, ethnic consumers were all but ignored. Instead, researchers were trying to tap into the "average American"—a label not applied to ethnic minority populations. Even while ethnic minority populations grew at a record pace, marketing researchers continued to overlook them. Now consumer research has indicated that blacks respond differently to advertising than whites (Hunter and Associates 1991).

Advertising, more than art, literature, or editorials, allows us to track our sociological history: the rise and fall of fads, crazes, and social movements; political issues of the times; changing interests and tastes in clothes, entertainment, vices, and food; and scenes of social life as they were lived. The only institution comparable in scope and magnitude was the Roman Catholic Church of the early Renaissance (Twitchell 1996, 229). Advertising is a powerful social force that commands the public's attention to, and faith in, a particular style of consciousness and consumption.

"The culture of consumption has replaced the culture of contrition" (Twitchell 1996, 230). Like Christianity, advertising afflicts the comfortable and comforts the afflicted. Advertising has become so absorbed by society that it has become the dominant culture. The culture of consumption was not always so pervasive. In the agrarian-based society that predated an economic system established on industry, other institutions such as family, community, ethnicity, and religion were the dominant mediators and creators of cultural forms (Jhally 1990). Their control dissolved in the shift first to industrial society and then to consumer society.

Branding

Branding—the process of differentiation—is at the core of advertising. What distinguishes similar products is not ingredients but packaging and brand names. Most shampoos, for example, are made by two or three manufacturers (Vinikas 1992). The major thrust of advertising is to remind shoppers to seek out and purchase a particular brand. Branding seeks to nullify or compensate for the fact that products are otherwise fundamentally interchangeable. Tests have shown that consumers cannot distinguish their own brand of soap, beer, cigarette, water, cola, shampoo, gasoline from others. In a sense, advertising is like holding up two identical photographs and persuading you that they are different—in fact, that one is better than the other.

Brand extension is introducing goods by adding the familiarity of a proven brand. Branding and brand extension have permitted discount retail outlets to "cannibalize the value of cooperative advertising" (Twitchell 1996, 251). These stores do little, if any, brand advertising (everyone already knows and can recall the brand products); rather, what little advertising they do is focused on claims to provide brand products at the lowest prices. They make their profits by buying and selling in large volumes.

Spending on Advertising

Advertising deconstruction is not trivial. Advertising is now a $180-billion-per-year industry (Moreno 1997, 57). Television commercials often cost as much as $264,000 to produce (Jhally, 1988). Advertising spending in 1950 was approximately $6.5 billion; by 1970, $40 billion; by 1980, $56 billion (Kellner 1988). Advertising expenditures nearly doubled from 1980 to 1986, suggesting a shocking development of advertising during the 1980s. All revenues for television and radio programming come from advertising. Eighty percent of newspaper and half of magazine revenues come from advertising (Jhally, 1998).

Advertising has colonized professional sports. Corporations spend almost $2.3 billion annually on sporting events (Twitchell 1996). (It's no wonder that they insist on dressing the athletes!) The average adult consumer is bombarded with at least 500 advertising messages daily (Bovee and Arens 1989). Other estimates are 1,500 (Kilbourne 1989), 3,000 (Landler et al. 1991), and 3,600 ads a day (Jhally, 1998). This makes advertising perhaps the most powerful educational source in society. In fact, we spend more money on advertising (at least 2 percent of our gross national product, according to the Association of National Advertisers [1988, 4]) than on public education (Kellner 1988).

Former NBA basketball superstar Michael Jordan of the Chicago Bulls was the best-paid and most recognizable product endorser in professional sports. He made approximately $40 million in 1997. Jordan was recognizable to 35.8 percent of the sampled individuals. Tiger Woods is the second-most-recognizable product pusher in professional sports; he was expected to earn about $20 million from endorsements in 1997. The 1997 Masters champion was recognized as a sports endorser by 8 percent of people surveyed by telephone over an eleven-week period, according to data compiled by

Stamford, Connecticut–based Sponsorship Research International and the *Sports Marketing Letter*.

The cost of a thirty-second commercial during the 2003 Super Bowl was $2.2 million or $73,333 per second. (In 1967, the cost was $42,000.) Moreover, numerous corporations opine it is no longer enough to simply market their wares and services on television's most watched event. People in more than 42.6 million homes watched the exciting Super Bowl in 2002, according to Nielsen Media Research. A typical two-month pre–Super Bowl public-relations project can cost advertisers about $150,000 to $200,000, in addition to the cost of commercial airtime (Vranica and O'Connell 2003). This tells us that advertising is very serious business. Although the amount of money is astounding, Super Bowl commercials are cost effective for reaching the estimated 140 million to 800 million viewers worldwide, many of whom watch only to preview the new commercials.

The advertising industry almost exclusively underwrites the mass media in the United States. "Newspapers obtain about 75% of their revenues from advertisers, general-circulation magazines about 50%, and broadcasters almost 100%" (Herman 1990, 70). It is clear that advertising is the economic lifeblood of the media (Kilbourne 1989). Companies that purchase advertising space and time affect to varying degrees the ideological content of all media forms (Dines and Humez 1995).

Corporate profits began to plunge in the early 1990s, and with the dive in profits came a decrease in advertising spending (Woods 1995). In 1991, network ad spending fell more than 7 percent over 1990 figures (Television Bureau of Advertising, in Woods 1995). Newspaper ad spending dropped by the same amount during the same period (Newspaper Advertising Bureau, in Woods 1995), and magazine ad budgets fell 5 percent (Landler et al. 1991, 67). Advertising may never again experience the boom that it enjoyed in the 1970s and 1980s, when revenues grew faster than the overall economy.

There are numerous reasons for the precipitous decline in advertising spending. Consumers are exposed to so many ads that they are conditioned to attend selectively to some ads while ignoring others. Consumers are remembering fewer ads. In one longitudinal study, viewer retention of ads dropped from 64 percent to 48 percent in four years (Landler et al. 1991).

Modernism and Postmodernism

> Advertising doesn't mirror how people are acting but how they are dreaming.
> —Jerry Goodis, advertising executive

Modernism has been characterized by an ideology that promotes control over nature and society, an illusion of rational order, the notion that constant change is inevitable and must be positively embraced, and increasing division and fragmentation. Modernism is dialectical, even paradoxical: unity versus disunity, standardization versus diversity, and centralization versus decentralization (Rojek 1995, 101). The essence of modernism is escape, disorder, restlessness, perpetual change, division, and uncertainty.

Some aspects of modernism are apparent in postmodernism: transition, fragmentation, circulation, instability, and discontinuity. Postmodernism may be either affirmative, signaling social responsibility and ethical open-mindedness (Bauman 1993), or nihilistic, beaconing primitive culture (Baudrillard 1988) or pathos and destruction (Jameson 1991). While modernism tries to impose rational control over the social and physical world, the proliferation of simulated environments (see Baudrillard 1988) indicates the accentuated appearance of fantasy and false elements in postmodern culture. Authenticity and meaning have vanished.

Bakhtin (1984) suggests temporary liberation from prevailing "truth" and established order and suspension of all hierarchical rank, privileges, norms, and prohibitions; dogmas and pomposity of official culture are ridiculed. It is worthwhile to make a distinction between postmodernity and postmodernism. "Postmodernity" refers to generalized change in social *conditions.* "Postmodernism" refers to generalized change in social *consciousness.* Rojek (1995) highlights the major events or developments that have contributed to postmodernism:

1. the rise of feminism, which challenged conventional authority structures installed under the male order of modernity

2. the expansion of the international tourism industry of mass communications (including advertising)

3. the transfer of cheap labor to the core industrial economies and the development in metropolitan areas of distinct ethnic enclaves that signify difference, contrast, and cosmopolitanism

4. the politicization of gays and lesbians, which exposed the restrictions of the heterosexual power order of modernity

5. the collapse of communism in Eastern Europe, which refutes the belief that social change can be rationally planned and managed

6. the development of ecological consciousness, or the belief that economic and industrial growth jeopardizes the ecological necessity of human survival, refuting the expansionist dynamic of modernity

7. the failure of world economic powers to manage effectively the global economy and combine high employment rates with low inflation and sustained economic growth

8. the explosion of information technology, which has increased the mobility and flexibility of data-retrieval systems and improved the speed and accuracy of communicating through networking and electronic mail systems. Technology has also dramatically altered the way in which some products and services are marketed. Computerized market research supplies detailed information about target audiences (e.g., ethnic minorities, college students, and women). Names, addresses, and telephone numbers can be matched with consumer habits.

Advertising as Culture Industry

The invisibility of Whiteness masks Whiteness itself as a category.
—Richard Dyer

Culture industry refers to the collection of entertainment industries dedicated to amusing the populace in their nonwork time: music, film, television, radio, and magazines

(Horkheimer and Adorno 1972). Marcuse (1964) maintains that the masses are no longer able to distinguish personal freedom from manipulation. However, one could argue that they are able to oppose, subvert, and neutralize codes of manipulation.

Rojek (1995, 117) identifies four sources of dissatisfaction (i.e., wishing, not having) in the psychology of the postmodern consumer:

1. incompleteness of market commodities on display (merely a sample of infinite possibilities)

2. arbitrariness of choice (commodities with no lasting value purchased by impulse, not free choice). "Food shoppers make almost two-thirds of their buying decisions when they set foot in the aisle" (Twitchell 1996, 57).

3. fragmentation. The individual experiences the world in fragments. There are fragmented relationships in private life.

4. indifference. The consumer becomes indifferent to commodity choice. "With more than fifteen hundred new items introduced to supermarkets each month, the need to inform and convince the querulous shopper is intense" (Twitchell 1996, 57).

The nostalgia industry is based on the embellishment or re-creation of the past by the use of artifice (device, deceit, ingenuity) for commercial purposes. Nostalgic representations (see figures 1.1–1.2) have nothing to do with history; they are merely "symptoms of the waning of our historicity" (Jameson 1991). "Advertising is not treated as epiphenomena of natural production but as the dream machines of everyday life" (Rojek 1995, 88).

The nostalgia industry represents one of the most opaque masks of white cultural dominance. The nostalgic illustrations of Norman Rockwell staged a comeback in 1989 mainstream commercial images to sell breakfast cereal and station wagons. These images

Fig. 1.1   Fig. 1.2

appear to show whiteness as lost innocence. Rockwell's compositions (see figure
1.3) symbolize some of the chief components of nostalgic mythology in the United
States: small towns, family rituals, mischie-
vous boys, flirtatious girls, and mainstream
institutions such as the Boy Scouts, the pre-
integration school, and church. The only
problem is that everyone is white.

Postmodern Advertising

> Magical thinking is at the heart of both
> religion and advertising.
> —James B. Twitchell, *Adcult USA*

Advertising promises instant access to
desire and love; consequently advertising
seems to assume a belief in magic. Postmodern advertising—characterized by a
rapid succession of visually appealing
images (the speed-up effect), repetition,
and high-volume, mood-setting music

Fig. 1.3

(see chapter 6)—is much more symbolic and persuasive than informative. Advertising
is an arena in which conspicuous role display and reversal, preening, and symbolically
enticing situations are evident.

Direct marketing has left its pejorative status as junk mail, expanding in scope and
often contending directly with advertising. Direct marketing has the advantage that it
is more focused or targeted than advertising. Specialized magazines, cable television,
and new media markets make it possible to cut the target market into narrow and more
clearly delineated slices (Woods 1995).

While modern advertising presented itself as an unquestionable authority figure—a
high priest of sorts—postmodern advertising presents itself as an insider, an ally of the
common person. Modern advertising used a paternalistic model; like your physician, it
knows what is best for you. Now advertising is trading in the semblance of godlike
knowledge for the role of a funny, self-deprecatory chum. Often there is self-parody
(Twitchell 1996). The point of parody, to be sure, is that the viewer detects the dupe so
well that it does not have to be explicitly revealed. Sometimes there is even the sugges-
tion of a secret agreement between the viewer and the advertising agency.

Postmodern advertising admits something to the public that its antecedents would
never have dreamed of admitting: that its goal is to grab our attention in order to persuade us to buy its brand. Advertising agencies have begun to acknowledge their true
raison d'être. Postmodern advertising is admitting that it can no longer manipulate
consumers as its predecessors once did. This is highly significant because it demonstrates that consumers interpret ads; they do not just accept them at face value. The
public is no longer "con" friendly; rather, it is more skeptical, cautious, savvy, and educated. Advertisers are starting to admit what Kuhnian scholars have known all along:
you cannot separate your "objective" judgments from your value-laden experiences.

In modern advertising, the image of the advertising executive was that of a manipulative liar or an evil seducer of the innocent. Now in postmodern advertising, the image is that of a slightly crazed fool. Nevertheless, this underestimation of the ad exec by the consumer guarantees the advertiser's success and makes advertising a very powerful social force.

Advertising has been stripped of its mystic authority. Postmodern advertising has recognized this and is now flaunting it as a technique to sell to those who have been sold out by the empty promises of advertising (e.g., if you buy the car, the sexy young woman comes with it; if you use our makeup, you become the perfect provocateur: youthful, beautiful, and, of course, sexy). The consumer has become very distrusting of the hard sell.

Now, in order to market a brand, advertisers usually have to use a very soft sell. It is so soft that the product is not the focus and is, in fact, often jettisonable. It is not that advertising no longer wishes to be authoritative; rather, ads and commercials get the consumer's attention by proclaiming their presence or participation and matter of factly admitting their ulterior motive—to sell their brand merchandise. When the Energizer Bunny tromps through the logos of other brand products, he is essentially saying, "Let's come clean; we know that you know that this is just a commercial!"

Advertising, again like early Christianity, was always at its purest, its most vital, when it was countercultural and confrontational (Twitchell 1996). Christianity was never a greater social force than when in conflict with another culture. "It has never been as vigorous as when it tangled with the Romans" (Twitchell 1996, 235). Advertising's new emphasis on self-mockery seems to take precedence over its mission to sell—and this may cause advertising to lose its competitive edge.

Advertising is no longer viewed as the manipulative villain. Instead, it has become the boy next door. In the process of shedding its depraved image, it has also oversaturated the public, leaving the consumer bored and unstimulated. In a tongue-in-cheek analysis of postmodern advertising, renowned copyeditor Howard Gossage comments: "The object of . . . advertising should not be to communicate with your consumers and prospects at all, but to terrorize your competition copywriters."

Since consumers know that material consumption does not bring happiness, successful advertisers connect their commodities to the elements of a valued social life (e.g., warm and happy family relationships, romance and love, meaningful friendships, relaxing leisure time, high self-esteem). Yet advertising pushes us to material consumption and pulls us away from meaningful relationships for happiness. Alternative strategies and values are not presented.

The Benetton Controversy Continues

The old law of an eye for an eye leaves the whole world blind.

—Martin Luther King Jr.

We are still human. We still have feelings.

—Edgar Ace Hope (death-row inmate)

I am not ready to die.

—Joseph Amrine (death-row inmate)

Benetton, a popular Italian clothing manufacturer, has created controversy through its graphic advertising, often depicting emotional scenes and contemporary social issues. In January 2000, Benetton, in a magazine-sized institutional advertisement, "We, On

Death Row," published photos of and essays on death-row inmates, some of whom had already been executed (see figure 1.4). Critics maintained that Benetton has exploited powerless inmates for profit. Nevertheless, two of the two-year project's contributors, Speedy Rice and Williman B. Moffitt, defend it for "bringing a human face to the individuals on death row."

Benetton has used "United Colors of Benetton" in its advertising campaigns since 1983. This appeals to racial harmony and a "global village" look (see figure 1.5). This type of ad displays people from a wide variety of cultural backgrounds to reflect society's greater acceptance of racial and ethnic diversity. (See the cultural attitudes model in chapter 4.)

Many of Benetton's ads do not even show its products. Instead, the photographs attempt to capture social issues

Fig. 1.4

that are on the cutting edge. Benetton has a reputation for provocative advertising, with shocking visuals to attract the reader's attention.

Postmodernity is a restless age in which new ideologies contest established traditions, making even more uncertain the highly uncertain environment (Hirsch 1972) that cultural producers, such as advertisers, face. The unspoken rules—a "business as usual" mentality of what is acceptable and appealing to the public, what consumers buy, and what award panels choose as "distinguished"—are often exposed and held up to scrutiny during times of social change (Pescosolido, Grauerholz, and Milkie 1997). Attempts to rearrange power, which are reflected in ethnic conflict, change the way in which cultural gatekeepers use their cultural "tool kits" (Swidler 1986). This is precisely what Benetton has done and continues to do in its advertising images.

Some of Benetton's ads are so controversial that they have been banned from publication. Take, for example, the ad (figure 1.6) showing a black woman nursing a white baby. This attention-grabbing photograph was considered too provocative for print advertising in the United States and Great Britain. The image harkens back to the antebellum era when house slaves often served as wet nurses for the babies of slave masters.

HIV and AIDS is a topic that is certainly socially relevant, political, timely, and controversial. The ad in figure 1.7 taps into this; the "H.I.V. positive" stamp shows us the stigma borne by persons who are HIV positive or have AIDS. Once

Fig. 1.5

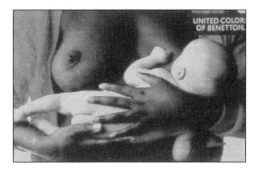

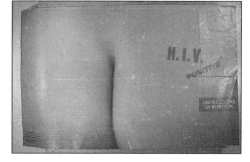

Fig. 1.6   Fig. 1.7

a person has been labeled HIV positive, he or she is symbolically branded with a new identity. This cultural representation is negative and often carries with it prejudice and discriminatory treatment. It perpetuates the myth that AIDS is transmitted only through anal sex.

The ad in figure 1.8 portrays a white man and a black man handcuffed together. The men are wearing identical apparel: denim jeans and jean jackets and light-blue shirts. This ad was published in the United States but was later pulled after civil rights organizations protested that the photo was racist because it implied that the black man was a criminal. But it is not clear in the ad which man is the criminal—the black man, the white man, or both.

Benetton continues to publish ads that tend to evoke emotional responses from viewers. For example, figure 1.9 shows a blood-stained T-shirt and camouflage pants. Figure 1.10 shows a priest and nun kissing.

Benetton's advertising provides a great example of the contested ideologies of postmodernism. The objective is still bottom-line profit. The method, however, is indirect: the product or service is ignored in favor of photographs that are

controversial.

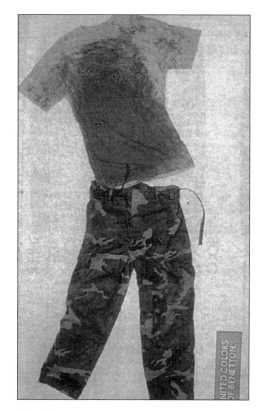

Fig. 1.8   Fig. 1.9

Fig. 1.10

Advertising as Social Life

> In a postmodern image culture . . . advertising becomes an important and over-
> looked mechanism of socialization as well as manager of consumer demand.
> —Douglas Kellner

The advertising industry essentially produces propaganda for commodities. Satisfaction is guaranteed with a purchase. Not only do advertising images try to sell a product by associating it with particular socially efficacious characteristics, but also they sell nothing less than an expansive worldview, a lifestyle, and system of values consistent with the imperatives of consumer capitalism (Kellner 1988).

Symbolic images in advertising develop a link between the product or service offered and socially desirable and meaningful traits to persuade the consumer that the product or service will produce a highly coveted lifestyle. Advertising obfuscates the manner in which a capitalistic system of economics creates and maintains a class-based society in which only a few can really afford to consume at the level depicted as the ideal in ads (Dines and Humez 1995).

"In the preindustrial world the object of advertising was often events, not objects" (Twitchell 1996, 9). Advertising sections of newspapers proclaimed the arrival of ships bearing new merchandise. In the modern world this process became commercialized. In the postmodern world there are now fifteen-second video ads while we wait for our cash transactions. Advertising is everywhere: on television and radio, in magazines, newspapers, and the mail; on billboards, buses, trucks, and subways—even in urinals. We are totally immersed in the messages—the pictures and words—of advertising. In postmodernity, advertising is pervasive. It fills up the spaces of our existence and is in the air that we breathe (Jhally 1990). We mistakenly tend to view advertising as a natural reflection of everyday social life. In decoding advertising imagery, I hope to attack the virtual invulnerability of the advertising industry in our society.

In our capitalist economy, profit is the vital pulse behind the production, distribution, and consumption of products and services. "Advertising legitimizes and even sacralizes consumption as a way of social life" (Dines and Humez 1995, 71). The major commodity being bought and sold is the audience for advertising, segmented along gender, ethnic, class, and age lines. Thus, any analysis of the role of mass media within a capitalist economic commodity system necessitates a look at advertising not only as an industry per se but also as discourse about cultural objects.

Advertising is indeed a very powerful social force. Nevertheless, it is clear to me that advertising caters to mass consumers much more than it actually changes their attitudes and behavior. Advertising does not function by formulating values and attitudes on its own; rather, it draws upon and redirects issues that the target audience or common culture already shares. Advertising packages our emotions and sells them back to us. It other words, advertising reflects (not affects) beliefs, values, and ideologies (cultural beliefs that serve to justify social stratification). Researchers in advertising agencies attempt to discover and expose our attitudes, moral judgments, and, sometimes, how we interact with others.

Ads then use images of these same attitudes, moral judgments, and social acts as cues to sell to us—sort of a cultural judo throw, using our psychological needs and desires and moral ideas to the advertiser's advantage. In other words, advertising uses elements of popular culture to which we are already sympathetic and empathetic. "Goods are knitted into the fabric of social life and cultural significance" (Jhally 1990, 80). In a sense, consumers participate in their own manipulation.

Advertising and Dramaturgy

Erving Goffman (1976) has studied gender images in advertising. He borrows terms from the theater (e.g., actor, role, cue, script, performance, offstage, onstage) in his *dramaturgical* model, which emphasizes the little details of daily life. Goffman's focus on social life as theater fits perfectly with a sociology of advertising.

Goffman's work pointed sociology toward a focus on interaction rituals and the self. His 1976 study of gender stratification in advertising, *Gender Advertisements*, reveals how gender distinctions inform our ceremonial life. Specifically, ads are highly manipulated representations of recognizable or institutional scenes from "real life." Ads tell us a lot about ourselves, about the link between fashioned image and "natural behavior." Ads tell us about the way self-image is developed and socially determined. Advertisements affirm existing social arrangements. In a social or public setting, the minutest behavior has meaning. Gesture, expression, and posture not only expose how we feel about ourselves but also construct a scene that embodies cultural values (Goffman 1976). Goffman's focus on gesture, expression, and posture ideally suits advertising analysis.

Model-development institutes teach models techniques with posture, facial expressions, body gestures, foot placement, and eye contact. These methods are designed to improve runway body movement and posing for still photographs. The institutes offer workshops on fashion, makeup, and hair design under the assumption that high fashion is both trendy and theatrical. Students must first pay the fee (approximately $100 for a several-hour course) because it is also claimed that a certain technique is required to accomplish this look. Other workshops are specifically designed to help models create several different appearances.

Ads try to tell us who we are and who we should be. Although advertisements appear to display real people, they are actually displaying depictions of ethnic and gender relations as they function socially. There are two basic points concerning gender here. First, ads tell us that there is a big distinction between appropriate behavior for men or boys and that for women or girls. Second, advertising and other mass media reinforce the notion that men are dominant and that women are passive and subordinate. In chapter 3, I use examples from a children's book to show how rigid and exclusive gender roles are set in early childhood. Moreover, while the masculine role is valued, the feminine counterpart is devalued.

Ads sell much more than products. They sell moral values and cultural images, such as concepts of success, love, and sexuality. Jean Kilbourne argues that advertising is a very powerful social force that should be taken seriously. Her videos (e.g., *Killing Us Softly: Advertising Images of Women; Still Killing Us Softly;* and *Calling the Shots: Women and Alcohol*) use print advertising as a vehicle to provide careful and cogent analyses of gender inequality.

Public and Private Pictures

Photographs are either private or public (Goffman 1976). Private pictures are those designed for display within an intimate social circle of friends, especially those featured in them. They commemorate occasions and rituals, relationships, achievements, and life-turning points in relationships, families, groups, and organizations. Private pictures are taken by hobbyists, enthusiasts, amateurs, or dabblers, not professionals. Public pictures are those intended to attract an extensive audience—an anonymous assemblage of individuals unconnected to one another by social relationships and social interaction, although they fall within the same market or political jurisdiction or have the same interests. Public pictures are mass produced in newspapers, magazines, books, leaflets, or posters. Public pictures are diverse in function and character. There are commercial pictures designed to sell a product or a service for an advertiser. There are also news photos related to matters held to be of current social, political, or scientific importance. There are instructional pictures—for example, illustrations in medical textbooks. Human interest pictures, anonymous and often candid, display otherwise unnoteworthy individuals who articulately (and presumably unintentionally) show some response, such as anger, fear, surprise, or puzzlement, or some inner state, such as hopelessness, innocence, or joy, or how we look and what we do when we think no one sees us. This type of picture, if done with sensitivity, acumen, and skill, is timeless and aesthetically appealing. Personal publicity pictures are designed to bring before the public an unusual or intimate portrait of a celebrity in some arena—political, religious, military, sporting, theatrical, literary, or social—where a class elite still functions. These photos are often taken by the paparazzi, who have come under increasingly sharp criticism after the death of Princess Diana. In short, public pictures are photographs or illustrations that are intended for display to public audiences. Finally, portrayals of people in children's books fit the definition of advertising that I borrow from Goffman (1976): something that is brought to the attention of the public, especially by paid announcement (see chapter 4).

The Structures of Racial and Gender Inequality

> That's part of American greatness—discrimination. Yes, sir. Inequality I think,
> breeds freedom and gives a man opportunity.
> —Lester Maddox, former governor of Georgia

Ethnic and gender representations in advertising are intricately linked to social arrangements and the power structure. The mass media are the strongest glue that bonds the diverse groups that compose a heterogeneous national and global community. Ethnic groups and social classes of all types share a great deal of common culture through the media. Yet ethnic minorities and the lowest social classes have little to do with the creation of mainstream culture.

The portrayal of unique subcultural groups in the media indicates that the groups have a type of power, a secure place in society, and a noted identity. Conversely, non-representation suggests the powerless status of groups that do not possess significant material or political power bases (Gross 1991). Those near the bottom of social stratification are kept in their powerless places in part through their relative invisibility in the media. When groups or viewpoints do achieve prominence, the way that prominence is illustrated will itself resonate with the inclinations and vested interests of the elite gatekeepers who set the public agenda. These gatekeepers are typically white, middle-aged, male, middle- and upper-middle class, and heterosexual.

Advertising is a very powerful force that articulates, develops, transforms, and elaborates these ideas of ethnicity, gender, and social class. Advertising (or the media in general), nevertheless, does not present a uniform conception of such complex issues. Nor does it typically consciously or deliberately conspire against members of protected classes. Such explanations are oversimple, accusatory, convenient, and misleading. Racism in advertising is more inferential or symbolic than overt.

As social importance is manifested through the appearance and varied performances of a social group, so too can the devaluation of groups be transmitted through *symbolic racism* (subtle ethnic stereotyping, trivialization of minority empowerment or racial equality, or the absence of ethnic representations). Symbolic racism involves seemingly fundamental illustrations of events and situations relating to race that have racist postulates and approaches built in as undisputed assumptions. This allows racist remarks to be presented without ever bringing into question the racist assumptions on which the assertions are grounded.

Racism cannot be treated as a simple product of capitalism. Historically, racist stereotyping has been documented at least since the propaganda of the Christian Crusaders (Said 1978). Racism has also been linked to the emergence of religious formations, ethnic identities, and nation-states that predate capitalism. For example, the Muslim trade in African slaves was well established in the first millennium A.D.

Racial images in advertising are important for at least two reasons. First, there is evidence that advertising and other media images help to shape attitudes about race and ethnicity. Thus, we can select the ethnic images that advertisements present to individuals. Second, ads can provide a barometer of the extent to which ethnic minorities have penetrated social institutions dominated by white males. That is, ads reflect in which arenas (e.g., business, politics, the economy, education, sports, entertainment, academia, art, the military, religion) the power of a white-male-dominated social system is challenged by minorities, including women.

The contemporary ethnic and feminist movements, with all their agitation about the meaning of the little details in daily life, have served as an electric prod to the work of many social scientists, giving new impetus and direction to their work, whose very substance is the observation of concrete detail in social life. Because of this, the most ordinary verbal or nonverbal exchange between white males and minorities now reverberates with new meaning (e.g., the notion of political correctness).

The simplest gesture, the most familiar ritual, taken-for-granted form of address, has become a source of new understanding, albeit not without occasional conflict, with regard to ethnic and gender relations, including the underlying social arrangements behind such relations. Operating out of a politics that originates with individual feelings, ethnic scholars and feminists have made clear what social scientists should have always known: It is in the details of daily exchange that the discrepancy between actual experience and apparent experience is to be found.

The minute details of social behavior are indicative revelations of how a sense of self is established and reinforced. That sense of self, in turn, both reflects and cements the social institutions upon which rests a culture's hierarchical structure. My point is that if one evaluates the details of social life from a highly critical stance, one learns profoundly who and what one is in the social lifeworld.

Social, Political, and Environmental Messages

Advertising sells more than products or services; it also sells values and attitudes. It attempts to persuade, build trust, and change or reinforce values, opinions, and attitudes on social issues. This section examines the following four types of messages:

Advocacy Advertising attempts to persuade or sell a value or attitude.

Subvertising uses brand recognition against itself.

Institutional Advertising tries to build lifetime trust or undo damage to a company's or government's reputation.

Hybritising combines two types of advertising. In this section, it refers to advocacy and institutional advertising.

Advocacy Advertising

Advocacy advertising attempts to influence public opinion on important social, political, or environmental issues of concern to the sponsoring organization (O'Guinn, Allen, and Semenik 1998). It often challenges conventional wisdom and presents alternative interpretations of social problems and political issues. Advocacy advertising essentially enhances participatory democracy, bringing issues into public view by attracting media attention. Advocacy advertising is sponsored by nonprofit organizations or companies that use nonprofit foundations to pay for ads.

The power of counteradvertising to attract attention and critique existing social arrangements is demonstrated in an incident from the 1940s. In 1942, the White Rose, an inconsequential bunch of German university students, began a humble propaganda campaign against the Nazis (Jacobs and Heller 1992). Members distributed anti-Gestapo proclamations and eyewitness exposés of atrocities on the Eastern Front. For over a year, the Nazis were frustrated by the band's knack for avoiding capture. Though inexhaustible, most members of the group were eventually arrested, prosecuted, and summarily hanged as enemies of the government.

Civil Rights. The stark image of many bullet holes in a metal sheet protests the police killing of a defenseless and harmless man. The copy reads:

> On February 4th, 1999, the NYPD gave Amadou Diallo the right to remain silent. And they did it without ever saying a word. Firing 43 bullets in 8 seconds, the police killed an unarmed innocent man. Also wounded that night was the constitutional right of every American to the process of law. Help us defend your rights. Support the ACLU.

Gun Safety. The grainy photo of a young blond child wrapped in a beach towel standing at the edge of a swimming pool provides an ominous visual for Cease Fire (figure 1.11). The organization is selling responsible parenting and gun safety. The copy delivers a tragic tale:

> Louis Taylor hid his .357 Magnum so well, it took his son 6 years to find it. Louis Taylor kept his handgun unloaded in a locked case. The bullets were kept hidden in another part of the house. How did his six-year-old son, Ron, end up dead? Like every child there was nothing in his house he didn't know about. If you think you can keep your handgun out of the hands of your children . . . please, think again.

Poverty. Poverty is correlated with changes in family structure (e.g., divorce, single women with children). In 1960, most poor families contained both men and women. By 2000, 53 percent of all poor families were female-headed (U.S. Census Bureau, 2000c). This has been referred to as the *feminization of poverty*. One-half of all children in the United States will live with a single parent at some point before reaching the age of eighteen (Macionis, 2002; Ellwood, 1988, 45–46). The increase in female-headed households is related to increasing rates of divorce, separation, and single parenting. These smaller households result in a large number of little, poorer households competing for a restricted number of affordable homes and decent jobs. The ad in figure 1.12 is sponsored by Dress for Success, a nonprofit organization that provides low-income women with used suits for job interviews and work.

Fig. 1.11

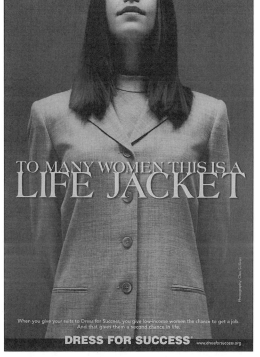

Fig. 1.12

Animal Rights

> I believe that mink are raised for being turned into fur coats and if I didn't wear fur coats those little animals would never have been born. So is it better not to have been born or to have lived for a year or two to have been turned into a fur coat? I don't know.
> —Barbi Benton, former Playboy bunny turned actress

This provocative ad (figure 1.13) was produced to persuade people like Barbi Benton to change their attitudes on the slaughter of mammals for the sake of fashion.

Homelessness. The poster "If Society Can Provide Housing for a Man Like This, Can't We Do More for the Homeless?" (figure 1.14) points to a glaring inconsistency in public policy. Why do we take better care of convicted mass murderers like Charles Manson than of the innocent homeless? Homelessness has now become criminalized in many urban areas.

Antiwar. The poster in figure 1.15 was used to protest the Desert Storm victory parade in New York City in 1991. The striking illustration is a photograph of the charred remains of an Iraqi war casualty. The copy reads: "On June 10th, the U.S. war machine that burned thousands of humans will get a 'victory' parade . . . It was right to resist the war. Resist this parade of shame." This antiwar message again became timely in the wake of what President George W. Bush called "The Battle of Iraq" in 2003.

Safe Sex. This advocacy poster sponsored by ACT-UP (figure 1.16), perhaps the most vocal AIDS advocacy organization, is entitled "Safe Sex Is Hot Sex." The poster was created for the "Red Hot and Blue Project" in New York in the 1980s. It is reminiscent of that time, with the dawn of the AIDS era and a presidential administration that refused to recognize the epidemic as a national health concern. Consequently, Ronald Reagan dragged his feet in funding research that would identify and treat the killer disease.

Fig. 1.13

Fig. 1.14

Fig. 1.15

Subvertising

Subvertising overthrows or subverts mainstream ads. It uses the power of brand recognition and brand hegemony either against itself or to promote an unrelated value or idea. It essentially turns rationalization on its head—a major theme in postmodernism. Subvertising has also been called "culture jamming" (Twitchell 1996) and "counteradvertising" (Henshel 1990). Subvertising uses the same motivational appeal as commercial advertising.

An example of the first type of subvertising is the sabotage of the Marlboro man (see chapter 6, "Segmentation in Cigarette Marketing"). The illustration in figure 6.3, with its two rugged cowboys on horseback, has the distinct look of a Marlboro ad. But the brief boldface copy—"Bob, I've got emphysema"—is startling.

Another example of the first type is the attacks on the use of sex to sell beer (figure 1.17). "Quit using our cans to sell yours" proclaims the copy of an ad showing disgruntled women, referring to the use of scantily clad women in Budweiser beer ads.

The ad's sponsor, the Dangerous Promises Coalition in Los Angeles, was prepared to pay the going rate for billboard space. Nevertheless, the ads were rejected by all of the mainstream billboard companies in the area. The coalition finally managed to purchase space on a portable billboard and arranged for it to be displayed in Hollywood at Sunset and Highland. With no additional promotion, photographs of the billboard appeared in the *Los Angeles Times* the day before the Wine Institute decided to revise its advertising code.

The San Francisco branch of the Dangerous Promises Coalition created the counterad shown in figure 1.18. A media firm originally agreed to sell billboard space but reneged two weeks later. The coalition was twice more rejected. It then

Fig. 1.16

Fig. 1.17

Fig. 1.18

used media refusal to accept its subvertising to
launch the Bay Area media campaign.

The second type of subvertising—the use of advertising to promote an unrelated value or product—is
demonstrated in the ad in figure 1.19; it exploits the
famous Tommy Hilfiger logo and copy on T-shirts,
baseball caps, and neckties to proclaim a message of
forgiveness and salvation.

Calvin Klein, one of the greatest purveyors of consumer culture in the late twentieth century, uses some
of the most sexually explicit advertising representa-   Fig. 1.19
tions to sell clothes. His famous "ck" logo has also been
exploited to advertise a different message of hope and good news. The logo is put on
sweatshirts and T-shirts underneath the copy "Christ is King."

Figure 1.20a, a World War II poster by J. Howard Miller, Westinghouse for War Production Coordinating Committee, features Rosie the Riveter, an icon and inspirational
symbol for women in the workforce during wartime. Figure 1.20b, an ad by Proctor &
Gamble, subvertizes this well-known image—only this time, Rosie has "Tampax was
there" tattooed on her flexed right bicep.

Institutional Advertising

> [Institutional advertising is] designed to remind consumers that this company has
> been a part of their communities for a long time and should continue to be a part of
> their lives.
>
> —Gail Baker Woods, *Advertising and Marketing to the New Majority*

Fig. 1.20a   Fig. 1.20b

Corporations, industries, and governments sometimes use advertising as bureaucratic propaganda, just as national governments use psychological warfare or religious cults use proselytization. Bureaucratic propaganda tries "to bring an audience around to the special viewpoint of a particular bureaucracy" (Henshel 1990, 61).

Institutional advertising attempts to persuade a public audience to adopt a certain attitude about a particular firm or institution (Henshel 1990). With traditional advertising, a company merely emits commercial messages to sell a particular brand of automobile. If institutional advertising is carried off successfully, it can be used to justify enormous profit.

Institutional advertising tries to create an emotional bond between consumers and the company. For example, Timberland's ad (figure 1.21) decrees: Give racism the boot. Institutional advertising sometimes subtly acknowledges the power of the consumer—an understanding that a company's success or failure is based on how consumers respond to the corporation. Institutional advertising is aiming for a long-term, loyal relationship with the consumer. Institutional advertising is sponsored by for-profit companies, government agencies, or national governments, often to undo negative publicity.

Hybritising

Hybritising combines two types of advertising. For example, the ad in figure 1.22 uses two sponsors: Mothers Against Drunk Driving (MADD) and Allstate Insurance. Both organizations benefit from the amelioration of drunk driving. Since MADD is a nonprofit organization, it is advocacy advertising. But because Allstate is a profit-seeking corporation, it is institutional advertising; since the ad combines both types, it may be referred to as hybritising. The ad is stirring: an auto key impaling an olive in a martini; the brief copy: Killer cocktail.

Fig. 1.21   Fig. 1.22

Overview

This book examines the ways in which cultural symbols, ethnic minorities, and women are displayed in advertisements. There is focus on print ads since they are a significant part of the advertising arena. Approximately 50 percent of advertising revenues are earmarked for various print media; 22 percent are spent on television commercials (Kellner 1988).

Consider how advertising, often unintentionally, reflects our values, belief systems, and behavior (in addition to shopping and purchasing). This is the *latent*, or unintended, function of advertising. This book is chiefly concerned with the latent consequences of advertising, not its manifest objectives and activities of selling brand goods and services.

This book expands Goffman's (1976) and Kilbourne's (1989) analyses of gender differences by examining images of minority men and women in advertising. The ideal images of men and women that advertising presents to the consumer in order to sell products or services are examined. The way that minority men and women are often held to the white standard of perfection is critiqued. This has significant implications for assimilation, identity, and racial integration. For example, the *copycat*: the concurrent production of two nearly identical ads except for the ethnic background of the models. This uses one approach for two different (e.g., black and white) target audiences.

Three possible models for the way minorities are presented in ads are examined. First is the notion of *equal presentation:* whites and minorities are shown in exactly the same way, regardless of any cultural, economic, or physical differences. Consequently, if whites are presented predominantly as middle-class persons in middle-class settings, ethnic minorities are portrayed similarly, regardless of actual differences in class distribution. Analyses of copycat ads (chapter 4) support this framework. Furthermore, since the structural obstructions to the procurement of wealth are not visible in the world of advertising, the tacit message is that a group's relative indigence is the outcome of inner failure, a notion compliant with the ideology of the American dream.

Second is the *social-reality* model. There is also evidence for this prototype. Since minorities are more likely to be poor or in lower-status occupations than whites, ads reflect any differences that currently exist in society. This realistic approach draws the public's attention to the very real inequalities in our society. However, both the equal-presentation and social-reality models ultimately fall short.

Finally, a case can be made that *cultural attitudes* toward ethnic minorities affect the way minorities are portrayed in advertising. Cultural attitudes held by whites toward people of color affect how they are depicted in ads and television commercials.

Chapter 3 focuses on the use of fear, intimidation, and violence in advertising. Advertisers have exploited, maintained, and developed women's fear of being pursued or sexually assaulted. Numerous ads reveal this disturbing trend of violent images. While some messages are meant to be subliminal, others are blatant. Goffman's concept of *mock assault* demonstrates this theme. Chapter 3 also analyzes visual representations of the child as sex object in advertising, another distressing trend.

2

Visual Attraction, Body Display, and Advertising

[Advertising gains] power as it colonizes distant aspects of life, making them part of a coherent pattern, [it is not] an oppressive dictatorship forcing innocent and helpless consumers to give up their better judgment in order to aggrandize some evil mercantile power.

—James B. Twitchell, *Adcult USA*

Commercialism is our better judgment.

—James B. Twitchell, *Adcult USA*

Successful advertising is able to manifest rich, intimate, and astute cultural and subcultural messages and representations as well as universal biological desires. This chapter borrows from the dramaturgy of Goffman (1976) and Desmond Morris's human zoology (1996) and visual anthropology (1986, 1977; Morris et al. 1979).

Morris's framework draws its material from three main sources: (1) the information about our past as uncovered by paleontologists and based on the fossil and other remains of our prehistoric ancestors; (2) the information accessible from the animal behavior studies of the comparative ethologists, based on elaborate observations of a wide range of animal species, especially monkeys and apes—our closest living relatives; and (3) the information that can be constructed by simple, direct observation of the most fundamental and widely shared behavior patterns of human specimens from contemporary cultures.

In deconstructing advertising from a postmodern perspective, there is special focus on visual cues such as expression, posture, and gesture. Three basic techniques used to establish superiority or power are size, attention, and positioning (Goffman 1976). Body language and nonverbal communication reveal an actor's mood or attitude. They are also important for corroborating or disconfirming verbal communication and speech patterns. Sometimes nonverbal communication clashes with the words that an actor utters. For example, signs of lying include blinking (to escape the stress of lying), covering the mouth with one's hand or an object (to "hide" the lie), and shrugging the hand—rotating the wrist so that the palm is facing up—(to plead ignorance or ask forgiveness). Human beings are complex creatures, but we still are animals. Just as a dog cannot conceal excitement (shown through wagging its tail) or fear (shown through curling its tail between its legs), a human being reveals a lot by a simple gesture.

Human Evolution

> The urge to have sex is in us because we are all descended from people who had an
> urge to have sex with each other; those who feel no urge left behind no descen-
> dants. Evolution is more about reproduction of the fittest than survival of the
> fittest.
> —Matt Ridley, *The Red Queen: Sex and the Evolution of Human Nature*

To understand the subtle nuances of human body language, we start with our human
evolution from apes. Apes originally lived in trees, eventually climbed down, and
finally began to walk upright. This produced a momentous characteristic change in
genetic evolution. Walking upright exposed the sexual organs. Sex in the animal king-
dom has never been the same!

In animals, courtship and mating are controlled by the female's estrous cycle. When
the female is ready to copulate, she sends out a pungent odor produced by her body's
chemistry. This is a signal to males of the same species that she may be approached. A
strong sex drive in animals guarantees the continuation of their genetic makeup. Lions,
for example, copulate every half hour for three days, dramatically increasing the
chances of pregnancy. Some lions mate for life, although most do not. Human beings
and other animals produce pheromones—chemical substances that serve especially as
a stimulus to individuals of the same species for sexual and other behavioral responses.

Some animals have complex and long drawn-out rituals of courtship. Others (goril-
las, for example) have no courtship at all, to speak of. The male of some species tries to
make the female notice him through preening, displays of strength, or direct confrontation with competing males. For baboons, intense courtship is abandoned in favor
of an unromantic yet efficient eight-second mating act. For some animals, copulation is
merely perfunctory. Chimpanzees, for example, display a general lack of interest in sexual behavior; they also tend not to have lasting partners. Humans, on the other hand,
are the sexiest animals alive. Unlike other animals, the human female doesn't advertise
when she is biologically available for mating. The male does not know when she is fertile. Unlike that of animals whose sexual availability is seasonal, humans' sexual activity is not seasonal; they can mate anytime.

Lust—the urge for sex—is an instinct that drives all species. Sex is a "genetic joint
venture" (Ridley 1994). Darwinian evolutionary theory maintains that certain characteristics evolve because they keep members of a species alive. Other attributes evolve
because they keep the species reproducing; for example, the peacock's brilliant
plumage attracts the peahen (Morris 1956). The evolution of characteristics because of
their reproductive benefits, rather than their survival benefits, is known as *sexual selection* (Buss 1994). In animals, males often tempt females to have sex with them by offering resources, such as food, while females flaunt their fertility. Among humans, too,
men and women use dozens of tactics to attract a mate. Men generally flash their
resources (e.g., money, designer clothes, expensive jewelry, and automobiles) and
their power (athletic prowess, work achievement). Women are more likely to display
evidence of their youth, health, and fertility in the way they dress and accessorize
themselves.

Advertisers use the display of material resources as a symbol of sexual selection.
Consequently, ads also sell cultural representations of success (figure 2.1)—the good
life, if you will. The Cutty Sark ad advises: "This is a glass of Cutty Sark. It won't make

you hip. It won't make you successful. And it won't change your life. And if you drink it simply because you like the way it tastes, your life is probably pretty good already."

Our sexual urges and our contemporary dating and mating behavior all have their roots in sexual selection. In the hedonistic pursuit of sexual conquests, men and women derogate their competition, deceive members of the other sex, and even subvert their own mates.

Fig. 2.1

Competition and Sexual Selection

Early afternoon television . . . used to be the entertainment ghetto for women.

—James B. Twitchell, *Adcult USA*

Symbolic of sexual selection, advertising sometimes pits women against other women as fierce competitors (see figures 2.2 and 2.3). There is typically conflict, albeit often subtle, between women. The message may instill in women, especially young women, an attitude of alienation from other women.

Advertising provides gender with a double standard with respect to youth. It is acceptable for men to age; a little bit of gray hair in men conveys an image that is considered to be distinguished. However, for women, gray hair is taboo and denotes an image considered to be unattractive. In fact, any sign of aging in women is not received favorably. Advertising delivers a commentary to women that, to secure the fascination and preference of men, they will relinquish the approval and sisterhood of women— and that the sacrifice is worthwhile.

Consistent with the notion of sexual selection, advertising also places men in competition with each other over the tribute of a woman. The copy in figure 2.4 urges, "Give her a diamond before someone else does."

Fig. 2.2

Fig. 2.3

Fig. 2.4

Male-Female Genetic Conflict

The differences between men's and women's bodies are a direct consequence of evolution (Ridley 1994). Women's bodies evolved to meet the demands of bearing children and of gathering plant food. Men's bodies evolved to meet the demands of competition within a male hierarchy, fighting over women, and providing food and shelter for their family.

For the same reason, men and women also have different minds. Sexually, these differences make men competitive and powerful, controlling wealth and seeking fame. Over time, women who chose rich and powerful men left more descendants, and, therefore, the urge to mate with wealthy, powerful men influences even some of today's women. The characteristic that a woman can most profitably seek in mates that will increase the health of her children is not more sperm, but greater resources (such as money).

A man, on the other hand, seeks a mate who will produce babies to carry on his genes—the more the merrier. Men are genetically programmed to prefer younger women, since they have health and years of fertility on their side. Those cues sexually arouse men. A pretty face and shapely legs, buttocks, and breasts signal youth and health and tap into the male's primary urge: to reproduce.

The instinct to keep the species going takes an interesting turn when men and women clash in their hardwired urges. Males reproduce best by planting their seed in as many females as possible. Females reproduce best by choosing the best male to father their brood—not just the male with the best genetic material but the most likely to remain and provide food and protection. Consequently, behavior that is in the male's genetic interest directly conflicts with the female's genetic interest (Diamond 1997).

Sexual Attraction

Human socialization processes are often segregated by gender. For example, boys and girls are often separated during various activities at school. Indifference and, sometimes, even hostile relations develop between groups of boys and groups of girls. Although they may be classmates or neighbors, boys and girls are often more strangers than friends. This changes, however, as sexual development and puberty approach. There is rediscovery; unfamiliarity and hostility are replaced by curiosity.

The male gang or group loses its power as the loyalties of its members shift outside the group to females. Members of both genders begin to preen and display courtship rituals. There is parading, visual contact, and cruising. The exposure of one's flesh seems to trigger primeval sexual motivations in members of the other sex (see figures 2.5–2.7). Advertisers are deft at displaying visual cues to stimulate sexual appetites (2.8–2.10).

Attraction is both socially constructed and biologically shaped to be an instantaneous decision. Whether a female is attracted to a male or vice versa is based on biological unconscious signals of sexual interest. Just as female animals are attracted to power and exhibitions of strength in males of the same species as signs of health and fertility, human females are also drawn toward masculine power and strength displays (2.11–2.12). Broad shoulders with a narrow waist define the classic triangular shape (2.13). Moreover, a thick muscular neck conveys a protector image. For females,

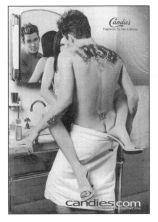

Fig. 2.5

Fig. 2.6

Fig. 2.7

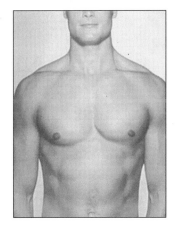

Fig. 2.8

Fig. 2.9

Fig. 2.10

Fig. 2.11

Fig. 2.12

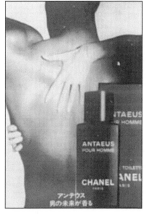

Fig. 2.13

a small waist (2.14) and a high-pitched voice are signs of vulnerability which appeal to a male's self-identification, through cultural transmission, as a protector.

Large pupils are sexually appealing, and this dilation occurs unconsciously during arousal (see figure 2.15). Youth is also a sign of health and sex appeal (see figure 2.16). (Youth is a major characteristic of the provocateur; see chapter 3.) Women use foundation makeup to hide small wrinkles, because eliminating any signs of aging contributes toward a more desirable and attractive image. Skin tones are warmed up in order to project a healthy sexual glow.

An exaggerated leg length appears to be more adult and, therefore, more sexual (see figure 2.17). Hair grooming is also an important component of attraction and gender display (see figure 2.18). A smile symbolizes approval or attraction (see figure 2.19). Unconscious blushing is considered to be very sexual. Blushing starts in the cheeks and spreads to the rest of the face and often to other parts of the head and body. Males are attracted to female blushing because it signifies innocence. Makeup mimics a blush, with an emphasis on red cheeks (see figure 2.20).

How female breasts are displayed is a key part of sexual attraction. The cleavage area

Fig. 2.14

Fig. 2.15

Fig. 2.16

Fig. 2.17

Fig. 2.18

Fig. 2.19

between the breasts is perhaps the epicenter of display and stimulation of interest. In fact, breast cleavage and the cleavage of the buttocks are considered to be very sexual. In truth, there is a great similarity between the appearance of the two types of cleavage (see figures 2.21 and 2.22).

In the ad shown in figure 2.23a, there is even an uncanny resemblance between the shoulder and buttocks cleavage. The carefully placed woman's shoulder in the foreground combines with a background figure to create an exact image of nude buttocks (see figure 2.23b). Also, in the insert photograph, the long-neck beer bottles are strategically located as phallic symbols emerging downward from the man's crotch area and upward toward the "buttocks" cleavage. Advertisers are the kings of soft pornography.

Fig. 2.20

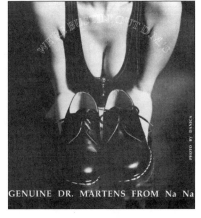
Fig. 2.21

Fig. 2.22

Fig. 2.23a

Fig. 2.23b

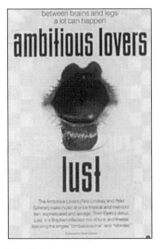

between brains and legs
a lot can happen

ambitious lovers

lust

The Ambitious Lovers (Arto Lindsay and Peter
Scherer) make music at once tropical and metropolitan, sophisticated and savage. Their Elektra debut,
Lust, is a Brazilian-inflected mix of funk and finesse
featuring the singles "Umbabarauma" and "Monde."

Fig. 2.24

Females color their lips in a symbol of sexual arousal (see figure 2.24). Large female lips mimic the female labia.

Cultural Variance in Attraction and Body Display

Although much of human sexual attraction and mating, as in other animals, is biologically based, there is one major distinction between human beings and animals: impression management. Humans are much more sophisticated; we can control what signals we give out and we are usually aware of how our body displays are being received or interpreted.

There is a great deal of cultural variance in sexual attractiveness. Although in many cultures, thin females are considered to be sexually attractive, in the South Pacific, heavier women are more desirable than thin ones. Standards of beauty often vary significantly between cultures. For example, for thousands of years, Eskimo women have tattooed their faces, arms, and bodies—a practice that some Eskimo women continue today. At the turn of the twentieth century, anthropologists dubbed this custom as "universal" within Eskimo culture.

Tattoos are painfully sewn onto the body, one stitch at a time. Skin-piercing is never pleasant, but nose and forehead punctures are excruciating. The tattoo designs are elaborate (e.g., an intricately woven Celtic knot) and require a full day's work to sew. The newly tattooed person takes a week to recover. Major swelling is not unusual. A high threshold for pain, not complaining, and a capacity for quick recovery are still venerated throughout rural Alaska. Extensive tattoos not only signify beauty but also advertise tenacity. The more pain a woman endured, the more beautiful she became, according to cultural values.

Sometimes cultural differences are subtle. What is obvious to an insider may go unnoticed to an outsider. For example, in some Asian Indian cultures, thick eyebrows in females are thought to be sexually alluring. In our culture, a lean, toned body shape for females is the mold. For males, a lean and muscular look is in.

Attraction and Courtship

> Human compassion springs from the fact that four to five million years ago, our ancestors became bipedal—existing on two legs.
> —Richard Leakey, paleontologist

Despite a wide variety of cultural standards of beauty and attractiveness, a healthy body with unblemished skin is nearly universally accepted as the archetype (see figure 2.25). (Flawlessness is also a chief characteristic of the provocateur.)

Perhaps one of the most fascinating aspects of cultural variance in mating and attraction is the social channels that provide opportunities for gender interaction and rituals of display and attraction. In our culture, opportunities seem nearly endless to meet and exchange information, whether visual or verbal, with a potential mate or sexual partner. Something as innocuous as walking a dog can provide a situation to bring two people together. The Masai in Africa leap up and down in dance to display attraction. Mate selection starts as early as age ten or eleven. The young male announces his personal interest in a girl by flicking her with a strand of his long hair. The flick and her reaction as revealed through facial expression, body posture, or gesture provide an exchange of information.

In some Chinese villages, in order to overcome shyness, groups of boys sing to groups of girls without facing them. The girls respond with an improvised song of their own. They may sing about something as innocent as the number of tractors in their village. What they sing about is not important; the point is that this is a ritual of expressing interest in those of the other gender and discerning their reaction.

Two events must occur: an initial display of interest (e.g., through eye contact) and an approving reply (e.g., a smile). If these occur, interaction can progress to the next step: verbal communication. Conversation, even mindless chatter, can lead to touch or other body contact. Laughter is affirmation and sure sign of interest (see figure 2.26).

As a relationship starts, the couple symbolically returns to childhood, even infancy, with expressions of intimacy, rocking, cuddling, and falling in love (see figure 2.27).

In courtship, the first time that a new couple spends together often involves the ritual of feeding. The couple, in sharing a meal, displays affection by smiling, leaning toward each other, touching, holding hands, kissing, and even feeding each other, a sign of intimacy. Food sharing is the basis of human society. Gifts, such as flowers, are offered. Courtship is exploited by business opportunities and seasonal holidays (e.g., Valentine's Day and Christmas) to provide gifts as displays of interest, affection and attraction, and intimacy.

Couples use rituals of display to show that the relationship is exclusive and to express trust: holding hands, putting an arm around one's partner's waist or shoulder, a double embrace, facing each other at close distance, touching one partner's knee or leg. Such displays often signal the beginning of intimacy (see figures 2.28–2.29).

In addition to cycles of fertility, several other biological traits make humans' sexual activities very different from animals'. Human beings are much less hairy than other mammals. More skin, which is very sensitive to touch, is exposed. This means that

Fig. 2.25   Fig. 2.26   Fig. 2.27

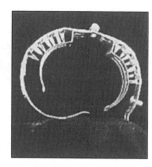

Fig. 2.30

Fig. 2.28   Fig. 2.29

Fig. 2.31

humans are more prone to sexual arousal than animals. Additionally, animal males have a bone in their penis, giving them an instant erection, and making sexual arousal unnecessary or superfluous.

Advertisers have capitalized on the nature of human sexual arousal. However, they have fed us mixed signals on the nature of our sexual desires. On one hand, sexual impulse is negative, something to be controlled and subdued. For example, at the turn of the century, wet dreams (spermatorrhea) were seen as an unconscious but energy-draining bad habit. In 1905 an aluminum collar with fourteen sharp spikes was marketed; it was designed to fit around a flaccid penis and awaken the wearer in case of erection (see figure 2.30). On the other hand, sex is viewed as pleasurable, stimulating, and invigorating (for men, at least). The prostate-gland warmer shown in figure 2.31 was advertised in 1918. The user plugged the device into an electrical outlet and inserted it in himself. This patented wonder, called the Thermalaid, heated to approximately 100 degrees Fahrenheit. This product was designed to stimulate the abdominal wall, in turn titillating sexual drive. The electrical cord was ten feet long—in case the user felt compelled to jump into the air. These objects are found in the Museum of Questionable Medical Devices in Minneapolis, Minnesota.

Subconscious Seduction

> An advertising agency is eighty-five percent confusion and fifteen percent commission.
>
> —Fred Allen

We are exposed at a minimum to hundreds of advertisements every day. Despite this exposure, we often do not actually notice or focus on them. Ads seem to seep quietly into the back room of our consciousness. Unobserved and tacitly approved, advertising socializes and conditions us without our even knowing it.

Provocative subliminal messages are used that are designed to influence and motivate consumers to purchase particular products and services. These are messages camouflaged within the ads. Evaluation of such ads shows us their use of a sophisticated applied psychology. It also permits us to deconstruct ads and view their concealed or secret messages and maneuverings.

Subliminal. Subconscious. Unconscious. Below the threshold of awareness. Advertisers know that you spend an average time of two seconds looking at an ad while flipping through a magazine. That doesn't leave much time to persuade you to buy a particular brand of product. The ad is meant to grab your attention. Even though you do not remember an ad, if it stimulates a desire, it may register on your subconscious. If an ad registers on your subconscious, the theory is that it will prompt you to buy that brand. Since you cannot be aware of your subconscious, by definition, there really is no way to determine whether subliminal ads are effective.

In the ad for More cigarettes shown in figure 2.32a, the woman's heel is positioned so that it becomes a phallic symbol thrusting toward her genital region (see figure 2.32b).

Lipstick ads often use lipstick as a phallic symbol to represent oral (figures 2.33–2.35) or anal (figure 2.36) sex. Phallic symbols connote particular meanings between actors (figure. 2.37).

Fig. 2.32a

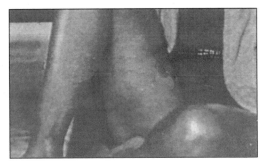

Fig. 2.32b

Fig. 2.33

Fig. 2.34

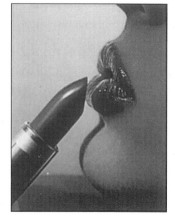

Fig. 2.35   Fig. 2.36   Fig. 2.37

Relative Size

Goffman (1976) uses the concept *relative size* as a visual indication of comparative power and authority. He found that men were characteristically pictured above women in ads (see figure 2.38). Male relative size over females in print ads reflects traditional cultural attitudes of male power and authority over females. Figure 2.39, a 1946 Chen Yu ad for women's cosmetics, exemplifies this. When women were shown being relatively larger than men, they had a higher social status than the men. In contemporary advertising, however, there seems to be an equivalent proportion of ads where women display relative size over men. For example, figure 2.40 displays couple intimacy with a woman as protector of a man. Goffman's finding that males always dominate females through relative size in advertising no longer holds.

Fig. 2.38   Fig. 2.39   Fig. 2.40

Multiple Meanings

> Advertisers, not governments, are the primary censors of media content in the United States today.
>
> —C. Edwin Baker

Advertisers often use multiple meaning as a humorous hook. Figures 2.41–2.43 contain copy with sexual innuendo. Figure 2.41: She went all the way; 2.42: Realign the troops; and 2.43: Hidden Agenda.

Advertising attempts to co-opt and commodify the very notion of "women's liberation." Perhaps the best known of this exploitative trend is the long-running Virginia Slims "You've Come a Long Way, Baby" campaign. It is paradoxical that an advertiser associates a "liberated" woman with smoking (Kellner 1988) and addiction (Kilbourne 1989). The campaign also tells women that they have come a long way, yet it calls them "baby"—in the same sentence! In fact, women have not come a long way. They still earn only fifty-seven to sixty cents for every dollar that men earn, given equal education and equal experience.

Advertising picks up the slang of popular culture, the dialect of ethnic subcultures, and the jargon of social movements. There is often a resulting deflation of the worth and importance of gender equality. For example, in the ad shown in figure 2.44, the copy says, "We believe women should be *running the country*" (emphasis added). However, the illustration of the woman jogging belies the copy's insinuation of women's political power.

The ad in figure 2.45 offers a similar innuendo. "We support radical movements," reads the copy. Yet the illustration merely shows women in various types of exercise. Again, a double entendre: exercise versus a radical social or political movement.

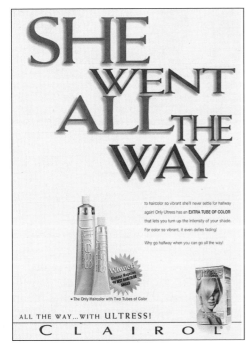

Fig. 2.41

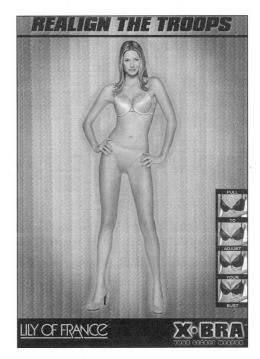

Fig. 2.42

Fig. 2.43

Fig. 2.44

Fig. 2.45

Fig. 2.46

In the Virginia Slims ad in figure 2.46, the copy proclaims, "The Sultan of Bundi had nothing against women—he thought everyone should own two or three." Here the enslavement of women is trivialized.

In 1984, when Democratic presidential nominee Walter Mondale chose Geraldine Ferraro as his vice presidential running mate, the Loveland, Colorado, *Reporter-*

Fig. 2.47

Fig. 2.48

Fig. 2.49

Herald published the headline "It's a girl!" (see figure 2.47). Though not an ad, the headline is clearly a public picture (Goffman 1976; see "Public and Private Pictures") and is in the same genre of language with multiple meanings used in the ads discussed here.

Figure 2.48 trivializes the glass ceiling, subtle discrimination that effectively blocks the movement of women into the highest positions in organizations.

Perhaps unintended meaning can be the most humorous or crude. Figure 2.49 is an ad for locum (note the lowercase "l"). The Swedish company intended a warm, embracing effect to celebrate the holiday season by replacing the "o" in locum with a heart. Instead, it can be perceived as a sexual fetish.

In sum, we see double meanings that contain sexual innuendo and trivialize the women's movement and use language for humor at the expense of women.

Body-Chopping/Dismemberment

Women's bodies are often dismembered or hacked apart in ads (see figures 2.50–2.55). When their bodies are separated into parts, women cease to be seen as whole persons. This perpetuates the notion that a woman's body is not linked to her mind, soul, and emotions.

Women's body parts are sometimes portrayed as inanimate objects: mannequin (figures 2.52–2.53), ice cream cone (figure 2.54), and flower (figure 2.55). Dismemberment or body-chopping appears to occur in advertising much more frequently for women than men. The implication is that women are objects and therefore less than human.

Advertising that depicts women's bodies without faces, heads, and feet implies that all that is really important about a woman lies between her neck and her knees. The lack of a head symbolizes a woman without a brain. A faceless woman has no individuality. A woman without feet is immobile and therefore submissive.

Fig. 2.50

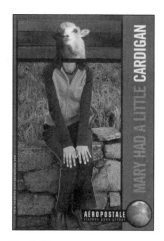

Fig. 2.51

Fig. 2.52

Fig. 2.53

Fig. 2.54

Fig. 2.55

Function Ranking

Goffman (1976) uses the concept of *function ranking* to denote a particular structure of gender inequality in which the male model in an ad performs the important role while the female model occupies a less meaningful role (figures 2.56–2.58). When children are photographed in print ads or shown on television commercials, the boy is usually active while the girl is passive.

The conscious or unconscious omission or underrepresentation of women and ethnic minorities in function-ranking activities in mass media constitutes symbolic annihilation. A classic example is the Marlboro Man campaign begun in the 1950s (figure 2.59). The icon of a Western image of ruggedness, masculinity, and independence (Kellner 1988)—a modern masculine archetype (Katz 1995)—is used in ads for other brands as well, including Camel Lights. The Marlboro Man (along with his clones—figure 2.60) is pervasive in contemporary advertising images of masculinity over into postmodern mass media.

Besides gender differences in function ranking, there are also racial differences. Using qualitative content analysis to study racial representation in advertising on children's television, Seiter (1995) found that black children tend to be shown as passive observers of their white playmates. This type of function ranking reveals that the

Fig. 2.56

Fig. 2.57

Fig. 2.59

Fig. 2.60

Fig. 2.58

underpinnings of white supremacy, even if in more subtle ways than in the past, still inform mainstream images of both whites and blacks.

Although Goffman (1976) did not use ads with women in function-ranking positions, they are not uncommon nowadays (2.61). Nevertheless, when women are displayed in function-ranking positions, men are absent rather than less passive. The ad in figure 2.61 is positive in the sense that women are displayed in function-ranking positions. Women in beachwear are portrayed as actually having interests and hobbies such as surfing rather than just playing the role of the provocateur. However, the ad also is problematic: it links alcohol consumption to a high-risk activity like surfing.

The ad in figure 2.62 also displays a gender-reversal spin on function ranking. The illustration shows a young, muscular man in the center of the frame with his girlfriend holding on to him with an approving expression. The copy reads, "This Coast Guard swimmer rescued a drowning fisherman at sea" (traditional function ranking). Then, in parentheses, it unexpectedly states: "Her boyfriend just dropped by to bring lunch" (gender reversal, function ranking).

In short, postmodern advertising sometimes uses the gender reversal of function ranking to catch the consumer's attention. Nevertheless, traditional function ranking remains a big draw for marketers.

Licensed Withdrawal

Advertising sometimes portrays people, customarily women, as psychologically removed from the situation, disoriented, or defenseless. Goffman calls this *licensed withdrawal*. The model is shown "spacing out," as in figure 2.63; the phone left off the hook symbolizes her unavailability.

Advertisements tend to show a woman drifting or in licensed withdrawal while in physical contact

Fig. 2.61

Fig. 2.62

Fig. 2.63

with a man (see figure 2.64). This symbolizes the woman's dependence on the man and the man's responsibility for the woman's welfare.

There are other ways to indicate licensed withdrawal. Goffman (1976) notes that placing the finger to the mouth, as in figure 2.65, also represents licensed withdrawal. Moreover, licensed withdrawal sometimes takes the form of surprise, remorse, or shock expressed by placing one or both hands over or near the mouth (see figure 2.66).

Body-Clowning

When men are shown alone in ads, they are often portrayed as secure, powerful, and serious, according to Goffman (1976). Even in their underwear, they usually look dignified (figure 2.67). Women, in contrast, are pictured as playful clowns (see figure 2.68), supporting the attitude that women are childish and cannot be taken seriously. They are often depicted with silly arm, leg, and head gestures. However, I have more recently been able to find many ads that depict men in body-clowning positions, as in figure 2.69.

Fig. 2.64

Fig. 2.65

Fig. 2.66

Fig. 2.67

Fig. 2.68

Fig. 2.69

Ritualization of Subordination

People in charge of their own lives typically stand upright, alert and ready to meet the world. In contrast, the bending of the body conveys unpreparedness, submissiveness, and appeasement (Goffman 1976). Even animals display rituals of subordination. A wolf, for example, bares its throat to concede a fight. This prevents the dominant wolf from having to kill the subordinate one. It also establishes a pecking order, or hierarchy. As a further example, a dog will automatically put its tail between its legs and lower its ears when it is afraid. In humans, a similar symbol of deference is lowering oneself physically (see figures 2.70–2.71). Head cant is also sometimes used as a ritual of subordination (see figure 2.72). Women are often shown in ads reclining or lying on objects. Nevertheless, contemporary advertising also shows men displaying rituals of subordination to women.

Feminine Touch/Masculine Grip

There are even gender differences in the way hands are shown in ads (2.73–2.74). Women are portrayed barely touching, delicately holding, or tenderly caressing men, objects, or themselves. On the other hand, men are depicted grasping, squeezing, clenching, manipulating, shaping, or gripping objects. Sometimes women are represented touching themselves, a sign that one's body is delicate and precious (2.75).

Gay- and Lesbian-Image Advertising

The Reverend Jerry Falwell, founder of the now-defunct political action group the Moral Majority, alerted followers to oppose an ad produced by Anheuser-Busch for Bud Light, in which two men are seen from the back holding outstretched hands (figure 2.76). The hullabaloo began when the beer company ran an ad April 22, 1999, in EXP, a bimonthly gay magazine in St. Louis. The ad was purchased to promote the company's sponsorship of a gay pride festival. Anheuser-Busch had planned to use the

Fig. 2.70

Fig. 2.71

Fig. 2.72

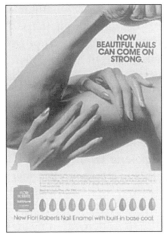

Fig. 2.73   Fig. 2.74   Fig. 2.75

ad of the men in a national campaign, but chose to test the waters first in St. Louis to gauge mainstream reaction.

"It is important that we get all of our friends and loved ones to call Anheuser-Busch immediately," Falwell warned on his weekly fax "Falwell Confidential."

"Please join me in opposing this advertisement as we work together to preserve Judeo-Christian standards on which this nation was founded. . . . Let's keep the heat on Anheuser-Busch so that they understand that pro-family Americans are terribly concerned about homosexual images coming into our homes through reckless advertising campaigns. Call today and have your friends and family call as well! Pastors, this Sunday please encourage your congregations to call. It is important that we all take action."

The swift and fervent disapproving reaction to this ad shows the hegemony of traditional gender images in the media. There is a range of masculinity and femininity in the postmodern media. Until recently, virtually all these images were at least implicitly heterosexual, especially in consumerism. The gay and lesbian communities face media that have traditionally been neglectful at best and often inhospitable. It is as if gays and lesbians are not even consumers.

According to the market strategies commonly used by advertisers, four criteria are used to develop target consumer

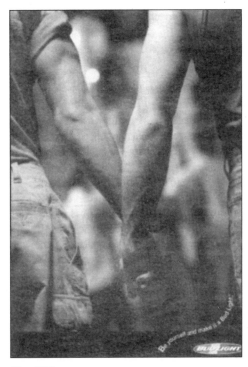

Fig. 2.76

groups. A population segment needs to be (1) identifiable, (2) accessible, (3) measurable, and (4) profitable (Astroff 1989). The problem is that advertisers do not know enough about the consumer shopping and spending habits of gays and lesbians, who cut across social class, ethnic, and age lines (three of the key characteristics used by advertising agencies to target population segments). To the degree that gays and lesbians are not recognizable or accessible, they are not calculable and consequently not predictable. If they are not predictable, they are not profitable.

Many gays and lesbians are not openly homosexual for a wide variety of reasons (e.g., discrimination in employment and housing, prejudice, family, religion). Such fear presents a further obstacle in reaching them. Moreover, advertisers know that if they appeal openly to a gay or lesbian market, their products and services will be negatively associated with homosexuality and may be avoided by heterosexual consumers (Stabiner 1982). Although gays and lesbians make up an estimated 10 percent of the general population—and up to 20 to 22 percent in major urban areas—advertisers have typically ignored them.

Despite problems in trying to market to the extremely internally diverse gay and lesbian communities, the basic meanings of masculinity and femininity are being redefined in light of both feminism and the gay and lesbian movement, including queer studies. Postmodern advertising has quickly reacted to shifting paradigms of gender ideology. Since the early 1980s, advertisers have become particularly interested in marketing to gays. Although a few ads target an exclusively gay audience, there is a more discreet method of reaching gay and lesbian populations through mainstream print media (Clark 1996). This is the best of both worlds for advertisers, who are able to reap financial rewards from both heterosexuals and homosexuals while avoiding alienating heterosexuals by being "so gay" and at the same time avoiding alienating gays by failing to recognize their existence. While advertisers aim to reach a larger market than just gays, they cannot afford to antagonize them either.

Advertising attempts to use a dual-market approach that will attract gays and lesbians in a subtle way that straight consumers will not notice. In short, advertisers try to reach gays and straights with the same ad, but in different ways. Because of the severe stigma that has historically been attached to homosexuality, gays have had to create coded behavior, using coded language and nonverbal displays of gesture, eye contact, expression, or posture (see figure 2.77).

This behavior informs the gay person for whom the message is intended—but not anybody else—that the messenger is gay. Now advertisers are trying to send these messages to gays. For example, these mainstream ads from Calvin Klein (figure 2.78), Versace (figures 2.79, 2.82–2.85), and Abercrombie and Fitch (figures 2.80–2.81) bear a striking resemblance to gay erotica.

This type of ad is much different from ads that directly court gay consumers (e.g., the Bud Light ad above). Here the intent is much more subtle or discreet. Advertisers typically do not own up to

Fig. 2.77

Fig. 2.78

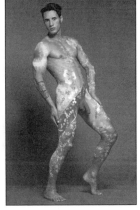

Fig. 2.79

Fig. 2.80

Fig. 2.81

Fig. 2.82

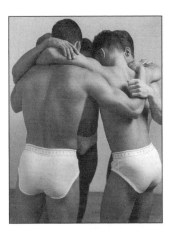

Fig. 2.83

Fig. 2.84

Fig. 2.85

this crafty type of marketing strategy. For example, marketing directors from Calvin Klein deny trying to appeal to gays (Stabiner 1982). Instead, they claim that they appeal to a much wider category of healthy, beautiful people interested in grooming.

Gay-image advertising displays same-sex couples or groups rather than heterosexual couples. This dual-marketing strategy has also been called *gay window advertising* (Stabiner 1982). In addition, advertisers sometimes use makeup and apparel to transform models into sexually ambiguous androgynes (figure 2.86).

Advertisers know that consumers interpret a particular ad on the basis of their life experiences, social position, and worldview. It is their hope that gays and lesbians will read into an ad certain subtextual elements that correspond to experiences with, or representations of, gay or lesbian culture (Clark 1996). If heterosex-

Fig. 2.86

ual consumers do not recognize these subcultural codes, advertisers can reach the gay and/or lesbian market without ever admitting their intent.

There is a trend in mainstream advertising to show apparent (yet usually subtle) images of gays and lesbians. Current ads court the gay and lesbian market with ambiguous visual codes and gay and lesbian style. For example, men are shown suggestively in the company of other men, instead of with women or by themselves. This, however, irrevocably deflates and directly changes the political meaning of a style of dress and presentation. What was once marginal, countercultural, and rebellious is now something chic, to be flattered through imitation. This market commodification quickly transforms the political arena into a fashion world of catwalks, photo shoots, and glamour. This certainly has consequences both for lesbian visibility in the social world and for lesbian identity politics.

Lesbians have a long tradition of resisting dominant cultural definitions of female beauty and fashion as a way of separating themselves politically from heterosexual culture and as a way of signaling their lesbianism to other lesbians (Clark 1996). This resistance to, or reformulating of, fashion codes traditionally accomplished two goals: it distinguished lesbians from straight women, and it simultaneously defied patriarchal structures. This lesbian-feminist antifashion was a potent symbol of refusal, an attempt to attack both capitalism and patriarchy in general and, more particularly, the fashion industry and the cultural images of femininity that fueled it (Stein 1989). The flannel-and-denim look is not so much a fashion statement as a counterstyle to replace the deception of fashion with an assumed freedom from gender expectations and materialistic pageantry.

Currently, nevertheless, not everyone in the lesbian community has adopted this "natural" look. Younger, urban lesbians, in particular, are defying this look and unmasking the contrived basis of counterfashion. They are showing us that one can be beautiful, ultrafeminine, and lesbian. Some lesbians are opposing the lesbian-feminist credo of political correctness that they view as stifling (Clark 1996). This is an attack against what is perceived as an intolerant fundamentalism within the lesbian community. This new "lifestyle" lesbianism sits in uncomfortable contrast with the old-style, politically correct strain of lesbianism. More important, this movement forces recognition and awareness of the diversity of lesbianism—lesbians of color, corporate lesbians, lesbian mothers, lesbian ministers, political-feminist lesbians.

During the past twenty years, advertisers have been trying to sell products and services mainly by linking them to personal values and lifestyles. Advertisers profitably connect demographic data (e.g., education, income, gender, ethnicity, age) to personal desires, self-images, and buying habits. In fact, in the case of yuppies, they actually helped to construct a lifestyle for consumers that was then marketed.

Advertisers are keenly aware that they are able to tap into the psyches of both straight and lesbian women who are fashion conscious and materialistic. Given lesbian feminism's countercultural, anticapitalist, antipatriarchal foundation, it is not surprising that the "traditional" lesbian community is highly critical of "lipstick lesbians," who are viewed as trading in their politics for self-absorbed materialism. However, one must look beyond the obvious: an irresponsible attitude toward spending or the virtually static character of the "natural look." Fashion-conscious lesbians are rejecting the assumed equivalence between fashion and identity. In this sense, fashion is indicative of personal freedom as well as political choice (Clark 1996).

Advertisers use a dual-market scheme, displaying gender innuendos that, in theory, indirectly appeal to lesbians. This dual approach of lesbian-image advertising refers not only to the two sets of interpretations by lesbians and heterosexual women but also to the multiple readings that exist among lesbians. Correspondingly, "lesbian verisimilitude" is the representation of general appearance, facial expression, and body language that are coded as "lesbian" according to current standards of style within lesbian communities (Ellsworth 1986). Lesbians are cognizant that they are not the principal audience for mainstream advertising. They also realize that an androgynous look, even on heterosexual models, is fashionable and therefore extremely marketable.

Gay- and lesbian-image advertising is like a Rorschach test that allows consumers to interpret "cultural forms in ways that are meaningful or pleasurable to them" (Fiske 1988, 247). The lesbian community delights in the way the dominant media try, but fail, to colonize lesbian space (Ellsworth 1986, 54). Even in images that exploit sexual ambiguity, specific parts of gay and lesbian subcultures remain isolated or unappropriated. In asserting such unarticulated psychological space as distinct and disconnected from mainstream heterosexist culture, gays and lesbians are no longer outsiders but insiders privy to the subtle nuances that produce a feeling of pleasure and solidarity among other discerning homosexuals.

In short, gay and lesbian communities have replied to the ostracism, neglect, and abasement detected in mainstream media dialogue by moving the arena of social pleasure to the core of their interpretive activities that reinforce their sense of individual and collective identity (Ellsworth 1986). There is a great deal of consensus about ads that contain coded messages discernible only to lesbians (Clark 1996). Given the preponderance of gay men and lesbians employed by major fashion publications, it is clear that gay- and lesbian-image advertising is more than a mere intellectual construct or classificatory exercise. The concept of gay- and lesbian-image advertising is theoretically significant because it sits in direct contrast to earlier heterosexist feminist conceptions of advertising.

Such previous analyses interpreted ads as endorsing the omnipotent male attitude that women are merely passive bodies to be incessantly ogled and sexually exploited for hedonistic purposes. "These conclusions were based on a conspiracy theory that placed ultimate power in the hands of corporate patriarchy and relegated no power or sense of agency to the female spectator" (Clark 1996, 147).

While gay men and lesbians may take pleasure in ads with unarticulated messages, advertisers play upon a material and ideological tension that concurrently appropriates segments of gay and lesbian subculture. Such ads position gay and lesbian interpretation in relation to consumer activities. This dialectic or simultaneous interplay between commercial exploitation and autonomous identity seems to be par for the course in any capitalistic economic mode of production. Gay-image advertising is a rational elaboration of capitalist development, one that likely will usher in more direct forms of marketing.

Targeting gays and lesbians, however, cannot be said to stem from a possible growing approval of homosexuality as an acceptable lifestyle. It is really all a matter of money. Capitalism creates tension; it weakens the bonds that once kept families together, but, ideologically, it drives people into heterosexual families (D'Emilio 1983). While capitalism has undercut the material foundation of family life, feminists, gays, and lesbians are demonized for the instability of the social system.

Both lesbians and female bodybuilders disturb the patriarchal and heterosexist values that are so fundamental to the dominant culture (Schulze 1990). The muscular woman who flaunts her muscles disturbs mainstream conceptions of sexuality, gender, and sex. Any discourse on the issue raises discomfort, ambiguity, anxiety, and tension. In order to justify it and make it palatable to mainstream culture, advertisers have painted female bodybuilding as a normative ideal of female beauty (see figure 2.87). As in all other versions of the perfect provocateur (see chapter 3), the image of the female bodybuilder promotes self-improvement and guarantees attractiveness to men. Discussions of bodybuilding in women's fashion magazines promise "women who are thinking about working out with weights that they need not fear a loss of privilege or social power; despite any differences that may result from lifting weights, they will still be able to 'pass'" (Schulze 1990, 63).

Both the muscular woman and the butch lesbian are charged with looking like men or desiring to be men. In this sense, muscles are a type of drag whereby women allegedly attempt to pass as men (Kuhn 1989). Lesbians are also accused of confusing gender by masquerading as men. Both bodybuilders and lesbians are subject to various forms of social control that either deny their physical or sexual "overindulgences" or otherwise try to tame their threat and force them into the dominant constructions of feminine appearances and role behaviors. In other words, both lesbians and female bodybuilders are strongly encouraged to pass as heterosexual women. This translates, for bodybuilders, into not flexing one's mus-

Fig. 2.87

cles in public spheres. For competitive bodybuilders, this means exhibiting the symbols of conventional feminine style—an unmistakable made-up look with styled hair and sexy bikinis. For lesbians, this means embracing more conventional feminine clothing or the stylish accessories or trappings of gender ambiguity.

Gay-image advertising invites the viewer—foremost as a consumer—to peer into ads and identify with particular components of fashion. As a consequence, gay men and lesbians are accepted as consumers but rejected socially. It also invites the viewer to be in vogue overall. "When gay sensibility is used as a sales pitch, the strategy is that gay images imply distinction and non-conformity, granting straight consumers a longed-for place outside the humdrum mainstream" (Brownski 1984, 187).

When "gayness" becomes chic, it glosses over political differences, potential tensions, and subcultural diversity. Gay-image advertising ultimately discourages gays from coming out of the closet by, at least thus far, suppressing any political identity. It also makes it easier to stay in the closet because fashion can blur superficial distinctions between gays and straights based on appearance and clothing style.

The advertising industry is interested in gays and lesbians only as consumers, not as a political force making waves and upsetting general-audience consumers. In a neatly packaged form sans its political implications, homosexuality is merely a sexual orientation whose characteristics can be incorporated into commodified images and sold back to gay and lesbian consumers, who are simply another population segment for target advertising. Gay-image advertising distinguishes sexuality from politics and links them both to consumerism.

As their visibility increases, lesbians have become the target of advertisers' continuous search for new populations to colonize (Williamson 1986). The fashion industry is reaching out for a potential partnership that will forever change political identity.

Fig. 2.88

Perhaps some lesbian images are presented merely for shock value. Advertisers use explicit symbols of homosexuality to do this. After all, advertisers know that we typically spend only seconds glancing at each page while flipping through a magazine. These ads do not target exclusively gay or lesbian audiences; they are ads in mainstream magazines that also target general audiences (see figure 2.88).

Conclusion

Advertising transmits cultural and subcultural representations and messages concerning sweeping, biological drives. This chapter employs the visual anthropology and human zoology of Morris and the sociological dramaturgy of Goffman, with particular emphasis on visual evidence such as gesture, posture, and expression, in order to deconstruct advertising. Advertisers use size, attention, and positioning as methods to convey social superiority or power.

Advertising sometimes promotes images of the nuclear family, supporting the idea of humans surviving in lifelong pair bonds. Nevertheless, advertising also displays sexuality as nonchalant and unplanned, glorifying lustful promiscuity. In short, advertising sends mixed messages about sexual desires. Marketers, to be sure, have profited through exploiting and subverting the character of human sexual passion. We have seen ads that depict sex as pornography, degrading people by portraying them as sex objects, ignoring human individuality. There is a striking lack of sexual imagery that shows sex as a core and profound human response.

One can certainly question advertising theories that portray women consumers as helpless victims. One may also caution against naively accepting the view that the mass media form a conspiracy against women. Yet one cannot overlook or condone the use of pubescent eroticism in selling products. If sex doesn't sell, it certainly catches one's attention. Advertising is the king of soft porn:

> The ad industry has managed to mainstream pornographic images and desensitize the populace into accepting the humiliation of women in advertising. Pornography implies the use of sexuality as if it were some kind of commodity for sale. (Strnad 1993, S6)

3

Constructed Bodies, Deconstructing Ads:
Sexism in Advertising

Feminist efforts to redefine gender ideals for advertisers . . . met with disbelief,
resistance and downright hostility.
　　　　　—Gail Dines and Jean M. Humez, *Gender, Race, and Class in Media*

This chapter focuses on gender representations in advertising. Ad deconstruction
reveals a pattern of symbolic and institutionalized sexism. *Sexism* is any attitude,
behavior, institutional arrangement, or policy that favors one gender over another.
Advertising sells much more than products; it sells values and cultural representations,
such as success and sexuality, as we have seen.

Gender Representations

What kind of representations does advertising produce? It creates a mythical, WASP-
oriented world in which no one is ever ugly, overweight, poor, toiling, or physically or
mentally disabled (unless you count the housewives who talk to little men in toilet
bowls) (Kilbourne 1989).

Advertising has a great deal to say about gender identity. Ads use visual images of men
and women to grab our attention and persuade. They are really projecting gender display—the ways in which we *think* men and women behave—not the ways they actually
do behave (Goffman 1976). Such portrayals or images are not reflective of social reality. In
advertising, for example, women are primarily depicted as sexual objects or sexual agents.

Because traditional gender roles are so easily recognized by consumers, they figure
conspicuously in the imagery of mass media. Gender images hit at the heart of individual identity. What better place to choose than an arena of social life that can be communicated at a glance and that reaches into the core of individual identity (Jhally 1990)?

In tracing the evolution of ad campaigns over time in relation to changing social developments and patterns of intergroup tensions, we are actually discerning the cultural codes
of gender, class, and race. It is important to expand media literacy in order to endure the
invasion of media images, messages, and displays that is flooding our senses.

Advertising images provide culturally sanctioned ideal types of masculinity and
femininity. Advertisers targeting women consumers subscribe to very limited notions

of what constitutes femininity (e.g., dependency, concern with superficial beauty, fixation on family and nurturance, fear of technology) and, consequently, "feminine" buying patterns (Kilbourne 1989; Steinem 1990). "Feminist efforts to redefine gender ideals for advertisers in the 1970s and 1980s met with disbelief, resistance and downright hostility" (Dines and Humez 1995, 73).

Advertisers sometimes attempt to control the editorial content of the media by trying to censor feature stories that might conflict with their interests. For example, an episode of *Little House on the Prairie* that featured a pack of wild dogs threatening children was pulled when the sponsor, a leading dog food manufacturer, objected. This shows the lengths to which advertisers will go to protect their financial stake in their products and services.

Boys are pilots.

Girls are stewardesses.

Boys are presidents.

Girls are First Ladies.

Boys are doctors.

Girls are nurses.

Boys are policemen.

Girls are metermaids.

Boys can eat.

Girls can cook.

Boys build houses.

Girls keep houses.

Boys invent things.

Girls use what boys invent.

Boys fix things.

Girls need things fixed.

Fig. 3.1

Two general patterns seem to emerge concerning gender and advertising. First, ads tell us that there is a big difference between what is appropriate or expected behavior for men and women, or for boys and girls. Second, advertising and other mass media inculcate in consumers the cultural assumption that men are dominant and women are passive and subordinate. Moreover, while the masculine gender role is valued, the feminine counterpart is disregarded or devalued. A few examples from a 1970 children's book (figure 3.1) show how rigid and exclusive gender roles are set, even in early childhood.

Ads portray women as sex objects (figure 3.2) or mindless domestics pathologically obsessed with cleanliness (figure 3.3) (Kilbourne 1989).

Perfect Provocateur: Young, Beautiful, and Seductive

> Her face was white and perfectly smooth . . . every blemish or flaw she ever had gone away, though what those flaws had been I couldn't have told you. She was perfect now. . . . She had the fullness of young womanhood.
> —Anne Rice, *The Vampire Lestat*

Advertisers have an enormous financial stake in a narrow ideal of femininity that they promote, especially in beauty product ads (Kilbourne 1989). The image of the ideal beautiful woman (see figures 3.4–3.5) may perhaps be captured with the concept of the *provocateur* (an ideal image that arouses a feeling or reaction). The exemplary female prototype in advertising, regardless of product or service, displays youth (no lines or wrinkles), good looks, sexual seductiveness (Baudrillard 1990), and perfection (no scars, blemishes, or even pores) (Kilbourne 1989).

The provocateur is not human; rather, she is a form or hollow shell representing a female figure. Accepted attractiveness is her only attribute. She is slender, typically tall and long-legged (figure 3.6). Women are constantly held to this unrealistic standard of beauty. If they fail to attain it, they are led to feel guilty and ashamed. Cultural ideology tells women that they will not be desirable to, or loved by, men unless they are physically perfect. Figure 3.7, an ad for Bijan, whose product line includes menswear, perfume, and jewelry, displays a fantasy: a nude obese woman is considered beautiful (the title of the ad is Bella) and worthy of an artist's careful work.

Fig. 3.2   Fig. 3.3   Fig. 3.4

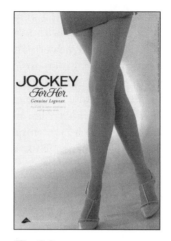

Fig. 3.5　　　　　　　　　Fig. 3.6　　　　　　　　　Fig. 3.7

This ultimate image is not real. It can only be achieved artificially through the purchase of vast quantities of beauty products (Kilbourne 1989). The perfect provocateur is a mere façade. Even the models themselves do not look in the flesh as impeccable as they are depicted in ads. The classic image is constructed through cosmetics, photography, and airbrushing techniques.

Although the feminist movement challenged this "beauty myth" (Wolf 1991), the beauty industries (i.e., cosmetics, fashion, diet, and cosmetic surgery) countered with a multidimensional attack. First, they simply increased the number of commercial beauty images to which women are exposed. More than $1 million is spent every hour on cosmetics (figure 3.8). Most of that money is spent on advertising and packaging (Kilbourne 1989). Only eight cents of the cosmetics sales dollar goes to pay for ingredients; the rest goes to packaging, promotion, and marketing (Goldman 1987, 697).

Through advertising, the face becomes a mask (something you put on) (see figure 3.9) and the body becomes an object (see figure 3.10).

Women spend a huge amount of money on cosmetics because of the "structural realignments in gender relations, as women [assume] a more public identity than [has]

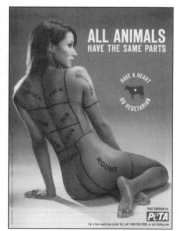

Fig. 3.8　　　　　　　　　Fig. 3.9　　　　　　　　　Fig. 3.10

been accorded them in the past" (Twitchell 1996, 149). This reinterpretation of the meaning of being female in the United States was signaled by suffrage, the birth control movement, the new conception of motherhood, and the development of new frameworks of opportunity for women beyond the confines of the home. It is only within the context of this fundamental change in the perception of the woman's place—the conditional acceptance of the "New Woman"—that the cult of feminine beauty becomes comprehensible (Vinikas 1992, xv).

Sexual Objectification, Eating Disorders, and the Waif Look

Twenty years ago fashion models weighed 8% less than the average female. Today, models weigh 23% less than the average female.
—Jean Kilbourne

The . . . influence of pageant competitions on young women's decisions about diet and lifestyle is . . . likely to have a strong . . . effect.
—S. Rubinstein and B. Caballero

What are the consequences of living in a society that sexually objectifies the body, especially the female body, through gaze or "checking out?" Although the social construction of gender is not fresh, this perspective has more recently been formalized in objectification theory (Fredrickson and Roberts 1997). Accordingly, being raised in a culture that objectifies the female body and sexualizes women leads them to internalize this objectification. This is called self-objectification. Such self-consciousness is characterized by habitual self-monitoring of one's physical appearance. Consciousness of one's body as an object has three components: body surveillance, internalization of cultural body standards, and beliefs about the controllability of appearance (McKinley and Hyde 1996).

Internalizing cultural standards of feminine beauty leads to increased shame and anxiety about the body and appearance, partly because societal images of idyllic beauty are virtually impossible to achieve. Moreover, continuous monitoring of one's physical appearance leaves fewer perceptual resources available for attending to inner body experience and results in a decreased awareness of internal body states. Self-objectification is hypothesized to be related to increased risk of psychological problems, including eating disorders, bipolar depression, and sexual dysfunction.

Objectification theory has empirical support. Body objectification is related to body shame and this, in turn, to disordered eating in college women (McKinley 1999, McKinley and Hyde 1996, Noll and Fredrickson 1998, Fredrickson et al. 1998). Body shame is tentatively related to body esteem, which is, sequentially, related to several dimensions of psychological well-being, including autonomy, environmental mastery, and self-acceptance (McKinley 1999).

One way to help girls and women resist the internalization of a passive, object-oriented sense of self may be to encourage sports participation and related forms of physical activity and risk-taking, thus promoting a more active, instrumental experience of the self (Fredrickson and Roberts 1997). However, participation in more "feminine" sports (those focusing more on female appearance) and/or physical activity is associated with higher body shame, indicating greater internalization of cultural standards of feminine beauty (Parsons and Betz 2001). Physical activity is also consistently related to both instrumentality (an assertive, self-determining, self-reliant approach to the environment) and internal locus of control (ability to view oneself as able to affect one's environment and one's fates to cope adaptively with stressful life experiences [Lefcourt 1991]).

In a study comparing former dancers and nondancers, Tiggemann and Slater (2001) found that former dancers scored higher on self-objectification, self-surveillance, and disordered eating. Self-objectification is a relatively long-term way of perceiving oneself. Even though former dancers are no longer exposed to a situation virtually requiring self-objectification, they still view themselves this way. The case studies in this section also support the notion that objectifying situations experienced at a young age may lead to the development of an enduring way of self-perception and worldview.

The rigorous physique standards demanded of fashion models and beauty pageant queens are extreme and often result in considerable weight loss and undernourishment. Using the heights and weights from most of the winners in the history of the Miss America Pageant, Rubinstein and Caballero (2000) constructed a Body Mass Index (BMI=weight divided by height squared) and found that many were undernourished. BMI has generally decreased over the years. In the 1920s, contestants had BMIs in the range now considered normal. But an increasing number of winners since then have had BMIs indicating undernourishment by standards set by the World Health Organization. In order to combat undernourishment and anorexia, pageant officials could use an eligibility requirement for a minimum body-fat percentage set by public health officials for all contestants.

The oppressive and draconian images of the ideal or perfect woman (see Andelin 1963) are hammered nearly continuously into countless little girls, adolescents, and women by the unrealistic representations in advertising. Advertising encourages not only fat-free diets but liposuction, anorexia, bulimia, binge eating, and cosmetic surgery and dentistry. Who gains by promoting this nonsensical image of the ideal woman? Cosmetic surgery is a $300 billion industry (Twitchell 1996). The diet industry rakes in $33 million per year; cosmetics, $20 billion.

Advertising is not a new type of lie. Today's women with ultrathin figures or breast implants are merely the contemporary version of females over the centuries who have mangled themselves in the name of feminine sex appeal. Feminist theories that portray women only as helpless victims of conspiracy plots are not accurate:

> The idea that women are so utterly victimized by the way they are portrayed in magazines that they starve themselves and become sick has a certain alluring simplicity.... But anorexia and bulimia are multifactoral disorders more attributable to biology, environment, and personality than to the appearance of scrawny models in Diet Coke ads. This is not to deny the sexist nature of much of the media, or the reflective and aspirational nature of images cast in that media, but only to deny that conspiracy is the explanation. (Twitchell 1996, 154)

More important than increasing the number of advertisements, the beauty industries revised the perfect provocateur so that it would be more arduous than ever for women to imitate, creating the anorexic-looking waif model (see figures 3.11a–3.11b) (Bordo 1993; Wolf 1991). This can only increase the anxiety that many girls and women feel about their own appearance. Advertising images simultaneously tried to co-opt and commodify the very notion of "women's liberation."

Jean Kilbourne, in her video *Slim Hopes,* offers an in-depth analysis of the role that female bodies play in advertising imagery and the resulting devastating effects on

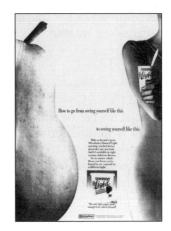

Fig. 3.11a   Fig. 3.11b   Fig. 3.12

women's health. There is a clear relationship between these representations and girls' and women's obsession with dieting and thinness (figure 3.12). The following three case studies of young women aptly illustrate the strong connection between media images of feminine beauty and life-threatening eating disorders such as anorexia and bulimia.

Case One: Megan

I didn't always hate my body. I thought I was doing so well, deflecting all the painful things that happened to me growing up, when all the while I was absorbing them. Each hurt pressed down, so deep inside I didn't know I was carrying them everywhere I went—a time bomb.

The women in my family bought into cultural standards of beauty so much that they felt they needed to save me from the fate of being overweight (size 14). I fought it for years, trying to ignore the comments and criticism from my family and the images in movies, magazines, and TV of the ideal woman's figure. After I entered college, I was diagnosed with anorexia and then bulimia. When I was anorexic I just refused to eat and lost so much weight that suddenly my family and acquaintances were so complimentary that I wasn't satisfied with my weight loss, but I was sick of starving, sick of being obsessed with the food I wouldn't allow myself to have.

My cousin taught me how to binge and purge so I switched to bulimia. I'm thirty-two years old now, and although I went through treatment for my eating disorders I know my recovery will never end. I have fought this battle for over eleven years now with varying success. I am currently in a relapse and meet the clinical diagnosis for bulimia [binging and purging three times per week or more, according to the DSM-4, an index used by psychologists and psychiatrists to diagnose bulimia].

When I was in elementary school I took a test called the Peabody Picture Analysis [a test of cognitive reasoning and verbal ability]. I was shown a picture and had to describe what was happening and why. I scored higher than anyone else in the history of the school—according to my mother. Over the years I utilized this ability by rationalizing and explaining away every bad thing that happened to me.

My father left when I was five and didn't keep in contact because he was too young and immature for the responsibility of a child. My grandmother was hard on me because she wanted me to develop to the best of my abilities. My mother moved out of state when I was a junior in high school to pursue a career because she had missed out on her childhood by having me, leaving me to live with my grandmother. I had an answer for everything.

All through junior high I was pretty happy with my body. When my grandmother offered me breast enlargement for a graduation present from high school (which I had never requested) I declined, and when I left for college, I felt free and full of hope. My struggle with my body image surfaced my freshman year. I had always been a size 12, but I gained the freshman fifteen and my weight kept creeping up.

When I went home for breaks, I noticed my mother and grandmother staring at me. They tried to throw money at the problem, trying to find clothes that would make me look smaller, better. The shopping expeditions were all failures. I looked fat in everything I tried. Then they began urging me to lose weight. I was uncomfortable but accustomed to hearing about this; I always kept silent until they finished and moved on to something else.

One time was different. My grandmother said, "Honey, I know you don't want to hear this, but you have gotten so big. Don't you know how much it embarrasses the whole family?" I was devastated. I walked away and tried to let it go, but it worked on me. I was a size 14 at the time, hardly obese.

My grandmother took me to a diet doctor who prescribed speed but I hated the way it made me feel—headaches, shaky, and with an awful dry mouth. I threw the pills away. I felt powerless and angry. I concentrated my anger on my body, which I felt had betrayed me. I wasn't strong enough to stand up to my family and their influence when they hurt me. Instead, the anger I couldn't express to them was unleashed on myself. It was so intense it allowed me to starve myself, to throw up what I did eat, to tell myself that I was ugly and undeserving of love and approval.

As the weight started coming off I had some satisfaction, but it was never enough. I got back down to a size 12 but kept going. I looked to cultural influences such as media images of the ideal body. Media influences eventually convinced me I wasn't worthy of unconditional love from my family and fueled my perfectionism about my appearance and the development of anorexia and bulimia.

By the time I got down to a size 2, I looked sick, but everyone was thrilled. (My family USED to say you can never be too rich, too thin, or too grammatically correct but that was before three of us developed eating disorders.) For two years my weight stayed the same and I didn't seek treatment. Once again I thought I was in control.

I got married in 1995 and right after our honeymoon my husband joined the Coast Guard and left for boot camp. While I waited the eight weeks he was gone, I dreamed about how exciting it would be to get his orders and move. My husband was stationed on a 270-foot cruiser. I was a little worried but figured I would adjust. I was terribly wrong. The only person I knew in the state was gone two months, back, then gone again. Newly married, I wanted so much to be with him, and I was crushed each time he left. The only person who I felt loved me unconditionally was forced to abandon me over and over again. Because my father left when I was little, my husband's leaving was tearing old wounds open, wounds I had refused to even acknowledge.

Each time my husband had to leave, I would tell myself it would be different, that I would be able to handle it. Going to the ship to say goodbye tore my heart out. We would arrive at the ship and sit with the other couples and families saying their good-byes. I would lean against him and hold his hand, trying to absorb as much as I could before they got under way, his smell, the way his arm felt around my shoulders. The further that ship got away from port the blacker I felt inside. The pain went so deep I didn't know how to express it. It was so much bigger than I was. I stopped eating; there was no reason to eat. The one thing I wanted was out of my reach. Each time the cycle repeated itself I got weaker and more depressed.

I had met some people, of course, but no one I trusted to tell such terrible things. My family knew I was lonely, but no one likes to hear bad news all the time, and I never told them how desperate my situation was. I held everything inside. My only comfort was my little dog, Nikki. I would hold him and cry and cry, knowing he would never judge me or think I was crazy. I did terrible things to my body, anything to take my mind off the pain: starving, throwing up, exercising, and cutting.

As much as I hated the Coast Guard, it was the Coast Guard that made it possible to get well. I went to the base clinic with a cold and the nurse practitioner knew something was wrong when she saw me. When she asked what was going on I told her. I am so thankful that she was there. I could tell she cared; it wasn't just a job to her. She didn't make me feel like a freak, and I will always be grateful for that. If she had, I wouldn't have sought treatment or had the courage to work to get better. Everyone at that base clinic was wonderful: the pharmacist who looked out for me, the cute young medic who ostensibly accepted my lame excuse about my cat scratching my arm, the physician's assistant who always encouraged me. They restored my faith in the military and myself.

I entered intensive outpatient treatment for my eating disorder, group and individual therapy, and it was draining. It's the hardest thing I have ever done in my life. I had to face all the things I had refused to acknowledge for years. There were so many rules, no talking about weight, no talking about food and diets, not looking at the scales when they weighed us. Eating the group meal every Wednesday was the most difficult part. Being forced to eat a balanced meal seemed like too much food. We were all so in the disease. Every meal was a struggle, and the mood in that room was dark, you would have thought we were going to be lined up and shot afterwards, all ten people facing their deepest fears at each meal. I used to get mad that alcoholics could stay away from alcohol, but we didn't have that luxury. We had to face our addiction three times a day or more.

It took me a long time to get better and it is an ongoing process. I have never cut myself again, and I don't throw up much anymore, although I still do it. In fact, I did it this week. I walked into a restaurant's bathroom and saw something chilling. Someone left a knife in the stall, and I knew just what she had used it for. I grieved for that person, whoever she was: a young girl trying so hard to be accepted, a woman trying to fit an impossible standard, we were connected. I thought about her concealing that knife, walking as quickly as she could, wondering if anyone noticed, desperate to get rid of the shame inside. I wish her love, acceptance, healing, and hope, all the things I wish for myself.

I am not trying to be dramatic when I say it is a daily struggle, and one I am currently losing. I wish I could just be happy with my body, but when I see idealized media images, or even very thin girls on campus, I find myself wanting. I want to look like that.

Case Two: Lori

I did not have to eat. Food was not nutrition; it was the enemy.

Holding out, pushing away, turning from desire was a main part of my eating disorder. There was a strong connection between self-control and anorexia nervosa. It was a form of power that I controlled over my eating habits. Second semester of freshman year in college, I felt so confused. It was at this time that everything seemed upside down in my life. I turned to the restraint of food to create something that I could hold stable. This was my grip for support, and I turned to the control of my body. By dominating over this one factor of restraint, my feet seemed to stay on the ground for a short while.

I did not have to eat. I would not let other girls see me eat. I could pretend I wasn't hungry. I would make my body do what I wanted it to do, not what it was supposed to do. Food was not nutrition; it was the enemy. I taught myself to hold out for long amounts of time. It took a while for my appetite to decrease, but my body slowly learned. I would ask myself how I would rather feel in an hour after I ate: full with an increased size in my belly, or would I rather feel hungry and eventually lose the weight? In my mind, I somehow viewed emptiness and happiness in a parallel world.

Right before I left school for summer vacation at the end of my freshman year was when people first started to notice that I looked different. People were saying I looked good. I started getting more people to pay attention to me and I received more compliments. When I came home for summer vacation, I weighed 120 pounds and was still losing weight. That may not seem like anything to worry about, but it was because of my height and bone structure. I'm a naturally tall and slender person, 5 feet 11 inches tall, and my normal weight was 135. I was dropping fast.

My mom remembered how I had gained weight during my first semester at college, so she assumed that I had just lost the pounds I had previously put on. She told me that I looked good, and so did my dad. I remembered how upset I was when my dad told me I looked fat when he came to visit for parents weekend. He thought it was funny. I was ashamed and shocked. So, when he saw me the next time, and told me that I looked beautiful, I felt a feeling of acceptance.

My friends, on the other hand, were worried. They watched me eat, told me I was too skinny, and would yell at me. One of them actually told me that I looked disgusting and I had to stop doing this to myself. Then my boyfriend became involved. He was pressured by my friends to tell me that I needed to start eating. So he would take me to dinner and lunch and yell at me to finish my meal. I never did. The strange thing is that he would also begin to tell me how good my body looked, and how I looked perfect. That just fueled my desire to keep doing this to myself.

It is obvious that society pursues the notion that self-control is a virtue, and a lean body is good evidence of self-control. Psychiatrists told me that depression originated my eating disorder, yet to this day I am still unsure whether my eating disorder caused my depression or vice versa. After these biweekly visits to counselors and psychiatrists, I could then see that an anorexic person's resistance to eat displays a distorted form of self-control. Restrained eating was never about the immediate results; it was about the delayed feeling of an empty stomach and smaller waistline, which never got small enough in my eyes. I never thought about the impact on my body until the weight started decreasing at rapid rates. I had trouble seeing the good form of self-control like creating a long, healthy life by putting vital nutrients into my body. Fortunately, I eventually realized anorexia wasn't a form of self-control; it was a lack of self-control.

Being skinny is an attention grabber, and it comes as a reinforcement to keep losing the weight. I am not going to lie and say that I did not gain attention from my smaller body. Guys commented by saying "You look good," which actually motivated the obsession to lose weight. While girls, on the other hand, would put on their questioning faces and inquire, "How did you get that skinny?" pretending to not have any assumptions of my eating disorder. Their eyes would burn holes in my back as they watched me walk away, analyzing my body, whispering to their friends about how anorexic I look, ironically followed by a comment about how fat they themselves are. The positive attention from males and jealous attention from females, were just reinforcement to keep losing the weight.

I assumed that choosing not to eat would make me feel good about myself in the long run. Little did I know, was that the disease increased a horrible feeling of weakness not long after the positive short-term feeling. In other words, long-term effects were not taken into consideration. I kept thinking about the time when I felt powerful. On the contrary, the long-term effects inhibited the ability to lead a well-rounded life. I was physically weak, my motivation was lost, and my mind started to play tricks with my body. Yet instead of gaining some amount of control or reward, I felt myself losing what I yearned for so badly—to be happy.

Before I experienced anorexia, I would always question infected girls and their actions. If their eating disorder seemed obvious to me, I would wonder how they could hold off eating for so long. It seemed to be a challenge of willpower, and as twisted as it is, I decided to take on this challenge. When in reality, it was not a goal at all. It was a weakness that I fell for. It is a disorder that so many young women, and now men, become slaves to and eventually regret.

Case 3: Jodi

I was 5 feet 5 inches tall and weighed 72 pounds.

I began dieting at the age of thirteen when I weighed 115 pounds. I was made fun of by family and friends for being chunky. For two years I restricted my food intake. My parents became worried about my eating behavior. . . . At first, I was encouraged by dieting; as time went by, I was able to suppress hunger pains by keeping my goal of losing weight in mind. As I grew older, I felt eating was the only thing I could control. . . . After a year of losing weight, my parents took me to the doctor. He was worried and put me on a high-calorie diet. I avoided this by lying about what I ate, or flushing food down the toilet. When I did eat, it made me sick. I felt guilty and would throw it up. At one point, I was consuming only 500 calories a day. When I got down to 72 pounds, I was placed in the hospital and fed by a tube. Today I'm sixteen years old and weigh 108 pounds. Now I'm able to look in the mirror and not be disgusted by thinking I'm fat. But I still sometimes struggle with eating and always watch what I eat.

A common theme weaving alarmingly through these three case studies is that cultural stress on young women produces an unrealistic standard of feminine beauty.

Advertising gives us a constant stream of representations of perfect—and, of course, unattainable—female beauty. The "waif look," epitomized by ultrathin supermodel Kate Moss, has colonized the dreams of young girls. However, the failure to attain such an unrealistic look has been more like a nightmare than a dream for girls who consider the waif look the only valid form of female identity.

Barbie Makeover

The well-known toy manufacturer Mattel has given Barbie, its curvaceous, best-selling doll, a major makeover. Barbie has been an icon for young girls since her birth in 1959. In fact, a woman in Great Britain has undergone numerous cosmetic surgeries on her face and body in order to emulate Barbie. Barbie's unrealistic shape has rankled feminists. Just how unrealistic is she? If Barbie were to be blown up to lifelike proportions, her measurements would be 38-18-34. The makeover has given her a more realistic figure. The new Barbie has slimmer hips, a thicker waist, and a smaller bust. She also has a new nose, softer, straighter hair, and a more youthful face with less makeup. However, the changes have not come without problems. She has already lost her waitressing job at Hooters and her boyfriend, Ken, has told her that he wants to start seeing other dolls.

Muscularity as Masculinity

> This omnipresent cult of the body is extraordinary. It is the only object on which everyone is made to concentrate, not as a source of pleasure, but as an object of frantic concern in the obsessive fear of failure or substandard performance.
>
> —Jean Baudrillard, *America*

Baudrillard (1990) states that only women are seducers, but empirical evidence on advertising suggests otherwise. Men, too, are seducers—a male version of the perfect provocateur. The ideal man in ads is young, handsome, clean-cut, perfect, and sexually alluring. Today's man has pumped his pecs and shoulders and exhibits well-defined abs (see figures 3.13–3.14). He has tossed away his stuffy suit and has become a most potent provocateur.

Not many years ago, the slick and refined look defined fashion's ideal man (figure 3.15). Now the muscular guy dominates the runways and magazine pages. The male provocateur is the image of the perfect athletic physique (figure 3.16). He is the most recent model of manhood to appear in advertisements, films, musical artists, and fashion.

Even in children's action figures, the muscular, athletic look has replaced the moderately lean figure. One only needs to compare the G.I. Joe of the early 1980s to the well-defined and brawny superhero action figures of today to see this pattern.

This contemporary warrior has become chic—not accidentally—as fashion has discovered a fresh male lead in the blue-collar

Fig. 3.13   Fig. 3.14

man. Fashion photographers help create and capture this ultramasculine image. In fact, 90 percent of male models are working class—rough around the edges and beefy, not as frail, thin, or chiseled as their predecessors.

The new ideal look displays muscularity, athleticism, and a blue-collar background. Some musical artists regularly do strength and aerobic training to maintain a lean, muscular physique and endurance for performing. Shirtlessness is part of a trend that corresponds to the rise of the beefy male model (figure 3.17). Designers have embraced the garb of the blue-collar man. For example, Italian designers have presented European blue-collar industrial boots, sweaters, and overcoats. In the same vein are the bold fashions of the late Gianni Versace, who pioneered a tight tank top or vest over the exposed chest.

This ultramasculine look from Italy and other parts of Europe has immigrated to the United States. It has been successfully marketed in stores such as the Gap, Banana Republic, and Old Navy that primarily sell cotton clothing. Out went the preppy look and in came lumberjack plaid and denim shirts and lug-sole shoes. The blue-collar man's wardrobe became mainstream fashion.

The male provocateur has become a symbol of our times. The rise of the blue-collar man has stimulated a return to an emphasis on a muscular, athletic body build. Advertising agencies and fashion photographers have seized the ultramasculine look, marketed it, and propelled its success in popular culture.

The beefy, muscular look has found a receptive audience in everything from beer commercials to clothing ads. It may have evolved as a need to compensate for the widespread violence in postmodern society. An overdeveloped body has traditionally been viewed as a sign of vanity (Morris 1996). Now men (and women) may be bodybuilding to produce a strong physical image or give the illusion of invincibility in hopes of being less vulnerable to random acts of violence. A strong physical image may compensate for a lack of economic security and control over one's work. (This is discussed in greater detail in chapter 5.) In other words, a physically powerful look validates masculine identity and provides a dominating image for safety and protection.

The increased popularity of bodybuilding has been associated with male insecurity (Klein 1993). There is an interesting parallel between the anorexic waif look in females and the muscular and athletic look in males. At the extreme of both is obsessive-compulsive behavior, which is believed to be due to a chemical imbalance in individuals. In addition

Fig. 3.15   Fig. 3.16   Fig. 3.17

to this biological chemical imbalance, cultural, gender, and subcultural forces guide and shape individuals as part of the processes of socialization and acculturation.

In females, obsessive-compulsive behavior may result in anorexia nervosa, in which girls and women starve themselves in an attempt to reach unrealistic cultural standards of feminine beauty. Similarly, in obsessive-compulsive men we may see a condition called muscle dysmorphia. These men are obsessed with achieving an unrealistic cultural standard of muscularity as masculinity. Like the anorexic who sees herself as fat and unattractive despite her emaciated appearance the man suffering from muscle dysmorphia sees himself as scrawny and inadequate despite his bulging muscles. Many of these men have made lifting weights the most important activity in their lives, at the expense of family, relationships, and career.

Anorexia nervosa in women and muscle dysmorphia in men are sad reminders of the debilitating dysfunctions of gender roles in postmodern society. In contemporary culture, muscles reflect more than merely men's functional ability to perform heavy labor or defend themselves, their loved ones, and their private property. Muscles are waymarks that distinguish men from each other as well as from women (except for female athletes and bodybuilders).

The discussion of muscles as a sign of power involves not only working-class men but also middle- and upper-class males (Katz 1995). Muscularity and strength are highly valued within the male sports subculture by men of all races and social classes. Muscularity as masculinity is a motif in ads that target upper-income men as well as those on the lower range of social stratification. Advertisers often use representations of physically rugged or muscular male bodies to masculinize goods and services aimed at elite male consumers.

Bodybuilding may be men's reaction to compensate for an increase in women's economic, political, and social power. It is the intimidation factor. If men can no longer dominate women economically, politically, and socially, they are developing their bodies to be even bigger and stronger than women's. Men are reconceptualizing their images as they lose control or influence over the wives, girlfriends, mothers, sisters, and secretaries who used to purchase most of their clothes. Now men are designing an image for themselves. There appear to be two key points. First is a strong interest in clothing styles. Second is the beefy image, a type of exhibitionism. The provocateur exhibits himself either by showing his body or by displaying his fashion sense.

Beefy male models understand that they have a look that is currently very marketable. Sexual allure sells everything from cars, clothing, calendars, and cologne to music. After years of depicting women as sex objects and troubled bimbos, advertising is applying those stereotypes to men (Foote 1988). Contrary to Baudrillard's (1990) contention, it is clear that advertising also portrays men as provocateurs or seducers.

As part of my research on advertising, I immersed myself in the acting and modeling industry. I modeled on runways and in print media (e.g., the nacho maker in the ad shown in figure 4.7a), played minor roles on several television series and commercials, and was a stand-in for a CEO in another commercial. Despite an emphasis on muscularity, thinness is still demanded of male models. The norm for fashion runway models is a very narrow range: six feet to six feet two inches in height and approximately 160 to 170 pounds. My agent, a former model of Asian descent, stood six feet tall and weighed only 160 pounds. He was so thin that he covertly wore thigh pads in his trousers to simulate muscular quadriceps.

Now in postmodern advertising, it is the man's turn to be the sex object—stripped and moist, promoting everything from underwear to women's fashion. Feminist theory and the women's movement have made it politically incorrect to portray women as potent provocateurs or desperate dullards. Public consciousness has raised awareness in advertising of how women can be delineated. The insertion of men into these traditional roles is good business.

The most noticeable archetypes of the male provocateur are in advertising. Men are depicted in ads as incompetent and sometimes as objects of ridicule (figure 3.18), rejection, anger, and violence. Predictably, men's-rights activists have protested the use of these types of images for commercial exploitation. The image of men as incompetent fathers, unfortunately, is consistent with the way men actually have been treated in divorce courts and child custody hearings.

Consumer surveys (Langer, in Foote 1988) have shown that some women simply delight in seeing foolish men in ads and commercials. The portrayal of men as foolish and incompetent has possible connections with general cultural presuppositions about men and women (Elliott and Wootton 1997). This is a better explanation for the images than conspiracy theories that claim that it is female ad execs retaliating for decades of ads that exploited females as sex objects. Typically, women, as an aggregate, are not yet in power positions as advertisers or clients to determine such marketing strategy.

Fig. 3.18

Advertising images of women from sexpots to airheads not only sold brand products and services but also helped to shape social attitudes on relationships and on the roles and status accorded to women. It follows that these images of men confirmed that some women increasingly view men as sex objects, jerks, or nerds. Yet if women were the target audiences for such ads, it made them seem malicious, indignant, and unjust. Advertisers realized that they had gone too far and toned down the male image from the blatant sex object to a more affectionate view (see figure 3.19).

Men appear to have a mixed reaction to the provocateur image, which is a definite change from the old-fashioned protector and provider images. In fact, partial nudity within a romanticized context of fatherhood has become a convincing marketing device. The hunky dad image (figures 3.20–3.22)—especially the seminude hunky dad (figure 3.23)—has been cited as among the

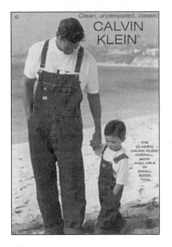

Fig. 3.19

Fig. 3.20

Fig. 3.21

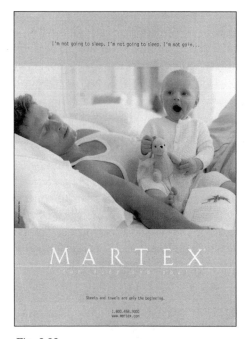

Fig. 3.22

Fig. 3.23

Fig. 3.24

most positive portrayals of men in advertising (Foote 1988). Men also have reacted favorably to images of vulnerability (figure 3.24). However, they seem to be most annoyed by the kitchen-klutz syndrome.

How long will the beefy look be hot? It has thrived for twenty years in a rapidly changing industry. Advertisers must shock us, it seems, to get our attention. We have become numb to their shock tactics. That is why postmodern advertising has sacrificed even its sacred brand logos to get our attention. Images of hunky but sensitive men cause us to pay attention. The postfeminist male in postmodern advertising (figures 3.25–3.26) hauntingly reminds us of the prefeminist female in modern advertising.

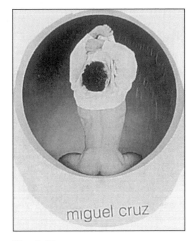

Fig. 3.25

Fig. 3.26

The Intrinsic Defect

> The promise of the commercial is not just "You will have pleasure if you buy our product," but also (and perhaps more important), "You will be happy because people will envy you if you have this product." The spectator of the commercial imagines herself transformed by the product into an object of envy for others—an envy which will justify her loving herself. The commercial images steal her love of herself as she is, and offer it back to her for the price of the product.
>
> —John Berger

To be successful, an ad must be persuasive on two levels. First, it should raise your anxiety level. It should persuade you that you need something; it should make you feel guilty, inferior, or somehow "less than." Second, an ad must provide the solution. If an ad captures you on both these levels, you are generally hooked.

Advertisers are constantly bombarding consumers, especially women, with the message that they are inherently flawed (see figures 3.27–3.29)—that what they are or what they have is not enough, too much, or not good enough (Kilbourne 1989). The ad in figure 3.28, for example, says, "Introducing the eyes you wish you had been born with." Women need change—specifically, eliminating what is wrong with them. There is an assumption, often explicit, that there is something wrong with their physical appearance, dress, or body odor. "Where did such widespread afflictions as body odor, halitosis, iron poor blood, gray hair, water spots, vaginal odor, dish pan hands, various small glands and muscles, and split ends come from?" (Twitchell 1996, 32).

Advertisers have cleverly poked fun at the way their own industry portrays women as needing substantial physical changes. The Michelob Light ad in figure 3.30 balances a group of exhortations to self-improvement with "Relax. You're OK. Improve your beer." This use of self-deprecation has been highly successful and has also come to characterize postmodern advertising, which no longer tries to come across as authoritative.

Ads also sometimes portray men as inherently flawed. There is plenty of room for improvement for men as well as women, the ads say. But advertisers don't seem to be as hard on men as they are on women. Nevertheless, ads target men's physical prowess

Fig. 3.27

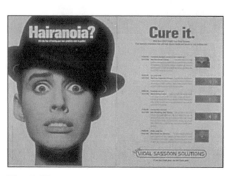

Fig. 3.29

Fig. 3.28

Fig. 3.30

in two areas especially, stressing a lean and muscular body (figure 3.31) and a healthy, thick head of hair (figure 3.32), without any gray, of course.

Child as Sex Object

There is a disturbing trend in advertising toward portraying children (figures 3.33–3.34), and sometimes even babies (figure 3.35), as sex objects. These ads combine a semblance of innocence with a heavy dose of sexual desire to tug at the emotions of prospective consumers.

The young girl in the four ads shown in figures 3.36–3.39 appears to be about five years old. But she's made up to look sexually mature. Note the serious facial expressions, the absence of clothing, the adult hairstyles and makeup, and body gestures and postures. These characteristics make the young model appear to be much older than she really is. In fact, in figure 3.39 she has the illusion of cleavage, created by body posture that creates a shadow in the cleavage area.

Fig. 3.31   Fig. 3.32   Fig. 3.33

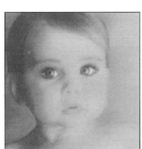

Fig. 3.34   Fig. 3.35   Fig. 3.36

Fig. 3.37   Fig. 3.38

Fig. 3.39   Fig. 3.40

One need not look further than the as-yet-unsolved murder case of young JonBenet Ramsey in Boulder, Colorado, to see a tragic consequence of transforming young girls into cultural representations of feminine beauty and sexual attractiveness. The cover of *Dallas Child* shown in figure 3.40 poignantly brings out the suffering caused by exploitation, inhumane treatment, and coercion that are sometimes involved in beauty pageants for tots and young girls.

Aggression, Violence, and Mass Media

> As a child, you see a Dirty Harry movie, where the heroic policeman is shooting people right and left. Even years later, the right kind of scene can trigger that script and suggest a way to behave that follows it.
>
> —L. Rowell Huesmann

On March 4, 1998, two young white men, aged nineteen and twenty-two, were charged with capital murder in Texas for the torture killing of a nineteen-year-old mentally challenged woman, Amy Robinson. After offering the trusting young woman a ride to work in their car, they drove her to a field. They first tried to shoot Amy with a bow and arrow. When she ran from them, the men chased her down and shot her with pellet pistols. Amy was finished off with a .22-caliber-rifle shot to the head. In their confession to detectives, the young men simply said that they were in the "mood to kill." One of the killers was recently convicted and sentenced to death.

Aggression is a learned behavior. Media violence teaches us aggression as children. Since aggression is learned, it is possible that it can be unlearned or, better yet, never taught in the first place. The mass media produce, reproduce, and distribute aggressive, violent, intimidating, or coercive "scripts," cultural messages that teach us how to behave. This pattern of media violence, continuously repeated and often extreme, creates a cumulative effect that often numbs us to human suffering and brutality. Advertising legitimizes such violence and in doing so glamorizes a form of violent masculinity (see figures 3.41–3.42).

"Violence refers to immediate or chronic situations that result in injury to the psy-

Fig. 3.41   Fig. 3.42

chological, social or physical well-being of individuals or groups" (Katz 1995, 140). This includes hitting, punching, kicking, beating, grabbing, pushing, slapping, raping, battering, sexually harassing, and threatening or trying to inflict injury with an object such as a gun, knife, or club. Interpersonal violence is "behavior by persons against persons that threatens, attempts, or completes intentional infliction of physical or psychological harm" (American Psychological Association 1993, 1).

Nearly all (90 percent) violent crime is committed by males (Federal Bureau of Investigation 1992), most of them young. If we deconstruct gender roles in our society, we discern how cultural definitions of masculinity and femininity encourage violence or receptivity to it. Since gender roles are so pervasive and deeply ingrained in our psyche through cultural transmission, cultural patterns of gender interaction often seem to be taken for granted as natural and, consequently, unchangeable. These cultural images of masculinity and femininity have a great deal of power over us.

Alcohol Use, Advertising, and Violence against Women

> The tragic abuse-affection cycle that many women are trapped in is too often glorified in advertising.
> —Barbi White, *Media & Values* intern

First, I would like to acknowledge that some of my readers are victims of domestic and sexual abuse. Others are undoubtedly abusers. All of us have our personal histories and, perhaps, intense feelings about issues such as sexism, violence, and alcohol abuse.

Domestic and sexual violence against women is widespread. A nationwide survey of over four thousand women indicated that three out of four have been treated violently by men (Consumers for Socially Responsible Advertising 1994). Yet many of these women will never talk about being battered (see figure 3.43). In 1991 half of the incidents in which women were victimized involved physical violence by an intimate male partner (Federal Bureau of Investigation 1992). One-fourth of all children will be sexually abused by an adult before they reach the age of eighteen (Federal Bureau of Investigation 1992). Girls are typically abused by a male within the family, boys by males

Fig. 3.43

Fig. 3.44

outside the family. Most of these sexual assaults are not committed by strangers. There is a strong correlation between domestic and sexual abuse and alcohol consumption (see Consumers for Socially Responsible Advertising 1994).

The cycle of domestic abuse has three stages: (1) tension, (2) abuse, and (3) repentance. If the cycle continues, repentance eventually dissipates and one of three events results: the abuser leaves, the victim leaves, or one of them is killed by the other. More women each year are killed or injured (badly enough to require emergency treatment) by their domestic partners than by car accidents (Consumers for Socially Responsible Advertising 1994).

Men who abuse their wives often grew up in environments where they saw their fathers abuse their mothers. Patterns of abuse are learned within the family. Scripting for the roles of both abuser and victim begins at an early age. Violence is often intergenerational, as the ad in figure 3.44 points out: "Men who abuse their wives often grew up in homes where they saw their fathers abuse their mothers. What horrible shoes for a son to fill." Children who grow up in violent homes are five times more likely to become batterers or victims themselves than are children from nonviolent homes (Straus, Gelles, and Steinmetz 1990). Forty percent of all perpetrators of spousal violence are also violent with their children (Consumers for Socially Responsible Advertising 1994).

Half of all battered wives report that their husbands were drinking when they were abusive (Frieze and Noble 1980). Besides the direct role alcohol plays in violence against women, some alcohol advertising involves gender representations that reinforce, justify, or trivialize violence against women (Consumers for Socially Responsible Advertising 1994). Alcohol advertisers' use of sex as the major marketing motif helps create a risky environment for both women and men.

Date Rape

> The boys never meant any harm against the girls. They just meant to rape.
> —Joyce Kithia, deputy principal of a Kenyan boarding school,
> commenting on a raid of a girls' dormitory by a gang of
> boys who raped seventy-one girls and killed nineteen

A rape occurs more than once every minute in the United States (Consumers for Socially Responsible Advertising 1994). While there is no single cause of sexual and domestic violence, alcohol use is one factor linked to its incidence and with our social response to it. One out of four persons, including both men and women, reports having unwanted sexual activities as a result of alcohol consumption at least once within the past year (Berkowitz 1992; Perkins 1992). Approximately three out of four acquaintance rapes involve alcohol consumption on the part of the victim, the assailant, or both (Koss, Gidycz, and Wisniewski 1987; Norris and Cubbins 1992) (see figure 3.45).

Many male college students have said that they drink alcohol to loosen their sexual inhibitions and to experience a sense of power; one in twelve said they would rape if they could get away with it (Benson, Charlton, and Goodhart 1992). Fifty-one percent of men in one study admitted to sexually assaulting a woman while in college (Berkowitz 1992; Muehlenhard and Linton 1987). Their typical modus operandi was simply to ignore the victim when she said no or otherwise protested.

People generally are less likely to believe that a rape has occurred when the assailant has been drinking than when he has not (Norris and Cubbins 1992). Moreover, victims of sexual assault receive less sympathy from juries if they were drinking alcohol in the same general time period in which the assault occurred. For example, three male students at St. John's University were acquitted of sexually assaulting a young woman. Jurors found "inconsistencies" in the story of a woman who was forced to drink alcohol and then gang-raped. The jury had doubts about the men's guilt (Goodman 1991). A student at the University of Richmond who was facing criminal prosecution for raping one of his classmates blamed the alcohol. His defense was that he was so drunk he couldn't tell whether she was consenting or not (Eigen 1992).

Sometimes laws have been passed in an attempt to bypass or compensate for this jury prejudice against victims of sexual assault who had also been consuming alcohol. In Texas, for example, the penal codes state that people under the influence cannot legally consent to sex. This is likely to result in higher conviction rates for "date rapes."

The copy in the ad for F. Scott's Nightclub (figure 3.46) reads: "If your date won't listen to reason, try a velvet hammer." In other words, using alcohol to force one's date into submission is perfectly acceptable. One can also visualize the dangerous image of hitting one's date with a hammer.

The copy in the Bacardi Black ad (figure 3.47) reads: "The best of the night's adventures are reserved for people with nothing planned." If we combine copy and illustration, we get an ambush. The illustration is set outside, perhaps in a parking lot. There are only two characters, a man and a woman. The woman appears to be off balance. Her

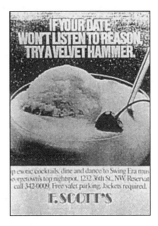

Fig. 3.45   Fig. 3.46   Fig. 3.47

legs are clasped together at the knees but spread at the ankles. She is wearing high-heeled shoes. A man has just appeared in front of her. He appears to be balanced and in control. His leg is visible between hers.

This ad perpetuates at least three myths about sexual assaults: (1) they are generally unplanned; (2) they generally occur in dark alleys or parking lots; and (3) rapists are usually strangers. The truth is that most sexual assaults are planned; they often take place in the victim's home; and they typically involve people who know each other (Consumers for Socially Responsible Advertising 1994).

Television and Movie Violence

> We are awash in a tide of violent representation such as the world has never known, and the consequences are very troubling.
>
> —George Gerbner

A television set is on in the average home in the United States seven hours a day. Before children start first grade, they have already spent more time watching television than they will spend in class in college. By the time a child graduates from high school, she or he will have seen eighteen thousand violent deaths on television. Children view approximately ten thousand acts of violence per year on television. Eighty-five percent of all movies contain violence, compared with 57 percent of all cable television shows and 44 percent of all broadcast television shows (*NBC Evening News* 1996).

In the United States there has long been concern about the social and psychological impact of increasing violence on television and in films, yet little has been done to slow its growth. The *modeling effect* perspective argues that viewing media violence teaches viewers to behave violently through imitation. Another perspective, the *catalytic effect*, maintains that if certain conditions are present, viewing violent media depictions may prompt real-life violence, but it is not a sufficient cause in and of itself (Curren and Renzetti 1996).

The V-chip, a relatively new technological marvel, has been proposed as a possible solution to the increasing violence on television. This innovation allows parents to monitor, screen, and censor what their children watch.

In the real world, women, ethnic minorities, and the elderly are disproportionately victimized. Abusers of credit cards are punished more severely than child abusers in our society. Eighty-four percent of all violent offenders see no pain or long-terms effects of violence, and 73 percent go unpunished. White males in the prime of life pay the smallest price for violence, being most likely to kill with impunity. In 1992, 94.5 percent of black homicide victims were killed by black offenders (Federal Bureau of Investigation 1992). Protest art has denounced black-on-black gang violence in Los Angeles.

In mainstream cultural images, whiteness is the norm vis-à-vis ethnic minority subcultures, which are excluded as out-groups. Whiteness is an invisible privilege, understood but not stated, unconscious but prevalent. Gender roles are complex, considering the diversity of life experience, worldview, social position, and individual identity. Concepts of masculinity and femininity are various, tempered by race, ethnicity, social class, and sexual orientation. The major cleavage is between the dominant white middle-class masculinity and the other, marginalized versions.

Despite all these differences, male roles in patriarchal cultures generally display a propensity for, attachment to, or identification with violence. Of course, Hollywood action adventure films supply a plethora of dominant masculine archetypal heroes, all of them violent. This breed of violent man emerged in the mid-1970s when white males faced increasing economic instability and dislocation due to a widespread recession, economic restructuring, and downsizing in the corporate world.

In addition, racial and gender preferences, through affirmative action policy, polarized white males vis-à-vis people of color and white women. White males began viewing their positions as challenged and themselves as victims. Big, muscular, violent men in the movies provided vicarious participation in "payback" for white men. Violence in films, like that in real life, is perpetrated overwhelmingly by males (Katz 1995). Males make up the majority of the audience for action films, as well as for violent sports such as football and hockey.

Structural transformation in postindustrial capitalism creates tensions in masculine roles (Brod 1987). The mass media tell us that men are supposed to be strong, aggressive, and in control of their work. Yet the dichotomy between mental and manual work prevents any man from attaining ideal masculinity. Moreover, men at various levels of employment are affected by the winds of macroeconomic forces that shape job availability, security, and salary.

Insecure in their identities and dissatisfied with the lack of control over their work lives, men use cultural images of muscular bodies as instruments of power, dominance, and control to validate masculine identity. Especially for working-class males, who have less access to more abstract forms of masculinity-validating power (economic power, authority on the job), the physical display of power, often through violence, is a way of asserting masculinity.

Men across social class and ethnic lines may be insecure about their masculinity, vulnerable to structural market forces, and unable to reasonably challenge revisionist gender relations. Men nevertheless continue to have leverage over women in terms of physical size and strength. Since advertising legitimizes and reinforces existing power relations, images that equate masculinity with size, strength, and violence have become more common.

Sexual Violence in Advertising

> Why is a little teasing about wife battering more objectionable than using conventional sexual images to stimulate conventional sexual appetites? Because it trivializes conduct that lacerates the bodies and psyches of unwilling victims, and obliquely excuses those who inflict the wounds. . . . Instead of being seen as deeply shameful, which it is, sexual violence has become chic.
> —Stephan Chapman, *Chicago Tribune*

Advertising is a continuous and fertile source of gender display. Postmodern ads depict violent, threatening, and dangerous-looking male ideal types (such as military men, football players, boxers, and bikers). In a period in which there has been a loosening of rigid gender distinctions, advertising, with the exception of the androgynous male look in fashion, emphasizes gender differences. This means that masculinity is defined in opposition to femininity. In short, masculine images are dominant, intimidating, and violent, while feminine images are subordinate, receptive, and passive. For example, figure 3.48 shows a young woman with an ostensibly hot iron pressed against the side of her face. In differentiating masculinity from femininity, images of aggression and violence (including violence against women) arm men with self-esteem, security, and a socially validated masculine role.

The efficacy of violent behavior for males, including its rewards, is coded into advertising in several ways, "from violent male icons (such as particularly aggressive athletes or superheroes) overtly threatening consumers to buy products, to ads that exploit men's feeling of not being big, strong or violent enough by promising to provide them with products that will enhance those qualities" (Katz 1995, 136). These codes are present in television and radio commercials as well, but I choose to concentrate on mainstream magazine ads.

Various recurrent themes in print advertising support the notion of white masculinity as violence. These include "violence as genetically programmed male behavior, the use of military and sports symbolism to enhance the masculine appeal and identification of products, the association of muscularity with ideal masculinity, and the equation of heroic masculinity with violent masculinity" (Katz 1995, 136). In short, in advertising violence becomes fashionable and urbane. Often ads equate muscles with violent power.

Violence is not limited to print advertising and television. A shoe store window prominently displayed a men's dress shoe resting on the throat of a female mannequin clothed only in a white shroud. In bold copy next to the shoes, "We'd kill for these!" "The relation of window dressing to modern culture is a chapter in art history still not written" (Twitchell 1996, 208).

Modern masculine archetypes in mainstream magazine ads normalize, legitimize, and excuse male violence. It's no secret that sex sells. Advertising has been using it for years. Now, however, violence has become foreplay (see *New York Times Magazine* 1984). Ads are trying to show us that fighting is playful and that intimidation and violence have become stimulating forerunners to intimate socializing and sex. The nonchalance of the message is startling in what it implies about our desensitization to violence and about advertising's role in promoting this numbness. White male privilege ignores or subjugates the perspectives and welfare of women, ethnic minorities, and even children.

Advertising not only makes this sexual genre of violent abuse tolerable but also unmistakably glorifies it. Sexual violence has become romantic and chic instead of being seen as grievously contemptible. Such ads are used by some of the most reputable manufacturers in mainstream magazines aimed at refined, stylish audiences (see, e.g., *New York Times Magazine* 1984). This is especially shocking. The eradication of domestic and sexual violence is not made any easier by such media images.

Ads show intimidated (figure 3.49) and fearful (figure 3.50) women and women as victims of violence (figure 3.51), potential violence, or the threat of violence (figure 3.52)—a clear extension of the structure of gender inequality. There is a fear of being pursued (figure 3.53) or raped. There are often representations of "stranger danger"—the male intruder (figures 3.54–3.55). Ads convey the explicit message that women should submit to the desires of the intruder (figure 3.56). The representation of the intruder reinforces societal myths that sexual violence is committed mainly by strangers, that women secretly want to be raped, and that women invite rape by their behavior and their attire.

A fuller understanding of the connection between the cultural construction of masculinity and the prevalence of violence may point to effective intervention to prevent violent behavior.

Fig. 3.48

Fig. 3.49

Fig. 3.50

Fig. 3.51

Fig. 3.52

Fig. 3.53

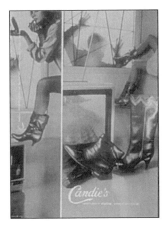

Fig. 3.54

Fig. 3.55

Fig. 3.56

Mock Assault

"Adults play mock assault games with children, games such as chase-and-capture and grab-and-squeeze. The child is playfully treated like a prey under attack by a predator" (Goffman 1976, 52). Of course, men play these games with women (and sometimes other men). Women often cooperate through a display of attempts to escape and through cries of alarm, fear, and appeasement. Underneath this roughhousing, clearly, is a deeper level—one that is perhaps more sinister. Although the man is just playing, there is an implication of what damage he could really do if he were at all serious. We are able to view the mock assault display in advertising (figures 3.57–3.59).

Cross-Cultural Gender Attitudes

Ideas about gender roles, sexuality, obscenity, and standards of physical appearance vary across cultures. Sometimes the differences are subtle, sometimes more blatant. Some European countries, for example, are much more open about sexuality and accepting of nudity than the United States. Figure 3.60a, an American ad for Yves Saint Lauren, shows a male model seminude (shirtless) next to a female model with shirt unbuttoned exposing the center of her chest and midsection. Figure 3.60b, an ad for a French audience, contains the identical photograph except the female's shirt is open wider, exposing both of her nipples.

Figure 3.61a, a French ad for Givenchy Hot Couture, shows a female model posing seductively, revealing cleavage, bare shoulders, and a leg all the way up to her hips. In contrast, figure 3.61b, also an ad for Givenchy Hot Couture, is directed at an Arabic audience (see text). Arabic culture demands more modesty in the public display of women. Consequently, she is posed less seductively, revealing no cleavage, bare shoulders, or legs.

Figure 3.62, a pair of ads for Givenchy Hot Couture, again contrasts French and Arabic culture. The top ad is for a French audience. The female model is wearing a snug-fitting sleeveless white dress opened at the center revealing most of the woman's chest and midsection. Her left hand cups her left breast. The bottom ad is for an Arabic audi-

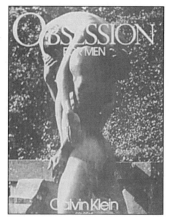

Fig. 3.57   Fig. 3.58   Fig. 3.59

ence and displays much less skin. The same model is wearing a similar white dress except it is long-sleeved and does not reveal any of the woman's chest or midsection. In addition to not revealing any skin, the model modestly covers both her breasts with her hands.

The Feminist Critique
of Advertising

We are in the midst of a violent backlash against feminism that uses images of female beauty as a political weapon against women's advancement: the beauty myth.

    —Naomi Wolf, *The Beauty Myth: . . . How Images of Beauty Are Used against Women*

Advertising has become sexual harassment.

                    —James B. Twitchell, *Adcult USA*

Fig. 3.60a

Fig. 3.60b

Fig. 3.61a

Fig. 3.61b

The feminist critique of advertising is a coherent indictment of advertising with a political following. It has produced real changes in the industry (Twitchell 1996, 142). Negative responses to advertising have undergone a remarkable transformation. At first, people merely complained about ads that offended them. Then consumers became braver; they started to deface ads, writing on them, for example, "This ad is racist!" or "That ad is sexist!" Now consumers are creating their own ads using companies' recognizable logos and symbols to ridicule them (see "Sub-vertising," chapter 1).

Advertising does more than sell products and services; it offers subjugation to consumption. The powerless and the marginal, especially ethnic minorities and women, are seduced into a commodifying system—what Marx called "false consciousness." Although the feminist movement freed women from an oppressive social structure through its campaigns for the control of reproduction, career possibilities, sexual freedom, and, most important, economic and financial independence, advertising regained lost ground in the arenas of the mass media, medicine, law, and cosmetics through unrealistic portrayal of the ideal woman (Wolf 1991).

Fig. 3.62

Although advertising affects the attitudes and behavior of individuals, behavior and attitudes are also affected by profound cultural forces. While it is true that advertising encourages women to "purge themselves, have breast implants, apply acid to their faces to peel off the wrinkles, go on innumerable, often dangerous, diets" (Twitchell 1996, 152), attempts by girls and women to beautify themselves, their bodies, hair, and faces go way back. They are no more novel than the ancient rites of passage carried out by adolescent boys.

Cultural and biological factors are at work here. The notion of the ideal woman is a social construct; it did not impose itself on an unwilling culture. Advertising reflects the traditional beliefs, myths, tales, and practices of our society and a culture based on commodities. Advertising articulates and channels cultural acts, but it does not create artificial desires nor mandate behavioral patterns.

It is true that advertising trends and strategies vary across generations. Products and services come and go. Technology advances. Cultures change, more slowly than not, over time. But the notion of the provocateur is as old as the concept of machismo. Cinderella, Cleopatra, Helen of Troy—I rest my case. "The face of a woman has been a commodity for some time" (Twitchell 1996, 152).

What are the effects of growing up and living within a cultural environment of ubiquitous, ritualized violent representations? The consequences are multifaceted, ranging from developmental to social, political, and psychological. I therefore reject the somewhat simplistic behaviorist model that holds that media violence causes real-life violence.

4

Symbolic Racism in Advertising

I can't get over saying "colored." I said it all my life. All the Negroes seem to resent it and I don't know why.
> —Martha Mitchell, wife of former attorney general John Mitchell

Beneath the surface of ordinary social behavior, innumerable small murders of the mind and spirit take place daily.
> —Vivian Gornick

Why study images of ethnic minorities in advertising? First, these images help to shape cultural attitudes about racial and ethnic minorities. Mass media are very powerful agents of socialization. Second, because advertisements are reflections of contemporary social relations and power structure, they serve as a type of barometer of the willingness of dominant groups to accept ethnic minorities into mainstream society. That is, ads are indicators of ethnic and racial secondary and primary assimilation. Finally, the judicious evaluation of ethnic and racial images in advertising will foster critical media literacy. Analytical reflection on advertising images empowers us to become more autonomous, capable of liberating ourselves from power configurations and becoming more vigorous citizens, keen on decisive social change.

This chapter addresses how ethnic images and race relations are presented in advertising and how such portrayals correlate with patterns of intergroup conflict and power clashes. Changing images in popular culture provide a dynamic view of the way that social relations and ideological challenges to them are represented in print advertising and other forms of mass media. We shall see that stereotypes of blacks and other ethnic minorities have not been eliminated but have changed in character, taking subtler and more symbolic or underhanded forms (Jackman 1994; Karins, Coffman, and Walters 1969; Pettigrew 1985). When social norms that characterize white-black relations are disputed and unresolved, portrayals of blacks may not mirror this decreasing subordination but rather may employ more qualified or subtler stereotypes or retreat from challenges to norms completely by limiting images, creating greater social distance (Jackman 1994). Advertising images, as cultural commodities and social constructions, are sites of struggle along racial fault lines in the United States' cultural landscape (Erikson 1976; Gamson et al. 1992).

In the early part of the twentieth century, popular cultural objects caricatured blacks, echoing their second-class citizenship and assisting as an instrument of social control. Prior to the civil rights movement of the 1960s, the mass media world was nearly all white. To be sure, some demeaning stereotypes of blacks (e.g., Aunt Jemima) served to reassure white consumers that an ideology of racial hierarchy was "natural." In other words, these icons helped to mitigate status anxiety among whites (Dubin 1987). Predominantly white media industries produced such overtly racist images during an era of customary (de facto) and legal (de jure) segregation in employment, residential housing, public transportation, and education.

The civil rights movement successfully challenged much of the racist ideology that had resulted in discrimination, legal segregation, and the social, economic, and political oppression of blacks (as well as of other ethnic minorities) in the United States. Such progress included higher educational and occupational attainment and increasing black voter registration. In doing so, the symbolic trappings of domination were also challenged and vanquished, or at least significantly altered. Traditional social stereotypes seemed to dwindle or perhaps even disappear. Consciousness-raising on issues of racial imagery also resulted in the appearance of many more black characters in mainstream media, including advertising, than in the past.

There are also more blacks employed as cultural producers within mainstream media industries (see Cassidy and Katula 1990). With increased numbers come efforts to produce more culturally authentic imagery of the black community. Nevertheless, minority-owned advertising agencies must walk a fine line between creating positive imagery out of a sense of community responsibility and securing the bottom line—making money. Unless there is profit, the agencies will not be creating any images, let alone positive ones.

Symbolic Vestiges of Domination

How much progress have we made in ethnic relations since the early part of the twentieth century? Have we become a "color-blind" society or do we remain polarized by race? On one hand, studies emphasize the steadily improving racial attitudes of white Americans, especially in terms of their attitudes toward African Americans. Such attitudinal changes are corroborated by more tangible indicators, most notably the rise of a black middle class. On the other hand, there is continual negative stereotyping of ethnic minorities, evidence of widely divergent views of the extent and importance of racial discrimination to modern race relations, and evidence of deepening feelings of alienation among black Americans. White openness to integration at the personal level is also very limited.

Blacks and Latinos continue to have low college attendance and graduation rates, high unemployment rates, and high rates of intraethnic violent crime. There are also new and subtle ethnic stereotypes. Stereotypes of blacks have not been removed from cultural products but have altered in character, taking subtler and more indirect forms (Jackman 1994; Karins, Coffman, and Walters 1969; Pettigrew 1985).

The Black Media Association protested against several advertisers in 1983 for "offensive" advertising (Woods 1995). For example, in a commercial for Dow Chemical's Ziploc bags, all actors had speaking parts except a sturdy black woman, whose reaction to the product was expressed with an excited "Ooh-wee!" Although ostensibly not blatantly racist, the commercial actually carries on the stereotype of the black mammy—

subservient, dark, heavy, asexual, and inarticulate. In Hollywood masterpieces like *Imitation of Life* and *Gone with the Wind*, mammy characters used outbursts instead of grammatical sentences to communicate.

Perhaps the most well-known mammy image is Aunt Jemima with her signature bandana. The original Aunt Jemima, Nancy Green (1831–1898), displayed acute business acumen in an era when few blacks or women operated businesses. This former slave from Montgomery County, Kentucky, was the world's first living trademark. She made her debut at age fifty-nine at the Columbian Exposition in Chicago, where she served pancakes in a booth. The Aunt Jemima Mills Company distributed a souvenir lapel button which bore her photograph and the caption, "I'se in town honey." The slogan later became the motto for the company's promotional campaign. Green was the official trademark for three decades. The mammy image can still be seen in today's advertising (figure 4.1).

Ronco was criticized for its Mr. Microphone ad, in which a black man sang and danced down a hill. This Sambo image is a vestige of "times when blacks were portrayed in Hollywood as minstrels, happy to entertain and serve whites despite their own ignorance, poverty, and lack of status" (Woods 1995, 31).

These ethnic images are closely linked to social relations and to power transformations through economic, classificatory, artistic, and judicial factors (Gans 1979; Griswold 1981; Peterson 1976). During turbulent times of intensified hostility, as social movements are struggling to gain power, gatekeepers confront the task of displaying cultural icons among the conflicts, skirmishes, and crises of accepted norms (Dubin 1987; Swidler 1986; Wuthnow and Witten 1988). When interethnic norms are challenged or unsettled, images may not directly mirror this sudden shift. Rather, cultural producers might use subtler or more limited stereotypes. Gatekeepers may also avoid the problem almost completely by restricting illustrations of interethnic contact, producing greater social distance between majority and minority. In the 1950s and early 1960s, advertisers did not use ethnic minority models because of unsubstantiated fears of retaliation from white consumers (Gould, Sigband, and Zoerner 1970). Despite his popularity as an entertainer who had crossed over from black to mainstream audiences, Nat King Cole could not find a national sponsor for his 1956 television show (Woods 1995). Though ethnic minority representation in advertising has clearly increased, how blacks are depicted and what they contribute to the product's image remain questionable.

As late as 1990, only 3 percent of people featured in national advertising were black (New York City Department of Consumer Affairs in Guy 1991). *GQ, Vogue,* and *Esquire* feature the fewest black models; *Sports Illustrated,* the most. When blacks do appear in ads, they tend to be athletes, entertainers, laborers, or chil-

Fig. 4.1

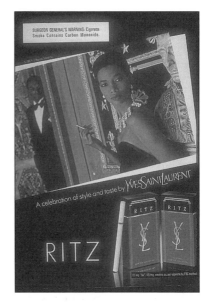

Fig. 4.2   Fig. 4.3

dren. The incidence of black women is even lower than that of black men. Fewer than 20 percent of all ads with blacks use black women (New York City Department of Consumer Affairs in Guy 1991). One study (Wilkes and Valencia 1989) found that blacks were featured in 17 percent of the 904 commercials seen but had major roles in only 31 percent of all ads with blacks. Like Latinos, blacks show up in groups. Group size, however, is considerably smaller for blacks (an average of 6.9 persons) than Latinos (an average of 8.1 persons). Blacks tend to be cast marketing beer or malt liquor (figure 4.2), cigarettes (figure 4.3), hair care (figure 4.4), automobiles, and electronic products.

Connecting ethnic images to periods of social change highlights more adequately and in a more nuanced way the social norms and cultural ideologies of a particular age (Williams 1981). Inspecting cultural continuities and changes that are an integral part of critical periods in history furthers our understanding of the interconnections between symbolic and social relations (Pescosolido, Grauerholz, and Milkie 1997).

Three Models of Minorities in Advertising

There are several possible explanations for the way minorities are presented in ads. Three are discussed in this chapter: equal presentation; social reality; and cultural attitudes.

Equal Presentation Model

In ads that follow the equal presentation model, whites and minorities are shown in exactly the same way, regardless of any cultural, economic, or physical differences. If whites are presented predominantly as middle-class persons in middle-class settings, African Americans are portrayed similarly (figure 4.5), regardless of actual differences in the class distribution. Copycat and racial assimilation ads also support the equal presentation model.

Fig. 4.4   Fig. 4.5

Copycat Ads. Minorities prefer to see images of people like themselves in advertising (Woods 1995). Consequently, advertising targeted at ethnic markets that uses ethnic models lends an aura of trustworthiness to the product or service. But this naive approach is risky if the marketer does not understand the nuances of ethnic culture.

In the early 1980s, advertisers began to replace white models with black or Latino models and translate English into Spanish. I call this technique used by advertisers to capture ethnic markets the copycat ad: an ad using a white model is duplicated with a black or Latino model (see figures 4.6a,b–4.9a,b). Although this pattern is ethnocentric and uncreative, it is also understandable, given that marketing corporations tend to assume that their general mass-media campaigns will reach minority audiences.

This copycat mentality mistakenly assumes that African Americans and Latinos are simply dark-skinned white people (figures 4.10–4.11). Some concepts and representations are not transferable across cultures (Lockhart 1992). Blacks and Latinos are diverse and large enough groups to necessitate distinctive and separate undertakings. Clearly, the copycat ad denies the uniqueness of ethnic subcultures and reveals a failure to understand important sociohistorical, racial, and cultural differences that affect the buying power of ethnic minorities. The behavior, attitudes, motivations, and mindsets of blacks, Latinos, and Asians are grounded in their particular sociohistorical backgrounds.

Unlike any other people in the country, blacks have been forced to leave their homeland and to endure the injustices and horrors of slavery. Latinos (with the exception of those who lived in what is now the southwestern United States before the Anglo conquest) and Asians have come as immigrants with hopes of better economic prospects. The black psyche still retains the wounds of slavery and the broken promises that ended it; lynchings, threatened lynchings, and other forms of racist intimidation; court-ordered segregation and other forms of discrimination; and the denial of basic human rights.

Racially, a high visibility factor usually prevents assimilation. Effective advertisers must understand what being black or Latino in the United States means. One's ethnic background has repercussions for consumption patterns, responses to particular advertising, and buying behavior. For example, an advertising campaign for Canadian Mist aptly

Fig. 4.6a   Fig. 4.6b

Fig. 4.7a

Fig. 4.7b

demonstrates cultural differences. Its general ad emphasizes scenery, wildlife, and a rural lifestyle. In trying to reach an African American audience, however, it refocuses on style, fashion, and other imagery that may interest African Americans because of their urban environment.

Fig. 4.8

On the surface, copycat ads tell us that minorities and whites are the same, there is racial equality, and acculturation is highly desirable. Beneath the surface, however, the message is that whites might not buy a product used by minorities. If it were not problematic, there would be no need to use both white and ethnic versions of the same ad. Why not use just one version, ethnic or white?

In one sense, copycat ads are more of a targeting afterthought. Mainstream marketing research tries to help advertisers reach the white, middle- to upper-class market. As ethnic minorities become socially mobile, they too are targeted, but often through copycat ads instead of those that play on unique subcultural images and symbols. The copycat technique often misreads Latino consumers, for example. A marketing campaign for fabric softener, for example, targeted at Latinas who are

Fig. 4.9a

Fig. 4.9b

Fig. 4.10   Fig. 4.11

recent arrivals to the United States is ineffective if they do not grasp the notion of two-step (wash and soften) laundry.

Which ad is the original and which is the copycat? They appear in print at approximately the same time. The difference is the target audience for the magazine or newspaper. The issue is not which is the copycat, but the bending of ethnic images into a utopian assimilated social context instead of using actual, unique subcultural values, images, and symbols. Despite the widespread use of copycat ads, their absence from advertising textbooks is notable. This may be due to a fear of facing the controversial nature of ethnic advertising (see O'Guinn, Allen, and Semenik 1998).

Racial Assimilation

> American culture is obsessed with blackness, but primarily in a commodified form that can than be possessed, owned, controlled, and shaped.
>
> —bell hooks

Through casting, print advertising exalts white standards of beauty: light skin, straight or wavy hair, and blue or green eyes. In other words, one must be as white as possible. When minority women appear in ads, they also conform to the generic ideal image: young, beautiful—often as defined by white standards—perfect, and sexually seductive (see figure 4.12). They are sometimes shown with light skin (figure 4.13), straight hair (figure 4.14), and Euro-American features (figure 4.15). The copy in figure 4.13 reads, "Fade to beautiful," indicating that cultural standards of feminine beauty demand lighter skin.

Fig. 4.12

Look at the notable difference in skin color in two photographs of a young black female model: a candid Polaroid shot (figure 4.16) and an advertisement (figure 4.17). With the use of a fair foundation makeup, she appears unrecognizably lighter complected in the ad. The racial assimilation model in advertising also applies to black men, as shown in figure 4.18.

Fig. 4.13

Social Reality Model

Second is the social reality model, in which minority life is presented as it is, not as a copycat of white life. For example, a McDonald's commercial displayed a single black mother whose son apparently didn't like his mother's date (Burrell 1992). Other examples of generalizable representations of ethnic minority life and subculture include extended families and fathers laboring at two jobs. Since minorities are more likely to be poor or in lower-status occupations than whites, ads (figures 4.19–4.21) exemplifying this model reflect any differences that currently exist in society. This realistic approach draws the public's attention to the very real inequalities in our society.

Advertisers recognize the disproportionately large increase in the population and buying power of ethnic and racial minorities. For example, figure 4.20, an advertisement for Jaguar, targets blacks. The ad's photo displays the face of a young black man; the copy: "The new

Fig. 4.14

Fig. 4.15

Jag generation." Figure 4.21 is an attempt to recruit Latinos as employees to UPS by appealing to bilingualism and international travel. The social reality model helps us to explain the rising prevalence of ethnic marketing, which is the focus of chapter 5.

Cultural Attitudes Model

The cultural attitudes of whites toward minorities also influence the way that minorities are portrayed in advertising. Social stratification is reflected in advertising. American society is highly stratified by race, ethnicity, gender, and social class. Advertising becomes an indicator of the readiness of influential groups to tolerate the mainstreaming of ethnic minorities in society. In short, advertisements are signs of ethnic secondary and primary assimilation.

Williams (1970) identifies ten values that are central in U.S. culture. In addition to freedom, democracy, science, progress, and the like, they include racism and group superiority. These values, including the negative ones, are passed to the next generation through cultural transmission (Macionis 1996, 34) (see figure 4.22). Cultural beliefs favor whites over people of color, males over females, and the privileged over the disadvantaged.

There are privileges that attach to white skin color that are often latent, invisible, or unnoticed. Although we would like to think of ourselves as a society where everyone is equal, like George Orwell's successful revolutionaries in *Animal Farm*, there is no doubt that some of us are "more equal than others."

The stereotypes and racist ideologies of dominant groups toward ethnic minorities are very revealing (Perkins 1979). These stereotypes depend on a connection of patterns that can be explained only in relation to each other (Carby 1987). Survey data indicate that whites are most willing to accept integration and equal treatment in the area of employment, less so in the area of close social contact and residential integration, and least so in the area of interracial relationships and marriage.

Fig. 4.16

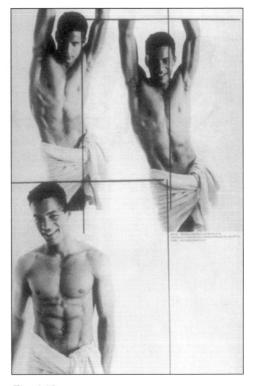

Fig. 4.18

Fig. 4.17

Fig. 4.19

Fig. 4.20

Fig. 4.21   Fig. 4.22

Secondary Assimilation

Let's look at these three areas in relationship to advertising. Humphrey and Schuman (1984) compared the frequency and social characteristics of African Americans and whites in ads from *Time* and *Ladies' Home Journal* in 1950 and 1980. During that thirty-year span, the occupational level of blacks portrayed has risen considerably. I have found some ads (e.g., figure 4.23) that support the finding that whites are willing to accept occupational integration and equality.

Despite positive reactions to minority representations in advertising, marketers have not been willing to feature them on a regular basis. In 1985, the Lawyers Committee for Civil Rights under Law assailed the *Washington Post* for a sharp underrepresentation of ethnic minorities featured in its real estate section ads. From January 1985 through April 1986, minorities were featured in fewer than 2 percent of the *Post's* ads (*Advertising Age* 1986). At the time, the population of Washington, D.C., was 90 percent black. The *Post* replied by establishing a 25 percent target for blacks in real estate ads. The paper further said it would refuse advertising that did not comply with the policy. This acute underrepresentation of blacks mirrors survey data that indicate resistance to close social contact and residential integration (Humphrey and Schuman 1984). More recently, a 1997 Fannie Mae ad (figure 4.24), published in *Hispanic* magazine, proclaims "the American dream should be open to everyone" and explicitly posits a commitment to "breaking down the barriers to home ownership, including discrimination."

Fig. 4.23

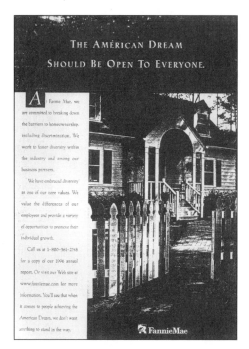

Fig. 4.24

Primary Assimilation

In the area of interracial relationships, I have found very few ads. Those that I have found depict the couples in nontraditional ways—in unusual attire, for example, as in figure 4.25. There has been a recent trend in advertising to show interracial friendships (4.26) and interracial socializing.

Not all differences between representations of African Americans and whites in ads can be readily explained by either of the first two models. Research on consumer responses to integrated advertising is inconclusive (Reid and Vanden Bergh 1980), perhaps because cultural attitudes toward ethnic minorities are contextually conditioned. Moreover, these cultural attitudes are mirrored in print advertising.

Ethnic Stereotyping

Another strategy in using minorities in advertising is to go completely in the other direction from equal presentation and play up or exaggerate the cultural and racial uniqueness of the role or the model.

Predator

One of the prevailing and enduring stereotypical images of ethnic minorities in the mass media has been that of the predator, someone who injures or exploits others for one's

Fig. 4.25

Fig. 4.26

Fig. 4.27

Fig. 4.28

own gain. A predator preys, plunders, destroys, or devours. Mass media have incessantly portrayed people of color as predators through their ethnicity or phenotypic features. The predator image has been around since at least the 1800s when American Indians were showed preying on stagecoaches in advertising for Buffalo Bill's Wild West shows.

The Chicano zoot-suiter was also stereotyped as a predator by California newspapers in the early to mid 1940s. The following illustrations are based on written descriptions of young Mexican American men by journalists (figures 4.27–4.29). This stereotype continues in contemporary images of young Latin men in advertising (figures 4.30a–4.30b). Figures 4.31a and 4.31b were posted adjacent to each other at Premier Operating Services

in Dallas, Texas, in 1998. Because they were placed side by side, it gave the impression that Spanish speakers were dangerous knife- and gun-carrying predators. The Equal Employment Commission successfully sued the firm for discrimination, driving it out of business.

Black men have also been exhibited as a predator (especially as a sexual threat to white women). This image can be seen in contemporary advertising (figures 4.32–4.33).

For women, the image is that of a sexual predator—a seductress. This image has been around since at least 1929 with Nina Mae McKinney's portrayal of a seductress who marries a revivalist in the feature film *Hallelujah*. The image of the sexual predator continues in contemporary advertising. Black women are sometimes portrayed as predatory, primitive, wild, or animal-like (figures 4.34–4.35).

Fig. 4.29

Fig. 4.30a

Fig. 4.30b

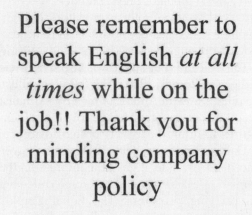

Fig. 4.31a   Fig. 4.31b

Fig. 4.32

Fig. 4.33

Fig. 4.34

Fig. 4.36

Fig. 4.37

Fig. 4.38

Fig. 4.39

Fig. 4.40

Fig. 4.41

Servant

In some ways, black representations in advertising have not changed much. Compare these illustrations from the 1930s and 1940s (figures 4.36–4.39) with contemporary advertisements (figures 4.40–4.41). Both the older and some of these more recent ads portray African Americans as servants who perform menial chores for a white person who has authority or political power over them. Black servants wear uniforms and always seem to be smiling.

Figure 4.42, a Versace ad, shows a Latina maid attending to a young white boy while he scowls at her.

Luscious Latina

Latinos are even more underrepresented than blacks in advertising. They were virtually nonexistent in ads prior to 1980 (Woods 1995). Even in the late 1980s, Latinos were featured in only 5.8 percent of all television commercials and as only 1.5 percent of the speaking characters on network television ads (Wilkes and Valencia 1989). When they do appear, Latinos are in background roles as part of a group. They are seen more often in commercials for food products, entertainment, alcohol, and furniture. Latinos typically are not represented in mainstream advertising hosting dinner parties, washing dishes, or drinking coffee (Woods 1995).

An exception to the vast underrepresentation of Latinos in mass media is the Latina sex object (figures 4.43–4.44). The cliché "Sex sells" seems especially applicable to the image of Latinas in advertising. The Luscious Latina, as presented by the mass media in film, television, and print advertising, has endured precisely because of its marketability (Fregoso 1993; Woll 1980). To sell its products the alcohol industry uses and reinforces representations that exploit and demean women. The liquor store poster

Fig. 4.42

Fig. 4.43

shown in figure 4.43, "Adelante con Budweiser," hints strongly at sexual availability. In fact, it bears a strong semblance to pornographic magazines. The luscious Latina is posed with her legs spread open. She is not relaxed; the balls of her feet rest on the floor as if she were wearing spike heels. Her shirt is coming off one shoulder. The copy means "Go Forward with Budweiser." The ad suggests that when a woman offers alcohol to a man, she is concurrently submitting herself to him. It also tells men that when women consume alcohol, they become sexually flirtatious and promiscuous.

The amalgam of genetic features characteristic of Latino populations provides an exotic and attractive look. At the same time, cultural factors and social stratification based on race have helped prevent Latinas from being assertive and self-confident. The passive role of Latinas corresponds to the complementary and active role of Latino men. The logic seems to be that since Latino men are macho, Latinas must be passive. This has resulted in a stereotype that portrays Latinas as inarticulate, subservient, passive, and gullible. This negative stereotype tends to limit mass media portrayals of Latinas to roles as either maids or sex objects.

Actresses in the past, such as Rita Hayworth and Delores del Rio, and today, such as Salma Hayek, sometimes present an image with both positive (e.g., powerful and sensuous) and negative (e.g., boisterous and oversexed) characteristics. Historically, del Rio broke the color barrier for Latinas in Hollywood in the 1920s. The exotic woman had her niche in movies. Lupe Velez, another breakthrough Latina actress, fell into the role of the comedic spitfire by "speaking with a heavy accent and resorting to rapid-fire Spanish when annoyed" (Menard 1997). Clearly, the spitfire, oversexed, and overly emotional woman was not an obsequious image. These images are present in today's media, including advertising. For example, figure 4.44 displays the Latina as a seductress.

Hayworth did not become popular in the 1930s and 1940s until her stereotypical image assimilated to Anglo standards. She dropped her image as a raven-haired, over-sexed Latina and transformed herself into an auburn-haired love goddess. Carmen Miranda, a contemporary of Hayworth, on the other hand, was never able to shake her image as a spitfire and was always typecast accordingly. Other Latinas pursued the trail blazed by these pioneers—Rita Moreno in the 1950s, Raquel Welch in the 1960s and 1970s, Charo in the 1970s, Sonia Braga in the 1980s, Jennifer Lopez and Hayek in the 1990s and the new millenium—though never quite breaking out of the sexually charged roles still retained for Latinas.

To be sure, advertising and film executives understand the allure and popularity of Latinas and have always found ways to profit from them. In fact, typecasting and stereotypes are perhaps the core of the modeling and film industries. Advertising agencies and Hollywood producers have always looked for "types." Unfortunately, Latina types seem to fit into one of three

Fig. 4.44

categories: Luscious Latinas, maids, or illegal immigrants. Young Latina models and actors, looking for visibility and a means to survive, are forced to accept jobs that cast them in these stereotypical roles.

Moreover, Latinas may also sometimes accept stereotypes because a role that requires physical attractiveness enhances notions of self-worth and self-esteem. The problem with this is that only a small proportion of Latinas are able to take advantage of this stereotype. Working-class Latinas are not afforded the opportunities to advance their careers or personal lives with this privilege. It is not always wise to stake one's self-regard on an attribute as ephemeral as physical attractiveness. It is crucial that Latina models and actors have access to playing everyday people, ranging from hard-working mothers to professional women.

Native American Stereotypes

Native American symbolism has not been used often in advertising. Marketers, however, have occasionally used it in their general marketing campaigns. Most popular is the Jeep Cherokee. A representation of an Indian woman is the logo for Land O'Lakes dairy products. Native American symbolism has not always been used by advertisers with cultural sensitivity. Sometimes it has been stereotypical and derogatory (see the Savage Code ad in figure 5.3.) The ad in figure 4.45, while ostensibly harmless, is a very stereotypical representation of a young Indian girl.

In 1991, much to the consternation of the Native American community, a brewer planned to introduce a new type of malt liquor dubbed "Crazy Horse" (Woods 1995) (see chapter 5). The namesake for the product was obviously the legendary Lakota (Sioux) war chief. Nevertheless, his descendants argue that Crazy Horse condemned alcohol because he regarded it as destructive to his people. These examples demonstrate cultural insensitivity and ethnic ignorance on the part of advertisers.

Asian Stereotypes

Figure 4.46 displays the traditional Japanese sumo wrestler. In figure 4.47, the image of a Japanese Kabuki performer with a brightly painted face is used to sell

Fig. 4.45

Fig. 4.46

tea. Kabuki is the traditional Japanese popular drama with singing and dancing performed in a highly stylized manner. Japanese men have historically played female roles in Kabuki theater.

Advertising stereotypes the Asian woman as a passive sex object. Asian women have been reduced to one-dimensional caricatures in Western representations (Espiritu 1997). In media, the Asian women is eroticized as exotic, sensuous, promiscuous, but untrustworthy.

Historical Representations of Blacks in Advertising

The image of African Americans in advertising has certainly changed, in some ways, in the last fifty or sixty years. Clearly, as educational and professional occupational levels have risen considerably for African Americans, this has been reflected in mass media, including advertising (see Humphrey

Fig. 4.47

and Schuman 1984). Moreover, the portrayals of blacks and black-white interaction increased between 1946 and 1965 (Kassarjian 1969). There was also an increase in the number of ads depicting blacks, and the roles that blacks portrayed changed by 1968 from chiefly unskilled in 1949 to skilled (Cox 1970).

The number of blacks featured in *Life, Look, Reader's Digest*, and *Ladies' Home Journal* increased in the 1960s, but the manner in which they were portrayed tended to confirm and perpetuate racial stereotypes (Colfax and Sternberg 1972). Later, however, "improvements" in the occupational status of black models in magazine ads were evident (Zinkhan, Cox, and Hong 1986). There was an increase in the use of black models between 1967 and 1974; they tended to advertise personal items, such as hair products, rather than nonpersonal products, such as automobiles (Bush, Solomon, and Hair 1974). Black models were also more likely to be found in public service announcements. Black media representations have increased over time; blacks are more often represented in television than in print advertising (Zinkhan, Qualls, and Biswas 1990). Blacks moved from background roles to minor roles, but there has been no substantial increase in their presence in major roles (Reid and Vanden Bergh 1980).

Cartoons and movie sound tracks utilize the threatening sound of drumming in the night, the hint of primitive rites and cults. Early ads, cartoons (figures 4.48–4.49), knickknacks, and movies depicted the simple, devoted female mammy figure with rolling eyes and the faithful, childlike, rhythmic, lazy, unreliable, clownlike, half-witted, unpredictable, and undependable male Sambo figure. This Sambo image continues today (figure 4.50). After the abolition of slavery, the urban coon or zip coon image of the black male as savage, cheating, cunning, barbaric, and violent was presented in an attempt to show the black man's failure to adapt to freedom. While these particular versions may have faded, their descendants are still present in popular culture, albeit reworked in many postmodern and updated images. One ad from Australia, for example, still depicts blacks as savages, primitives, and natives (figure 4.51).

Fig. 4.48

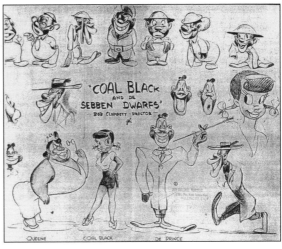

Fig. 4.49

Fig. 4.50

Fig. 4.51

Representations of Black Children in Advertising

Pay attention to the young and make them
just as good as possible.

—Socrates

Symbolic racism includes subtle ethnic stereo-typing, trivialization of minority empower-ment or racial equality, or the absence of ethnic images. There are mass-marketing advertising campaigns in which children of color never appear. Positive stereotypes are as significant as negative ones in terms of what ads reveal about race relations. Positive stereotypes of white children and negative stereotypes of ethnic minority children are part of a larger set of racial attitudes. The American dream begins at infancy for whites, at least as seen through the lenses of print advertising (Seiter 1995). Their pricelessness is stressed by reference to their future economic value. For example, an ad showing a white baby's bare bottom reads: "One day this little bottom may sit on the board of directors." A common stereotype of white infants and small children in ads is the go-getter (Seiter 1995). This image is not available for children of color, who tend to be shown in advertising as passive observers of their white playmates. (See the discussion on function ranking in chapter 2).

Fig. 4.52

The same trait or behavior may be judged to be either positive or negative depending on the race of the model. For example, if black children are illustrated in the same aggressive poses displayed by white boys, they are viewed as pushy bullies or bruisers.

We are part of a culture where white skin and blond hair define what is attractive. A dominant group's status is comparatively fixed and clear. This is why the images of blond children in the media have remained markedly stable over the years. Note the sharp racial contrast in the ad shown in figure 4.52.

Whiteness is the norm for media images; it reflects what is perceived as "natural": "White is not anything really, not an identity, not a particularizing quality, because it is everything—white is not a color because it is all colors. This property of whiteness to be everything and nothing, is the source of its representational power" (Dyer 1988, 45).

In a predominantly white media world, it is easy to notice ethnic minority children when they appear in ads. From a white perspective, it is also easy not to notice their omission from mainstream advertising. Advertisers may use a black child to represent all minority children. At the same time, white children are portrayed as endlessly varied, individual, even quirky and idiosyncratic (Seiter 1995). Commercial messages ignore or do not recognize the tremendous diversity between and within ethnic minority groups such as blacks, Latinos, Asians, and Native Americans.

Colfax and Sternberg (1972) note advertisers try to make advertisements less threatening to whites by using black children instead of black adults. But even when black children are used, there is still an element of symbolic racism that ensures that even black children are not threatening to whites. In the three-page Benetton ad in figures 4.53a–c, the first frame shows a close head shot of a blond-haired white child who faces the viewer; the second frame displays a silhouetted profile of a young black girl; and the final frame features a black boy with the back of his head toward the viewer.

Blacks have sometimes been portrayed as dependent on whites, with white authority figures aiding blacks or supervising black children (figure 4.54). However, I have also found ads with blacks aiding white children (figure 4.55). Black children are often shown without parents, as token members of peer groups, or as "neighborhood kids," as Mattel named one of its genres of multiracial dolls. Black children are not typically in commercial messages dealing with fantasy images of home, safety, love, and family.

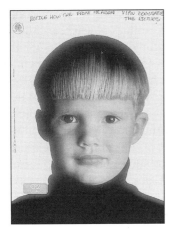

Fig. 4.53a

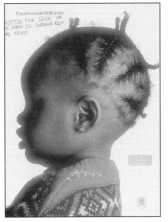

Fig. 4.53b

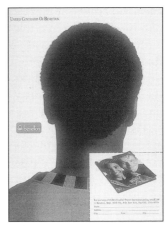

Fig. 4.53c

They do not appear to share the utopian visions of their white counterparts. When black children are visible in ads, they are on city streets, outdoors, or sitting in fast-food restaurants.

These are all examples of what I call symbolic racism, a term that is not dissimilar from the term symbolic annihilation (Gerbner and Gross 1976; Tuchman 1978). Blacks have been omitted, stereotyped, or debased in advertising images. These representations are important because the mass media's portrayal of blacks is likely to influence white attitudes. Because mainstream society develops many of its views about ethnic groups through advertising and other forms of mass media, stereotypical representations can lead to stereotypical attitudes (Woods 1995). Ads help to shape racial images. Ethnic stereotypes in advertising can actually interfere with the acculturation and assimilation of ethnic minorities (Wilkes and Valencia 1989).

Many fourth- and fifth-grade white children reported that television is a greater source of information for them about blacks than are

Fig. 4.54

Fig. 4.55

friends, parents, and even personal contacts (Greenberg 1972). Thus, the representation of a black person in a television commercial is more likely to influence a white child's attitude about blacks than actual interracial contact (Humphrey and Schuman 1984). Exotic adults of color are sometimes seen in television commercials (Seiter 1995) or children's books (Pescosolido, Grauerholz, and Milkie 1997) that feature fantasy or magical themes. In short, minority adults are relegated to the roles of supernatural companions and helpers, playing roles very similar to those of animated animal figures (Seiter 1995).

When integrated groups of children are depicted in commercial messages, whites always outnumber blacks, who are often nearly pushed out of the frame by the other youngsters. Black children are rarely given speaking parts or shown in close-up facial shots. They are usually in group shots with white children. Black boys are stereotyped as clowns, in contrast to the multidimensionality of moods, expressions, and traits depicted in the white child. This code guides the portrayal of children in commercial images across an extensive array of advertising techniques. They are also very similar to black images in children's books (Pescosolido, Grauerholz, and Milkie 1997).

Representations of Blacks in Children's Books

Although the focus of our analysis is advertising, I have chosen also to compare the images of blacks in advertising with the portrayal of blacks in U.S. children's picture books (Pescosolido, Grauerholz, and Milkie 1997) for two reasons. First, historically speaking, there has been a parallel development in the nature of black representations in advertising and in children's books. Second, both ads and illustrations in children's books are public pictures (see chapter 1).

Racial Images, Gatekeeping, and Conflict

Pescosolido, Grauerholz, and Milkie (1997) studied patterns in the portrayal of black characters in children's picture books and the substantive nature of these images over time, from 1937 to 1993. They documented changes in racial images and examined the relationship between culture, gatekeeping, and conflict in society. They demonstrated a declining number of black images from the late 1930s through the late 1950s, virtually no images from that point through 1964, a sharp increase from the late 1960s to the early 1970s, and a leveling off after 1975. Moreover, the nature of these images varies over time. For example, in award-winning books, black characters reappear during the late 1960s in "'safe,' distant images" (Pescosolido, Grauerholz, and Milkie 1997, 443)—examples of symbolic racism. In addition, the portrayal of intimate, egalitarian, interracial interaction and the depiction of black adults as central characters are scarce.

Pescosolido, Grauerholz, and Milkie (1997) also found that increases in multicultural depictions were not sustained consistently across the three different sets of children's books that they studied. Prize-winning books are more likely to depict blacks. The researchers linked these patterns to gatekeeping activities and to conflict in black-white relations in the larger society. Ads from publishing houses were more likely to include black characters than were award panel selections or editorials in leading professional journals.

Prize-winning books continue a trend toward increased representation of blacks, accounting for most of the books with exclusively black characters. When challenges to the dominant societal norms were strongest (as measured by the number of conflicts, protests, and legal actions), blacks virtually disappeared from children's illustrated books published in the United States.

Previous studies of children's books show that portrayals of blacks have been stereotyped and narrowly focused (Klein 1985; Larrick 1965; Sadker and Sadker 1977). African Americans tend to be relatively invisible in children's literature, and when they do appear, they are shown in negative ways, especially prior to 1945 (Children's Literature Review Board 1977). Magazine advertisements, films, novels, cartoons, television, and newspapers typically indicate lower visibility and more restricted representations of black characters than white ones (Humphrey and Schuman 1984; Merelman 1992; Thibodeau 1989; Van Deburg 1984).

Pescosolido, Grauerholz, and Milkie (1997) hypothesized that there would be a more complicated account of symbolic racism throughout more recent U.S. history. This hypothesis was based on a dialectical rationale that social and cultural gains are often followed by countervailing recessions. For example, one can paint a positive account of racial advances if one considers a retreat of traditional racial stereotypes, higher educational and occupational attainment, and increasing voter registration and participation in the political process. On the other hand, one could argue for a gloomier picture considering the rise of hate crimes, new subtle racial stereotypes, high unemployment, high rates of intraethnic violent crime, and relatively low college attendance and graduation rates.

Pescosolido, Grauerholz, and Milkie (1997) expected that the period from World War II to the mid 1960s—a time of high uncertainty and radical social change—would present a crisis in symbolic representation. Cultural gatekeepers, those who set the images for public consumption, are to some extent affected by racial conflict in society. One avenue is to look at advertisements and the selection by editors of images in specialized professional journals. The authors used time-series analysis to examine whether the trends in cultural representations over time are significantly different from chance fluctuations and to test for the effects of the racial conflict and cultural gatekeeping variables. They hypothesized that the symbolic representation of blacks would follow a systematic but nonlinear pattern depending on the roles of cultural gatekeepers and the kinds of minority-majority intergroup relations and tensions. Gatekeeping was determined by comparing award-winning (Caldecott Medal or Caldecott Honor) books with other "quality" books from the librarians' reference Children's Catalog and the "popular" Golden Books line.

Data on racial conflict were based on descriptions of events involving blacks mentioned in the New York Times Index for the years 1926–1993. This index was chosen on the basis of previous analyses of ethnic conflict (McAdam 1982; Olzak 1992). The number of racial conflicts, protests, and legal actions each year is an indication of the struggle for the redistribution of economic, political, and social power between blacks and whites. Conflicts include acts of violence, physical confrontations, and arrests. Protests include actions related to racial tensions that do not involve direct confrontation. Legal actions refer to black-initiated litigation. These types of racial tensions often involve education and schools, colleges and universities, labor, housing, the Ku Klux Klan and other white-supremacy organizations, and assaults and disorderly conduct.

Images mirrored the subordinate status of blacks and the dominant position of whites. Ads and children's books stressed physical appearance and social status. They also depicted the behavior of blacks as role-determined. No intimate relationships between blacks and whites were shown.

Images in the Early Years

Not surprisingly, there is a parallel pattern between what I found in print advertisements and what Pescosolido, Grauerholz, and Milkie (1997) found in children's picture books. From 1937 through the mid-1950s, blacks appeared in minor, marginal roles. They occupied subservient positions such as menial workers, maids, porters, bellhops, servants, or slaves. During this era, black-white relations can be characterized as depicting "surface contact" (Levinger and Snoek 1972). In addition, in both early ads and children's books, black dialect is stereotyped. Take, for example, an excerpt from a 1945 Children's Catalog book, *Little Fellow*. The book features a black stablehand who says, "An a thororbred ef I evah seed one! De white folks gwine be might proud ov yo baby."

Children's books during this era showed black characters in multiracial clusters of children (and sometimes adults). This trend was especially evident in religious books during the 1930s and 1940s (Pescosolido, Grauerholz, and Milkie 1997). These children's books contained portrayals of children of diverse ethnic backgrounds, although there was no particular reference to race, culture, or ethnicity. Moreover, a white child was typically the central character of the story.

The inclusion of black characters in most of these books reveals "unilateral awareness" (Levinger and Snoek 1972). There is a shared proximity but no interracial interaction. However, in some books (e.g., *Small Rain: Verses from the Bible*, 1944), there is no one major character, and the depiction of black children throughout the book goes beyond superficial contact. Such rare images suggest mutuality or egalitarian and intimate relationships that focus on shared experiences (Levinger and Snoek 1972).

The Disappearance of Black Characters

From the late 1950s to the mid-1960s, we see a distinct second phase. Virtually no blacks appeared in children's books. In ads, black characters were also infrequent, appearing only as servants (such as Aunt Jemima). These kinds of stereotypes represent symbolic racism or symbolic annihilation. For example, *Boats*, a 1958 Little Golden Book, shows over two hundred whites and only three blacks. The black characters are posed on the top deck of a large paddleboat while whites mingle below. One black character eats watermelon, another plays the banjo, while the final one is asleep.

The Reintroduction of Black Characters

From the mid-1960s through the 1970s, the proportion of both ads and children's books displaying black characters increased sharply, owing to black economic, political, and social empowerment and the costly success of the civil rights movement. Moreover, black commercial images improved substantially from the earlier blatantly stereotypical depictions (Humphrey and Schuman 1984). For example, there were often both black and white versions of the same ad (see the analysis of copycat ads in this chapter). Similarly, in several children's books, blacks simply replace some whites (Pescosolido, Grauerholz, and Milkie 1997).

The Caldecott Award books included some that featured only black characters (Pescosolido, Grauerholz, and Milkie 1997). While these awards certainly legitimized black authors, they also represented another form of symbolic racism. All of the Caldecott Award books that depicted only black characters published from 1965 through the mid-1970s showed only "safe" and distant portrayals of blacks in Africa. Others have observed the conspicuous absence of contemporary United States blacks in a wide range of cultural products (Larrick 1965; Thibodeau 1989, 489). Sociologically, this demonstrated whites' continued rejection of blacks in mainstream social institutions and continued social inequality. Even though strong community and family life was depicted in several of the books with African themes, family structure was often difficult to discern in either text or illustrations (Pescosolido, Grauerholz, and Milkie 1997). Furthermore, there are no central characters throughout the books; the characters are not even singled out and given names.

Post-1975: Stabilization at New Levels

The representation of blacks in children's books seems to have leveled off after 1975 (Pescosolido, Grauerholz, and Milkie 1997). Blacks appeared in thirty of the fifty books that featured human characters. The symbolic racism continued; the books displayed surface contact, such as crowd scenes on playgrounds or city streets or in classrooms. The Little Golden Books series had a smaller percentage of books with black characters during this period than the previous one. This phenomenon is market driven; blacks spend proportionately less than whites on this type of book. In the Caldecott series, three patterns are evident (Pescosolido, Grauerholz, and Milkie 1997). First, books depicting only blacks focus on both Africans and African Americans. Second, since the 1990s, clear-cut interracial themes and political issues are included. Finally, there is racial ambiguity in characters, which allows more depth and resonance.

Transgressions of Omission

Symbolic racism both in advertising and in children's books points to a lack of progress in majority-minority relations. Throughout the entire period and across the three series, there is a noticeable lack of "mutuality" or intimate, egalitarian relations central to the story lines (Pescosolido, Grauerholz, and Milkie 1997, 455). Moreover, most of today's books are not interracial. When they are, images are similar to the group images in the early religious books (i.e., background scenery).

Interracial childhood friendships seldom appear, and interracial adult relationships are even rarer. When such relationships occur, they appear to be merely the result of chance. Black adults rarely appear as central characters, perhaps because black adults are perceived as more threatening to whites than black children. When black adults are found, they are "safe," distant images in African and African American folktales or fantasy characters. It is particularly telling that not one Caldecott book features a contemporary black man (Pescosolido, Grauerholz, and Milkie 1997).

Ethnic Representations and Ethnic Relations

The larger question is whether ethnic relations in society can explain trends in the images of ethnic minorities. The rise and decline of ethnic conflict suggests an inverse relationship to the greatest change in the visibility of blacks in children's books. The data demonstrate a slight rise in conflict starting in 1945, corresponding to a gradual decline in portrayals of black characters; a sharp increase in conflict between 1955 and

1965 corresponding to the disappearance of blacks in illustrations and story lines; a sharp decrease in the late 1960s, paralleled by the dramatic reintroduction of portrayals of blacks in books; and a return to earlier low levels of conflict, corresponding to stabilization in the images of blacks in overall trends.

As ethnic conflict escalated, black characters and interracial images were systematically removed from children's books. This pattern held across all three sets of books. While the overall pattern indicates an increase in books that feature only black characters, the Caldecott books largely account for the trend (Pescosolido, Grauerholz, and Milkie 1997).

Ethnic conflict has cultural as well as social consequences that are revealed in the changing images of blacks in children's books. At the period of greatest uncertainty in ethnic relations, a period marked by increasing legal and social protest and conflicts, blacks virtually disappeared from children's books, suggesting indecision or unwillingness to portray racial contact in new and radical ways. Pescosolido, Grauerholz, and Milkie (1997) found two major patterns. First, stories and illustrations in which intimate interracial relationships are central appear rarely in early and later phases. In the books, black and white characters may stand beside one another; much less often, they interact in intimate egalitarian ways central to the story. Second, contemporary black men and women are less likely than black children to play a central role in the stories. In general, blacks were secondary, peripheral, and subordinate characters from the late 1930s through the 1950s.

Thus, the amount of interracial tension in society is significantly and inversely related to the images of blacks in children's books. When black-white relations were stable before and after the sharp increase in black insurgency, black characters were more visible, whereas during the time of contested black-white relations, blacks and black-white interactions were virtually removed from books.

Data on gatekeeping indicate that books chosen for awards are much more likely to feature only black characters than are children's books more generally. Cultural gatekeepers, who grant enormous prestige (and income) to illustrators, authors, and publishing houses through the Caldecott Award, appear to prefer African folktales. It is extremely ironic that the selection of African folktales, which are an important part of the African American cultural heritage, remunerates books removed from contemporary U.S. society and from whites.

Ethnic crises push cultural producers to avoid books about troublesome issues and groups. Although the direct response by predominantly white publishers during periods of racial tensions can only be inferred, the awareness that early depictions of blacks as subordinate were unacceptable is apparently coupled with a reluctance to portray new racial norms to young children (Thibodeau 1989). The political provocations of the civil rights movement left cultural producers without socially acceptable modes of portraying blacks. Blatant racist stereotypical images clearly were not in step with the ideological challenges to a social system stratified by race. Conversely, portrayals of racial equality or mutuality were distasteful to a powerful sector of individuals who were not comfortable with the implications of primary structural assimilation.

Blacks were reinserted into children's books in a variety of ways. The Caldecott Award books used full representations of black family, community, and history outside of the United States. The ever-popular Little Golden Books avoided racial controversy by simply adding black characters to preexisting stories and illustrations.

Why do blacks reappear in children's books in more positive portrayals even though substantial racial tensions persist? It is not so much the simple decline in racial conflict, per se, as gains in recognizing blacks as artists and writers and a greater responsiveness among whites to issues of racial equality. In short, racial conflict has resulted in a shift in social power for blacks. Such redistribution of power among blacks and whites propelled the changes in advertising images as well as those in children's books.

The conspicuous increase in distant and safe images of blacks in the Caldecott Award books may be interpreted as a remembrance and commemoration of blacks' unique cultural heritage. However, it may also be interpreted as symbolic racism in which the cultural representations of blacks do not include contact with whites or portray contemporary African American adults. The overall underrepresentation, especially in more recent years, of depictions of significant intimate relations between whites and blacks or of strong, contemporary adult images of blacks may testify to the persistence of a symbolic status quo in which black equality is viewed as threatening to whites (Humphrey and Schuman 1984).

In the era of shakiest ethnic relations in the United States, contentious power relations resulted in a vacuum in cultural images. A swift increase in black opposition quickly influenced advertising images and children's books and finally modified the portrayal of black characters into more positive depictions. However, the underrepresentation of images of contemporary black adults and of interracial reciprocity throughout the twentieth century conceivably indicates the continuation of social distance between blacks and whites.

Representations of Ethnic Minorities in Advertising

Eventually, social change dramatically reversed images of ethnic minorities in advertising as well as in children's books. People of color became much more visible and were portrayed more favorably. Four points about the images of ethnic minorities in advertising are notable:

1. Until the 1980s, there were virtually no ethnic minority fashion models on the runways or in mainstream print media. This historical omission of positive ethnic minority images in advertising represents the persistence of a symbolic status quo in which minority equality is viewed as threatening to whites (Humphrey and Schuman 1984).

2. Now ads are changing color and are becoming an ethnic rainbow. The saturation of ethnic minority images in mainstream broadcast and print media tracks racial advances, such as higher educational and occupational attainment; recent black economic, political, and social empowerment; and a retreat of traditional racial stereotypes.

3. Despite the large increase in ethnically diverse models, problems remain with how their images are marketed to the public. Ethnic minority models in ads often conform to standards of white beauty. This conformity is similar to the conspicuous increase in safe images of blacks in books.

4. At other times models are exploited through their ethnicity or phenotypic features. This trend of playing up unique ethnic characteristics is similar to the form of symbolic racism seen in books in which minorities are portrayed with distant images, commemorating their particular cultural heritage, but without contact with whites.

Perhaps multicultural ads are now popular because they are a reflection of social reality as a global village (recall figure 1.5). Ads using only white models risk appearing stiff or dated. Similarly, using only one token person of color in a white crowd or group is a thinly veiled attempt to appear sensitive to ethnic minorities. Now minorities are used to sell products and services to all people. The use of black models in advertising grabs the attention of both black and white viewers (Burrell 1992).

The use of minorities in ads first emerged in Europe. Couturiers, notably Givenchy, began using black women as runway fashion models (Scott 1989). There was a negative response to this; some French felt that the jobs should not be given to immigrants. *Elle*, a top French fashion magazine, assisted in the development of the multicultural look in its editorial pages. The global-village look entered the United States in 1985 when the American version of *Elle* was introduced.

One of the original advertisers to adopt the global-village look was Benetton (see chapter 1, "The Benetton Controversy Continues"). The Italian knitwear producer initiated its United Colors of Benetton campaign in 1984 (Scott 1989). The ads show ethnically diverse, good-looking teens and youngsters, often arm in arm. Benetton's goal is to project a sense of brotherhood and sisterhood as well as appeal to ethnic consumers. Also in the 1980s, Esprit, a San Francisco–based sportswear enterprise, took a step further in this direction by using actual employees in ads. Today Wal-Mart does the same with its ethnically diverse workforce.

Advertising across the globe has become increasingly ethnically diverse. Japan, a country whose advertising has reflected an obsession with blond hair, blue or green eyes, long legs, narrow noses—the Western provocateur—has shifted to using more Latinos, blacks, and Asians. Ethnically diverse advertising images provide a unique

Fig. 4.56   Fig. 4.57

alternative to sterile white ones and are more representative of the real world. Model-ing agencies now recruit internationally in order to meet the ever-increasing demand for fresh faces and the ethnic look. The shift toward more ethnically diverse fashion models is a big step in social change and offers a cultural opening to a previously closed arena. Multiculturalism represents a cultural strength instead of racial conflict or divi-sion. The biracial look is in vogue in advertising. The process of changing racial defin-itions continues, and dramatic new developments may be on the horizon. These poten-tial changes may be attributable to increasing rates of interracial marriage and the new ethnic classification in the census that finally recognizes multiracial individuals.

Conclusion

There has been considerable growth in the use of ethnic representations in advertising. However, sometimes advertisers merely "color" mainstream ads. Copy-cat ads are prevalent. Ethnic stereotypes remain. In other marketing campaigns, ethnic themes are tastefully done (4.56). Sometimes explicit reference is made to dark skin color, as with the "Ebony and gold" copy in the ad in figure 4.57.

It certainly remains debatable whether ethnic representations in advertising have improved. They are important because through visual and sound imagery, one is able to understand how mainstream culture views ethnic subcultures.

5

Ethnic Advertising

Mass marketing is dead. Marketing segmentation is the way of the future.
—Gail Baker Woods, *Advertising and Marketing to the New Majority*

Ethnic advertising has always been aimed at specific audiences and therefore, is at
the forefront of what we call target marketing.
—Tom Burrell, chairman and CEO, Burrell Communications Group

Cultural diversity has always been a hallmark of our society. Ethnicity has been a part
of the social character in the United States since its inception. For persons of color, as for
other population segments in society, subcultures play a significant role in individual
identity, as well as in group unity and cohesiveness. A *subculture* is "any cultural pat-
terning that preserves important features of the dominant society but provides values
and life styles of its own" (Berkman and Gilson 1978, 11). "Subcultural behavior is a
means through which heritage and pride can be openly communicated" (Woods 1995,
6). In short, a subculture serves three major functions: (1) it provides a psychological
source of group identification; (2) it offers a patterned network of groups and institutions; and (3) it serves as a frame of reference for viewing the new culture (Gordon 1978).
  The use of language or dialect, the celebration of events, and certain types of attire
and hairstyles sometimes believed to be unacceptable in mainstream culture can be displayed within the subculture without fear of rejection. Membership in subcultures has
become a method of protecting and preserving what is unique and distinct about specific groups of people (Woods 1995). These are people who refuse to give up their
native culture in order to be considered American.
  Today ethnicity is also an important characteristic in both culture and consumer
behavior. How a product or service is constructed, how it is positioned, where it can be
bought, and what it costs are quite important issues for ethnic consumers. As a result,
they are also key considerations for product and service advertisers attempting to reach
these ethnic groups. Yet there probably is not an area in consumer behavior where
research is more deficient (O'Guinn, Allen, and Semenik 1998). What is attributed to ethnicity is often instead due to an extraneous variable associated with ethnic background.
  From the late 1970s to the present, there has been a growing body of literature on ethnic advertising and marketing (Woods 1995). Generally, there have been three foci of
studies: (1) ethnic representations in advertising; (2) the proportional representation of

minorities in advertising; and (3) consumer behavior effects of advertising on minorities. Although the foci are conceptually distinct, they are connected with respect to trying to understand what strategies function successfully in reaching an ethnic minority target audience. While marketing research tries to measure what techniques are able to persuade an ethnic minority consumer to buy a particular brand of goods, the ethnic (and gender) representations in advertising fall within the purview of social responsibility.

Ethnic marketing is actually a type of segmented advertising. There are several urgent incentives for examining ethnic marketing. First is sheer numbers. As the size of ethnic markets increases exponentially, so does their spending power. For example, in 1992, ethnic minority shoppers, predominantly Latinos, blacks, and Asians, spent $600 billion on everything from toothpaste to shoes to cars (McCarroll 1993). This represents an 18 percent increase in two years. Second, because markets for products change, die out, or shift priorities, marketers must discover new ways to sell products. For example, the Listerine ad from the 1940s shown in figure 5.1 pushed the product as an astringent, not a mouthwash. Third, economic instability has created a trend toward careful segmentation, minimizing costs and maximizing profits. Major firms such as Sears, Wal-Mart, and PepsiCo are competing for minority markets, using minority marketing experts who speak each group's language and understand their customs. This is truly the age of ethnic marketing.

Latinos and blacks, for example, are said to have greater brand loyalty than whites. However, people of color live in areas where there are fewer product and service choices (O'Guinn, Allen, and Semenik 1998). If income disparity between ethnic minorities and whites is controlled for, the differences in brand loyalty disappear. Nevertheless, ethnic groups do have subculturally related consumption tastes. In order to tap into such preferences, high-quality consumer research must be undertaken. Ethnic marketing applies the basic postulates of segmentation. Moreover, advertising agencies must seek a deep understanding of ethnic identity and subcultures. It wasn't until the mid to late 1980s that many companies in the United States tried to court the black consumer (Dates 1990). Endeavors to serve the Latino communities have been erratic and sometimes inappropriate.

Black Culture and General Marketing Campaigns

A brief look at the history of popular culture reveals a pattern of the way that ethnic subcultures, at times, sway mainstream culture, which in turn activates general market advertising. The producers of mainstream culture have shown a strong interest in, and curiosity about, black culture (Burrell 1992). Black culture is viewed as being at the cutting edge.

Fig. 5.1

Clothing styles seen on black youth are often copied by their white counterparts. Marketers have used black cultural representations (e.g., Gatorade and Nike television commercials) to convey a variety of themes and to appeal to a wider audience.

Various African American musical artists have produced, recorded, and performed jazz, blues, rap, soul, rhythm and blues, and other types of music that have successfully crossed over to mainstream culture. These types of music are now a prevalent fixture in television and radio advertising. Even when blacks are not featured in the visuals of ads, their music can be heard (Woods 1995).

From black music and dance to Ebonics, marketers have employed black culture or black celebrities in some of their most lucrative campaigns. Black music has been easily embraced and exploited by the advertising industry to sell products and services. "Black people have traditionally set trends in fashion style, language, and particularly, entertainment," as they did in the 1980s (Lewis 1992).

The popularity of black music in commercials is perhaps exceeded only by the marketing industry's extensive use of endorsements by black athletes such as Tiger Woods, Kevin Garnett, Reggie Williams, Allen Iverson, Serena and Venus Williams, Grant Hill, Shaquille O'Neal, Kobe Bryant, and Emmit Smith.

The use of black athletes to endorse products and services is not a novel idea. Jackie Robinson, the first black player in major league baseball, was used in the 1950s in cigarette advertising targeted at blacks (Woods 1995). And who could forget O. J. Simpson running through airports for Hertz rental cars?

The use of black athletes to sell goods has not occurred without undue delay and criticism. In 1988, Doug Williams, of the Washington Redskins (pardon the racist stereotype), became the first black quarterback to win the coveted Super Bowl. Yet afterward, commercial endorsements were nowhere to be found. Marketers believed that mainstream advertising was not yet ready for a black spokesperson.

There are accusations that the use of black athletes promotes and maintains stereotypes of the black jock and the black stud. Athletic prowess is not the only representation of black culture borrowed by marketers. Black images are often used in advertising to impart what is considered "cool," stylish, "hip," or insurgent. Black representations and black music, so prevalent in postmodern advertising, are being used increasingly to market products and services to mainstream consumers. The jury is still out on whether the same outlooks and methods used on the mainstream population are interchangeable with ethnic minority advertising.

At least until the late 1960s, the history of advertising in our society can be characterized as "One message fits all." However, like the homogenized 1950s-era households to which they were targeted, the methods of mass marketing are changing dramatically. Waves of immigrants from Mexico, Latin America, Asia, and Africa, added to an already rapidly growing minority population, are radically reshaping the face and buying habits of the traditional American consumer. Minorities are not persuaded to buy by ads that display only whites or represent ethnic people in stereotypical, unrealistic, or unlikely roles. Because of the enormous variety of merchandise and services, consumers of color will simply make their purchases elsewhere.

Mass marketing was used heavily when the United States was viewed as a cultural melting pot. Now postmodern advertising uses a distinct approach to fit the tastes, worldviews, ideologies, and spending habits of each group. Corporate America in many ways is at the cutting edge of multiculturalism. Nearly half of all Fortune 1000 companies had some kind of ethnic-marketing campaign in 1992 (McCarroll 1993). That is up from only a handful in 1980. In 1992, corporations spent $500 million on advertising and promotions to reach ethnic minority consumers (McCarroll 1993). This included bilingual or Spanish-language-only billboards, mailings, sweepstakes, and parades. Expenditures on advertising and promotional campaigns aimed at ethnic groups have increased steadily since the 1980s.

Minority-targeted advertising has been around since the 1960s, when McDonald's and Coca-Cola advertised to Latinos in Spanish. However, the benefit of ethnic targeting was not fully acknowledged until the 1970s, when corporations realized that blacks were spending close to $250 million a year on consumer products. Corporations such as Quaker Oats and Philip Morris began to permeate the market, gradually succeeding with African American consumers by portraying blacks in positive and nonstereotypical roles. Corporate America invested heavily in ethnic marketing research in order to do its homework on black consumers.

Demographic Changes and Social Characteristics

The vast movement of blacks from the South to the North after World War II, a sharp increase in immigrants from Mexico and Latin America, and a constant flow of Asian newcomers, especially South Koreans and Filipinos, have greatly changed the racial makeup of the population in the United States. To be sure, such ethnic groups stand in contrast to the white majority population, yet they, too, consider themselves American.

Dramatic Ethnic Minority Growth

The face and color of America's cities have greatly changed in the past fifty years. By 2000, Latinos became this country's most numerous ethnic minority (35,305,818, U.S. Census Bureau 2001, table 1.1). This represents 12.5 percent of the total U.S. population.

Data on Latinos are conservative since they do not include undocumented immigrants who cross the border illegally—by some estimates, 46.2 percent of all Latino immigrants (Woods 1995). Nevertheless, they are consumers who work and purchase U.S. products and services. African Americans (34,658,190) are the second largest ethnic minority category in the United States, with 12.3 percent of the total population (U.S. Census Bureau 2001).

Both the black and Latino populations are younger than the white population. Latinos and Asians are the fastest-growing minorities. Since 2000, half of all elementary school children in the United States are now ethnic minorities; nearly half (44 percent) of all residents in the United States under the age of twenty are nonwhite (U.S. Census Bureau 2001).

The United States has undergone racial change throughout its history but never at the current rate and in the present way. Within the next fifty years, whites as a share of the total population will decline from 75 percent to just over 50 percent. The black population will increase in size but remain at about 12 percent of the total population. The Latino population may increase to more than one-quarter of the total.

Latinos. Latinos are the fastest-growing ethnic group in the country. The Latino population was only 4 million in 1950 (Woods 1995). It grew to 6.9 million in 1960, 9 million in 1970. Between 1970 and 1989, the Latino population increased from 9 million to 23.7 million, a 163 percent increase (Berry 1990).

Latinos include Mexican Americans or Chicanos, Puerto Ricans, Central and South Americans, and Cubans. The Latino population is predominantly young, with a median age of twenty-four, six full years younger than the general population (Woods 1995). Cubans are an exception, with a median age of 39.1 in 1987, markedly older than the overall population.

Chicanos constitute 60 percent of the Latino population and are predominantly (83.3 percent) located in the Southwest (Texas, California, New Mexico, Arizona, and Colorado) (Saenz and Greenlees 1996). Chicanos grew at a record pace during the 1980s. In fact, they account for approximately one-fourth of the total growth in the U.S. population during that decade (Saenz and Greenlees 1996). The Chicano population increased 55.4 percent during that period, about 5.5 times faster than the U.S. total population.

The growth of the Chicano population has been due to three factors. First, Chicanos are relatively younger than other ethnic groups in the United States. While the baby boom generation begins to approach retirement age, the Latino population is getting younger, on average. Such youthfulness in the Chicano population signifies greater potential for growth, since low proportions of group members are in age groups with high death rates, but high proportions are in the younger age groups that are correlated with childbearing and family formation. Second, Chicanos have higher birthrates than other ethnic groups. Thirty-seven percent more Latinos are born each year than die (U.S. Census Bureau 1993). Finally, the growing number of Chicanos is augmented by a large influx of immigrants. Immigration accounted for approximately half of the growth in the Latino population during the 1980s (O'Hare 1992).

The second largest group is Puerto Ricans, with an estimated 3 million people (U.S. Census Bureau 2000a), many living in New York City. There are more than 1.7 million people in the United States from South and Central America. Another 1.4 million Latinos are Cubans, who are heavily concentrated in Miami and the rest of South Florida. More than three out of every four Latinos (76 percent) live in only five states: Texas, California, Florida, New York, and Illinois (Woods 1995). Latinos, like blacks, are more urban than the general population. Los Angeles has the largest number and the highest concentration of Latinos, with 5.3 million people, a full third of the area's total population. The next largest numbers of Latinos are found in New York, Miami, and San Francisco.

By 2050, the Census Bureau predicts, Latinos will be about a quarter of the U.S. population, and blacks, less than a sixth. Latinos are also the least educated ethnic group. Only 7.1 percent of all Latinos have college degrees, compared with 15.4 percent of all blacks (U.S. Census Bureau 2000a). Retailers cannot endure unless they are able to draw from this dominant economic force.

Asian Americans. Asian Americans are a diverse category, including Koreans, Indians, Vietnamese, Filipinos, Chinese, Japanese, and Pacific Islanders. They have been considered *middlemen* (Bonacich 1973) and *model minorities* (Woods 1995) because they tend to occupy an intermediate economic position within American society. They are "strongly motivated to work hard, to be thrifty, to take economic risks, and concentrate their funds in businesses that may easily be converted into money" (McLemore and Romo 1998, 190). Frugality, honesty, and an entrepreneurial spirit have helped to make Asian Americans prosperous and powerful (Woods 1995).

By 2050, Asians may increase from their present 3.6 percent (U.S. Census Bureau 2001) to 8 percent. Filipinos are expected to be the largest Asian group, representing 21 percent of the total Asian American population. Chinese are expected to be 17 percent, Vietnamese 16 percent, Indian 10 percent, Japanese 9 percent, and "other" 14 percent.

Asian American households, like their Latino counterparts, are larger than those of other Americans (U.S. Census Bureau 2001). There is typically more than one worker in the household, resulting in higher household incomes (U.S. Census Bureau 2000b). Asian Americans, like blacks and Latinos, are more urban than the general population. Fifty-six percent of all urban Asian Americans live in California or Hawaii (U.S. Census Bureau 2001).

Asian Americans have relatively high educational and income levels. They have the fastest-growing rates of college enrollment of all ethnic groups. Thirty-six percent of all Asian Americans have college degrees, compared with only 25 percent of all Americans (U.S. Census Bureau 2000a). Ninety-six percent of all Japanese males receive their high school diplomas, while 94 percent of Koreans complete high school (Greenberg et al. 1987).

Native Americans. Native Americans, with an estimated two and a half million people, are the nation's smallest minority group, constituting 0.9 percent of the total population (U.S. Census Bureau 2001). Native Americans are a rural people, generally living on reservations. They have the lowest median income of all Americans ($30,784, U.S. Census Bureau 2000b); nearly 26 percent (U.S. Census Bureau 2000c) of all Native Americans live in poverty. They are the only ethnic minority group that is not expected to grow rapidly at the beginning of the new century.

Black-White Inequality

Although the ethnic market and the general market overlap somewhat, there are also ample differences. Considerable income gaps remain between ethnic minorities and whites. The unemployment rate for blacks is among the highest in the United States, hovering at about 10 percent in 1994 (Woods 1995). In major urban areas where most blacks reside, jobless rates are much higher than the national average.

The consumption behavior patterns of blacks must be considered against a backdrop of their overall economic situation. Blacks are nearly the poorest ethnic minority group in the United States. The median income of all black families is only $31,778, compared to that of all American families ($48,950) (U.S. Census Bureau 2000b). However, married-couple black families in which both husband and wife were wage earners took in 84 percent of the income of similar white families ($49,752 versus $59,025).

Household Composition. Another factor affecting the black market is household composition. The married couple is the rule among white families and the exception among blacks. Nearly 83 percent of white families are built around married couples, compared with 46 percent of black families. There were more black families headed by single women than black married couples in 1996. Half of all black households are headed by women (Deloitte & Touche Trade Retail and Distribution Services Group 1991). Female-headed households are most likely to live in a seemingly endless cycle of poverty. Nearly 24 percent of all blacks live beneath the poverty level (U.S. Census Bureau 2000c). Black households are larger than white households. Twenty-eight percent of all black households are composed of five or more people (Woods 1995). Larger households, to be sure, spend more money on food. Blacks as a group spend an estimated $30 billion annually on food (Smikle 1992).

Education. Blacks achieved significant educational progress from 1960 to the mid-1970s. By the beginning of the 1980s, however, the number of blacks attending college began to slip (Woods 1995). This slippage may be due, in large part, to the sharply rising costs of college tuition, fees, books, and room and board. Income differences sometimes narrow as education and family stability increase. For example, college-educated black women have nearly closed the income gap with their white counterparts. Black women with bachelor's degrees made 98 percent of what white women with the same level of education did in 1995. College-educated black men's income was 73 percent of that of similarly educated white males. Women of both races still make less than men.

Income. Black per capita income overall was 56 percent of white income in 1995. However, the steady economic growth of the mid-1990s apparently benefited black families; 10 percent of all black households had an annual income of $50,000 or more (Woods 1995). The 24 percent poverty rate for black families, while still four times the rate for white families, represented a continuing decline from the 31 percent level at the beginning of the 1990s. These are the lowest poverty rates since the mid-1960s. Clearly, the black middle class has grown considerably since the mid-1970s. At the same time, the black underclass has swelled in numbers (Woods 1995). It is clear that there is an increasing financial gap between middle- to upper-middle-class blacks and their economically disadvantaged black counterparts. It is difficult to commercially target all blacks because of this disparity.

Ethnic Marketing

This is the era of ethnic marketing.
—Gary Berman, president of Market Segment Research

As ethnic minorities increase in number and purchasing power, their share of the U.S. consumer market draws increasingly more attention from producers and retailers alike. *Buying* or *purchasing power* is the total personal income of consumers that is available, after taxes, for spending on goods and services. This may also be thought of as disposable income. In other words, as the ethnic minority population increases and the majority white population proportionately declines, there will be greater chances for target marketing to reach the homes of Latinos, blacks, Asians, and Native Americans.

Because of their unique status as subculture members as well as Americans, it is possible to market to ethnic minorities on two separate levels. Advertising messages with cultural allure appeal to their strong adherence to the tradition and heritage of their ethnic group. Because they also view themselves as Americans, representations of unity, participation, nationalism, and patriotism can be persuasive.

At the turn of the century, long before the sophisticated study of consumer behavior, decades before it was in vogue to target specialized segments of the marketplace, prior to the rise of strategic marketing, a black beautician known as Madam C. J. Walker produced and marketed a line of beauty products designed to eliminate the curl from black hair. Within twenty years, she was the first self-made female millionaire in the United States (Logan and Winston 1982). Without benefit of education, research, or demographic and psychological data, Madam Walker initiated one of the first comprehensive advertising and marketing campaigns aimed at an ethnic audience (Woods 1995). She provided the guideposts for future ethnic advertisers.

Aside from the efforts of Madam Walker (and perhaps a handful of others), ethnic advertising is still relatively new, having its unofficial beginning in the mid-1960s (Kovach 1985; McCarroll 1993). Textbooks started to incorporate minority subcultures and people. Ethnic groups were eventually earmarked as marketing targets with enormous potential for growth in buying power. By the 1970s, a "new" black middle class had been "discovered." These individuals had an annual average income of $33,000 (McAdoo 1979). Within the black middle class, there are significant differences in consumer patterns, lifestyles, and education. The black middle-class market is as diverse as the white middle-class market (Mellott 1983, 140). In fact, the consumer behavior patterns of black middle-class people, in many ways, are similar to those of their white counterparts.

Estimates of the absolute size and rate of growth of markets are significant factors of market potential. Market share is important because the higher the share, the lower the cost of reaching potential buyers. The more diffuse the market, the more difficult it is to target a particular consumer, although selective media or zip-code mailings can lower the unit cost of reaching individuals.

The black and Latino buying power estimates mentioned below suggest that targeting one basic advertisement, product, or service to all consumers misses many potentially profitable market opportunities. As the consumer market becomes more diverse, advertising, products, and media must be tailored to each market segment.

African Americans

Consumer research has indicated that blacks respond differently to advertising than whites (Hunter and Associates 1991). The minority status of blacks has led to subcultural differences in the marketplace that persist even today. The motivation of blacks to purchase products is different from that of whites. Blacks shop more frequently, because traditionally they had less money (Burrell 1992). For economic reasons, blacks were forced to eat grits, collard greens, and chitterlings. They were inexpensive foods that could be stretched to feed large numbers of people. Such products remain a part of African American cuisine. Historically, blacks also bought smaller quantities since they had less space for storage. Because blacks sometimes internalized the cultural stereotype that they were inferior and dirty, they buy more cleaning supplies. This indicates that psychological oppression is perhaps the most invidious and effective form of social control.

Blacks read advertisements more literally than whites. African Americans tend to favor a direct correspondence between visuals and copy. Blacks also prefer ads that convey lifestyles and contextual attractiveness. They prefer realistic ads that show people in authentic circumstances. African Americans like multicultural ads that depict people of various skin tones, hair types, and personalities. They are attracted to positive representations of black life.

Black households had $631 billion in earned income in 2002, an increase of 4.8 percent over the $602 billion earned in 2001 (Target Market News, 2003). In 1997, blacks' share of total U.S. buying power was 8.2 percent, up from 7.5 percent in 1990. It is estimated that advertisers spend $700 million each year to target blacks (Hume 1991), yet there are few comprehensive studies on blacks and black culture that connect demographic data (educational level, occupation, income, gender, age) with consumer-oriented data (brand use, lifestyle). A major weakness of both social scientific and marketing research, historically, has been the mistaken assumption that ethnic minorities such as Latinos and blacks are homogeneous.

Blacks are diverse, despite their shared ethnicity. There are significant economic, social, and regional differences. Younger blacks, those who did not directly experience the civil rights movement of the 1960s, are often dramatically different from their parents and grandparents with respect to their consumption patterns and buying habits (Woods 1995). Affluent blacks tend to buy products that showcase their high status, such as designer labels and luxury automobiles. Nor does limited disposable income necessarily predict the purchasing patterns of blacks at the lower end of the socioeconomic range. For example, many poor black consumers purchase high-priced designer-label athletic shoes and stereo systems.

In developing a product for a particular market segment, advertisers must satisfy a unique consumer need. For example, Johnson Products introduced a line of Afro-Sheen hair products in the late 1960s (Woods 1995) in direct response to the black community's emphasis on its African heritage in displaying personal identity and subcultural membership through grooming and fashion. The Afro hairstyle was essentially a cultural representation, a way of showing the wearer's ethnic background. Johnson Products introduced a line of products that supported two important functions for black consumers: good grooming and ethnic fashion imaging. Afro-Sheen ads used African dialect and developed a campaign that focused on the phrase "Wantu Wanzuri" (meaning "beautiful people" in Swahili) (Woods 1995).

The availability of a line of products at places where blacks shop is also significant. For example, most blacks reside in densely populated urban areas. They frequent fast food establishments. Consequently, chains such as KFC (formerly Kentucky Fried Chicken) and McDonald's are concentrated in urban areas, often within walking distance of customers. Suburban consumers, conversely, are more likely to drive a short distance to their local fast food restaurants.

Blacks listen to the radio more than whites, especially during the evenings and on weekends (Deloitte & Touche Trade Retail and Distribution Services Group 1991). Blacks also watch television more than other ethnic groups; black households view an average of 71.1 hours per week. Black consumers also look at magazines more than their white, Latino, or Asian counterparts (Woods 1995). Black local newspaper readership is low, but a higher proportion of blacks than whites read *USA Today*. Blacks are heavy consumers of cigarettes, compact discs, soft drinks, and orange juice. They account for 20 to 25 percent of all domestic beer sales, 15 percent of all cola sales, and 9 percent of all domestic car sales (Woods 1995). Black women spend 6.5 percent of the family income on clothing, compared with 5 percent for white women (Smikle 1992).

Alcohol-related illness and death are prevalent in African Americans. Cirrhosis of the liver, which is linked to alcohol consumption, is 70 percent higher among blacks than among whites (Center for Science in the Public Interest 1990). While the life expectancy for the mainstream population continues to rise, it drops each year for blacks (Woods 1995). This decrease is attributed to cigarette- and alcohol-related illnesses, homicide, and AIDS.

There have been complaints about the sexual nature of liquor advertising aimed at black consumers. Typically such ads show men using malt liquor to conquer women who are sexually aroused by black men who drink alcohol (Woods 1995). The media representations are based on power, sexuality, and masculinity. It is the stereotypical and sexual nature of the representations that is the most disconcerting. They tell us that black men are studs, while black women are sexually available. Blacks consume half of all the cognac purchased in this country (Center for Science in the Public Interest 1990); advertisers heavily target them for this costly liquor. Consumer activists charge that connecting expensive liquor with an affluent lifestyle is, in essence, deceptive advertising. Black consumers who cannot afford the upscale lifestyle represented in ads attempt to compensate by vicarious participation through the purchase, display, and consumption of prized liquor.

There are two key concepts in black advertising: psychological distance and positive realism (Cassidy and Katula 1990). *Psychological distance* is the feeling of separation between the black consumer and a mainstream product. In order to compensate for this assumed distance, advertisers link the product or service with displays of black people at their best—engaged in productive work or well-rounded family life; as good parents and thoughtful people caring about other people; as good neighbors; as people with ambitions, dreams, and aspirations. This is *positive realism,* and this advertising displays the social ideals and values of the dominant culture. Advertising does not represent social reality as it really is but as it should be. Advertising's symbolic system is based on stereotypical social categories and values (Schudson 1984, 215). These values stand in sharp contrast to negative stereotypes of blacks in the media: the violent, unemployed gangster; the ghetto drug dealer or pimp; the deadbeat dad; the welfare mother; and the lazy Sambo.

Latinos

The Latino market became a topic of interest and study in the 1970s when its numbers began to increase substantially. Advertisers finally began to recognize the economic potential of Latino consumers by the mid-1980s, but lacked an understanding of their culture and reliable data on consumer behavior patterns. Latino advertising expenditures doubled between 1983 and 1988 (Balkan 1988). Approximately $550 million was spent in 1988, nearly half of it (45.8 percent) in Spanish-language television, the fastest-growing segment of the television industry.

Because Latino households are generally larger than those of other ethnic groups, they purchase more goods more often, purchase larger quantities, and shop for groceries more than other groups (Woods 1995). In 1992 Latinos spent $107 a week on groceries, in contrast to $90 a week for non-Latinos (Conill Advertising 1993).

Latinos are a challenging marketing task, necessitating tight and exact segmentation. It is no coincidence that the four largest Latino markets (in terms of money spent on Latino advertising) are the most concentrated pockets of Latinos: Los Angles, Miami, New York, and Chicago. This heavy concentration of Latinos in only a few major markets makes national advertising inefficient (Woods 1995). Latinos are quite diverse in terms of cultural identities, consumer interests, lifestyles, and attitudes. Such diversity provides some indication as to why segments of the Latino market respond differently to ads targeted at them (see Woods 1995). In short, indisputable differences in occupations and income within the Latino population translate into different consumption and lifestyle patterns, which make sweeping advertising campaigns wasteful at best.

Choice of language in advertising is an important issue. Less than half of all Latinos (43 percent, or 10 million people) speak fluent English (*U.S. Hispanic Market Survey* 1991, 174). More than three out of every four (83 percent) Latinos speak Spanish in their homes, where they receive many of their advertising messages. Even fewer are able to read English fluently. More prosperous and younger Latinos favor English over Spanish; less assimilated older Latinos, of course, choose to communicate in Spanish (*U.S. Hispanic Market Survey* 1994, 55).

Latinos are brand loyal (Woods 1995). Brand loyalty is believed to be a factor of family dynamics. Latino consumers tend to shop to satisfy the brand desires of family members. Product history, reputation, and consistency are important issues for Latino shoppers (Saegert, Hoover, and Hilger 1985). Latinos try to learn as much as they can about the goods they use. They tend to be familiar with only a few brands but want current information about these products (Rossi 1993).

Latino consumers favor promotions (Woods 1995) and place trust in a company that shows interest in them and in their families. The strong sense of *familism* in Latinos cuts across socioeconomic divisions (DeAnda 1996). Latinos make purchases from firms that are sensitive to their language needs and are involved with Latino community events (Fry 1991). Consequently, J. C. Penney has sponsored major promotional campaigns around five Latino holidays, including *Diez y Seis* (Mexican Independence Day), *Cinco de Mayo*, Columbus Day, Three Kings Day, and Puerto Rican Day (Fry 1991). Domino's Pizza, American Express, and Campbell Soup have used major Spanish-language campaigns targeted at Latinos. Coca-Cola, Procter & Gamble, Kraft Foods, and Pillsbury have also targeted Latinos. Coca-Cola used well-known major league pitcher Fernando Valenzuela, a Mexican American, to endorse its beverages. Coca-Cola's major competitor, Pepsi, whose advertising targets younger consumers, used popular Cuban American singer Gloria Estefan as a company spokesperson.

Latino culture, like black culture, has trickled gradually into mainstream advertising. Besides visual representations, marketers exploit commodities with a particularly Latino character to differentiate and situate their goods and services. This marketing technique has been used successfully for several products. For example, in 1991, picante sauce outsold ketchup as the top condiment in the United States (Woods 1995). Latin music can be heard in the background of Pepsi commercials. The image of Juan Valdez adorns advertisements for Colombian coffee (figure 5.2). McDonald's developed breakfast fajitas in 1991 (Woods 1995). "Run for the Border" was a theme for a popular Taco Bell television commercial campaign.

In 1992, Latinos spent $180 billion on purchases (McCarroll 1993). In only five years, that figure grew to a massive $300 billion (Jaramillo 1997). In a mere ten years (1983–1992), spending on Latino media, such as Telemundo, a Spanish-language television station, and *La Opinion*, a Spanish-language newspaper, more than tripled (to $224 million).

Marketers are anxious to take advantage of this awesome purchasing power. The buying power of Latinos reasserted

Colombian Coffee is now on board **AmericanAirlines.**

Café de Colombia
The richest coffee in the world!

Fig. 5.2

itself in a recent incident involving HBO and its corporate parent conglomerate, Time Warner Communications, which had more than $20 billion in revenue in 1996. Time Warner's domain is wide and deep and includes Time Inc., publisher of twenty-five national magazines; Warner Brothers, an immense film production and distribution corporation; Turner Broadcasting System, an arrangement of cable television networks; and numerous others.

HBO boxing commentator Larry Merchant's televised comments about mariachi music before the Oscar De La Hoya–Pernell Whitaker bout in April 1997 struck many Latinos as overtly racist. The incident tarnished not only HBO, which aired a vague apology by Merchant a week later, but also Time Warner. The fact that Time Warner is an increasingly important player in the U.S. Latino media market made this event even more significant; clearly, any marketer catering to Latinos must be sensitive to cultural issues.

During prefight introductions of the original broadcast of the fight on April 12, 1997, on TVKO, HBO's pay-per-view branch, a mariachi band performed in the ring. Merchant called the mariachis a "marketing ploy" by the fight promoter that was designed "to get Mexicans, not Mexican Americans, to support De La Hoya, but slights the fans of the champion whose title is at stake. . . . As wonderful as this music is, . . . in this setting, it sucks. Unless they follow it with some soul music." (Whitaker, the champion, who is African American, did, in fact, use soul music for his ring entrance.)

Was Merchant so ignorant that he failed to realize that Mexican Americans, as well as Mexicans, adopt mariachi music as a source of ethnic pride? During the HBO rebroadcast a week later, Merchant's remarks were edited out of the commentary, but, ironically, they were published in *Sports Illustrated*, another member of Time Warner. By the first business day after the fight, correspondence from indignant fans, including many Latinos, gushed into Internet bulletin boards, local media, *Hispanic* magazine, Time Warner Sports, and HBO Sports. De La Hoya, who received a private apology from Merchant, indicated that mariachis will continue to play before his fights.

HBO Sports executives confirmed that Merchant was admonished for his regrettable comments. Yet neither HBO nor Time Warner issued an official apology. And Merchant's apology was negated by his reference to "misunderstood remarks"; he did not even take responsibility for his actions. Even though Time Warner has decided to court the Latino market, it still must overcome an insensitivity to cultural issues.

In October 1996, on the heels of the phenomenal success of the issue of *People* that featured the tragic death of Mexican American singer Selena, Time Warner launched *People en Español*. Essence Communications, the black magazine empire, also seeing the potential of the Latino market, introduced *Latina*, which one may call an *Essence* for Latinas. *Men's Health*, *Playboy*, and *Newsweek* are also trying out Spanish-language editions. Will mainstream heavyweight publishers push out traditional Latino and Spanish-language publications? While Latino-owned publications stress the relationship between their service to traditional Latino communities and reader loyalty, mainstream publishers are tempted by potentially enormous profits generated by demographic changes in the Latino population.

People en Español has contained advertising by Philip Morris, Toyota, Kraft, and Ford, all enterprises that have had an extensive presence in the Latino market. Thus, it could be argued that the multinational media conglomerates like Time Warner are taking advertising away from Latino-owned publications.

Alcohol advertisers have also targeted Chicanos. In one study (Gilbert and Cervantes 1986), 41 percent of Mexican American men who died of alcohol-related illnesses did not live to the age of fifty, as compared with 30 percent of whites. Latino activists have protested the explicit sexual content of liquor ads targeted at them, as well as the use of religious symbols for commercial ends (Woods 1995).

Asian Americans

There are 10 million Asian Americans in the United States (U.S. Census Bureau 2001). They spend an estimated $35 billion annually (Wright 1989). Asian Americans are the only ethnic group with a higher median income and lower unemployment rates than whites. Moreover, they save 20 percent of all earnings, a rate considerably higher than the national average (Woods 1995).

Such choice characteristics should make the Asian American market an advertiser's paradise. The tricky part is that, like Latinos, they are concentrated in only a few states: Hawaii, California, New York, Texas, Illinois, and New Jersey (U.S. Department of Commerce 1990). In addition, Asian Americans are unique among ethnic minorities regarding exposure to particular types of mass media and consumer buying patterns. Their use of media is more similar to that of the white consumer than other ethnic minorities.

Asian Americans prefer to read business-related magazines (Delener and Neelankavil 1990). They also read newspapers more than Latinos and blacks and listen to the radio less than Latinos. Television was considered to be the most influential marketing mode, followed by newspaper, magazine, radio, billboard, theater, and flyer. Asian Americans are especially targeted by advertisers of electronic goods and financial services because of their strong interest in business and technology.

Buying decisions are often made by both wives and husbands in Asian American households. Though Asian Americans receive advertising messages from a variety of sources, word of mouth is an important source of product and service information. Eighty-five percent of the respondents in a consumer behavior study (Greenburg et al. 1987) indicated that a friend's recommendation was their primary source of product information. Advertising was second (48 percent), followed by previous experience with product (38 percent) and by *Consumer Reports* magazine (24 percent).

Asian Americans are not as loyal to brand names as Latinos (Woods 1995). Still there are major product categories (e.g., automobiles, electronics, major appliances) in which brand name is an important criterion in making a purchase. Both Asian and Latino markets are strongly connected with family and culture. Nevertheless, there are major differences in subcultural rituals of celebration and demarcation, often the focus of such advertising. Asian Americans, for example, are less likely than other groups to entertain at home or in a restaurant (Greenburg et al. 1987), and they tend to celebrate less often than Latinos.

The Asian American market did not become a distinct market until the 1980s, a decade following unprecedented growth in its numbers (Woods 1995). The population grew by 42 percent between 1970 and 1980 (mainly through immigration). It is no surprise that now advertisers are also targeting Asian Americans, especially Vietnamese and Koreans. They are among the fastest-growing and most successful newcomer immigrant markets.

Asian American households earn an average income of $56,316, in contrast to an average income of $48,950 by all Americans (U.S. Census Bureau 2000b). In 1992, Asian households spent $120 billion on products and services. Clearly, the Asian market has become fertile ground for advertisers because of this relative affluence.

Asian Americans, like Latinos, are a segmented population composed of autonomous subcategories, including Koreans, Vietnamese, Filipinos, Indians, Chinese, and Japanese. In addition, there is diversity within each of these subgroups. Both recent and longtime immigrants typically travel back to and call their country of origin. This makes them excellent consumers for the travel, communications, and shipping industries. Asian Americans call overseas three times as much as the average consumer in the United States.

Savvy advertisers target specific products and services to particular ethnic groups. For example, Hormel & Company arranged some of Spam's grocery-store promotional displays in Korean communities, because Koreans consume more Spam than any other ethnic group. In addition, Remy Martin and Courvoisier (cognac producers) regularly target Chinese Americans, who drink nearly twice as much cognac per person as the general population (Woods 1995), by using both Cantonese- and Mandarin-dialect ads in Chinese print media. At over $100 a bottle, Remy Martin XO is out of the price range for many alcohol consumers. However, the firm has created a campaign to link the prized brand with special occasions or times when price is not an object.

If done correctly, ethnic targeting in advertising is lucrative. Three out of four Asian Americans prefer to communicate in their native language (McCarroll 1993). So it is not surprising that Asian Americans spend 60 percent more on products that are advertised in Asian American broadcasting and print media than those in general media. Perhaps a security or trust factor is at work here. Asian representations are also used in mainstream advertising but not with the same regularity as their black and Latino counterparts. With a few exceptions, mainstream marketing has still not assimilated Asian American cultural representations into its commercial messages.

In sum, Asian Americans are rapidly increasing in numbers, although the actual numbers are relatively small. Tremendous diversity prevents a single approach for targeting all of them. Four patterns nevertheless emerge: (1) Asian Americans have strong ties to family and culture; (2) older Asians like to see advertising in their native language; (3) newspapers are a powerful medium for reaching Asian Americans; and (4) Asian Americans have a strong need to please and impress their families through the products they purchase (Woods 1995, 49).

Native Americans

Native Americans are the most destitute of all ethnic minority groups. Their median income is more than $18,000 less than the national average (U.S. Census Bureau 2000b). The unemployment rate for Native Americans is a staggering 35 percent. Nearly 26 percent live below the official poverty line, in contrast with 11 percent of the general population (U.S. Census Bureau 2000c). Besides their disadvantaged economic position, Native Americans are so geographically isolated from the rest of the population and are so few in number that they are targets of few marketing endeavors. Alcohol advertisers, however, have targeted Native Americans, as they have other ethnic minorities (Woods 1995).

Native Americans have also protested liquor marketing allegedly targeted at them. In 1991, Hornell Brewing Company introduced a malt liquor named after the famous Sioux war chief, Crazy Horse (Woods 1995). The company denied that the malt liquor was targeted at Native Americans. Nonetheless, its introduction was questionable. The historical Crazy Horse, a spiritual as well as military leader, opposed alcohol consumption among his people since he was keenly aware of its devastation. Moreover, alcoholism rates are particularly high for Native Americans—as high as 80 to 90 percent in certain areas, according to some estimates (Schlaad and Shannon 1994).

How Not to Do Ethnic Advertising

While mainstream advertisers have successfully tapped into major ethnic markets, they sometimes do not do their homework, or, at least, not correctly—and they suffer the negative consequences of cultural insensitivity. Social scientists and advertising agencies along with their clients often ignore the diversity within an ethnic group or marketing segment. They also often misunderstand the nuances of ethnic subcultural interaction and communication. Such misunderstandings can lead to ethnic stereotyping by outsiders.

One classic example of the advertising blunders that sometimes occur is the infamous Frito Bandito. In 1967, one of the top advertising agencies in the United States (Foote, Cone & Belding) developed a Mexican cartoon character called the Frito Bandito to promote Frito-Lay products (Woods 1995). The Frito Bandito was far from a positive cultural representation. He was unfriendly and unshaven, and he conned Anglos out of their Fritos. The Mexican American Anti-Defamation Committee protested the marketing campaign because of the clearly negative stereotype that it presented. The advertising agency at first did not budge, because its marketing research showed that Mexican American consumers liked the image (probably for its comic value). Nevertheless, the campaign was eventually pulled in 1970.

Mistakes have also occurred in Asian American target marketing. For example, a New York Life Insurance Company advertisement targeted at Koreans fell far short of expectations because it used a Chinese model instead of a Korean. In another case, Citibank opted to pull a New Year's holiday commercial targeted at Chinese Americans after viewers protested that the way corks popped out of champagne bottles was too risqué. Advertisers conservatively replaced the suggestive spot with the culturally traditional dragon.

Woods (1995) offers other examples of advertising blunders in marketing to Latinos:

- The copy for a Coors campaign also targeting Latinos stated: "Turn it loose tonight!" The Spanish translation, however, meant "loose bowels."

- In the 1970s, General Motors tried to market the Chevrolet Nova in Mexico without realizing that "Nova" translates into "no go" in Spanish.

- Braniff Airlines' copy "Fly in Leather" translates into "Fly naked."

- Young & Rubicam's Bravo division almost used "polvo Johnson" instead of "talco Johnson" to advertise baby power. In some parts of the Caribbean, "polvo" means "sexual intercourse."

- The English copy for a campaign targeting Perdue chicken to Latinos read, "It takes a tough man to make a tender chicken." However, something was lost, and gained, in translation. The Spanish version read like a case of bestiality: "It takes a sexually stimulated man to make a chicken affectionate."

It is clear that merely translating English advertising copy into Spanish can result in sending the wrong message or no message at all.

Even English has its pitfalls. A leading bug-spray producer aired a commercial in which a group of roaches, wearing untied athletic shoes, was attacked by a woman with a can of bug killer. Her rejoinder to their intent to devour her crumbs was, "Think again, home bug!" "Home bug" is obviously a parody of "home boy," a term used by blacks to refer to a neighbor or member of one's own community. Black urban youth pioneered unlaced athletic shoes, though it was a style copied by white youth and became part of the fashionable grunge look. The copy and visuals implicitly associated blacks with something as dirty, disliked, and annoying as roaches.

Such flagrant cases of ethnic insensitivity are not difficult to spot. Less obvious are acts of omission, another form of symbolic racism. Not a single ethnic woman was chosen for Revlon's 1987 "Most Beautiful Women" campaign (Woods 1995). Two years later, however, a Vietnamese American from California was selected as Revlon's "Most Beautiful Woman."

Native American symbolism has sometimes been stereotypically insulting and derogatory. For example, the rifle ad in figure 5.3 is basically calling the Native American a savage. The National Football League's Kansas City Chiefs outfitted defensive star Derrick Thomas in an Indian warrior headdress for a publicity poster (Woods 1995). The Native American community was indignant, since the headdress is to be worn only by those who have earned the status of warrior.

It is clear that the social environment has changed, and will continue to change, the way that advertisers treat ethnic minorities. For example, a national restaurant chain vowed to hire more minority employees after picketers protested discriminatory service. Additionally, a major insurance company hired a black advertising agency to help improve its image among blacks in the midst of a lawsuit over auto insurance rates.

Now an advertiser cannot simply choose a target audience without first carefully weighing political implications, social concerns, health issues, and the like. Businesses must weigh the benefit of potential profit to be gained from ethnic consumers against the risk of permanently alienating such large consumer markets. In the past, boycotts by ethnic consumers were successfully used for social change. Today's activists are much more hostile and bold. Demands that particular goods be taken off retail shelves have become more intense.

Community activists have sometimes resorted to sabotaging property. Billboards, a dominant feature of the postmodern urban landscape, have especially come under attack. In Dallas, New York, and Chicago, Catholic priests and their parishioners painted over billboards to protest the selling of cigarettes and liquor to black consumers (see "Segmentation in Cigarette Marketing,"

Fig. 5.3

chapter 6). Cigarettes and alcohol accounted for approximately one-fourth of the spending ($163 million out of a total of $696 million) on outdoor advertising in 1993 (Davis 1994).

Culturally Insensitive International Advertising

Advertising in foreign countries often leads to embarrassing situations for U.S. multinational marketers. In a spot that ran briefly on Peruvian television, Africans are seen getting ready to devour some white tourists until they are appeased by Nabisco's Royal Pudding. Nabisco initially responded that although the commercial was "inconsistent" with company values, the Peruvian audience saw it as "a fantasy situation that was humorous in nature, and effectively communicated people's preference for Royal Desserts over all else."

After realizing that its explanation of local taste tests as justification for a racially insensitive ad was feeble, Nabisco quickly moved to consolidate control of its international advertising under Foote, Cone & Belding in New York in an effort to keep ad campaigns more uniform. The firm wanted to "ensure that the quality of our ads meet the standards we set for our brands" (Wynter 1998, B8). The pudding commercial was called "a mistake."

In a similar incident, a sketch on a popular Peruvian television show featured a Michael Jackson character complaining that his son plays in "blackface" and, having a tail, looks "too black," prompting him to beg a doctor to bleach the boy's skin and cut off his tail (*Advertising Age* 1997). The show was sponsored by such major corporations as Cheseborough-Ponds, Procter & Gamble, PepsiCo, and Quaker Oats. Moreover, the characters of the show are featured in a commercial for Goodyear Tire & Rubber Co. shuffling around and stating that "Goodyear tires are as strong as a black man's lips." Goodyear quickly pulled the ad after its U.S. executives saw it and fired the Lima, Peru, agency that produced the tire ad. It also promptly issued an unsolicited apology to the NAACP even though the ad ran only in Peru for one week. Although the company determined it would be impractical to impose central review of all international advertising from its U.S. base, as Nabisco did, it stepped up sensitivity training for local managers and suppliers around the world.

Like many multinational companies, Nabisco and Goodyear were forced to address concerns about how to adapt advertising campaigns to foreign markets without violating domestic sensibilities. Such situations shed light not only on how far some ad agencies will go to create eye-catching messages but also on how a lack of internal controls at agencies can cause problems. Because local units of international ad agencies are not typically required to consult with parent companies when creating ads for domestic audiences, racially insensitive or otherwise controversial ads, such as those for Nabisco's Royal Pudding and Goodyear tires, sometimes slip through.

Ethnic Advertising Agencies

Historically, ethnic minorities have been sharply underrepresented in advertising agencies and in the international marketing divisions of corporate America. Blacks, who make up 10.1 percent of the total workforce, are only 5.2 percent of the advertising industry (Winski 1992). For Latinos and blacks, this underrepresentation may be due in part to inadequate formal education, high high-school dropout rates, and relatively few members with business degrees.

Ethnic advertising agencies are companies with particular expertise in developing marketing campaigns for ethnic minority audiences. They have been in existence for less than forty years (Woods 1995). Despite ethnic consumers' increasing share of the marketplace, ethnic agencies have not prospered like their general market counterparts. Approximately 105 agencies deal exclusively or in part with ethnic minority consumers (*Standard Directory of Advertising Agencies* 1993): 69 Latino, 24 black, and 12 Asian agencies. Such firms are typically smaller and less successful than white agencies; they are also more vulnerable to economic recessions.

Firms operated and owned by ethnic minorities also suffer from the misconception that all they can do is create marketing campaigns for ethnic consumers. This tends to discourage major manufacturers from using them. But ethnic agencies are not unidimensional; they provide clients with several unique services. They understand the subtle nuances of ethnic culture and ethnic minority psychology. Ethnic agencies can also prevent clients from making significant errors in creative strategy usually due to cultural insensitivity. Since they focus on market segmentation, ethnic agencies are able to dissect and penetrate any target population (Burrell 1992).

Advertising clearly is a reflection of culture. Will advertising mirror an increasingly ethnically diverse society? Doing so will require the industry to go beyond its current boundaries for talent and skill.

Conclusion

The dramatic growth of Latino, black, and Asian populations is a sign of changes in the marketplace that cannot be disregarded. New consumers are born every day, bringing needs that will expand into desires and expectations. Ethnic background affects consumer behavior patterns, and consumption patterns shift as family size increases. There is meaningful lifestyle diversity between, and often within, ethnic markets. Advertising representations that stereotype or otherwise do not take into account the diversity of consumer behavior among ethnic groups are fated for failure. Often, products fall out of popularity within mainstream culture, and new markets need to be discovered if the producer is to prosper. Ethnic minority markets are a fertile source of new consumers.

Ethnic markets are a potentially rich reservoir of untouched consumer dollars. Demographic data suggest that ethnic markets are growing rapidly. As ethnic minorities attain higher levels of education, they are becoming more affluent and refined in their consumer tastes. There are consumer patterns shared by most, if not all, ethnic groups; there are also ethnic differences that affect buying power.

Advertising agencies that specialize in, or deal exclusively with, ethnic groups are becoming more popular. Many of the top Madison Avenue companies have either developed ethnic targeting divisions within the firm or acquired separate firms. Young & Rubicam owns the Latino-market specialist Bravo Group. Grey Advertising, Leo Burnett, and Foote, Cone & Belding have Latino marketing divisions in their corporate structure.

The methods of attracting potential consumers from ethnic minority populations have differed from those aimed at mainstream audiences. Advertisers have decreased the use of more conventional types of mass advertising, such as mainstream magazines and network television. Instead they have become more specialized, using subject-oriented magazines and cable television. This has dramatically altered the marketing game. Advertisers have also adopted more sophisticated uses of direct mail, such as zip-code targeting.

The successful incorporation of ethnic targeted marketing within large mainstream firms has not come without a high price. Tensions of a multicultural workforce are evident in miscommunication and cultural insensitivity. Workshops in cultural diversity in such firms are used to increase sensitivity and enhance communication.

The dramatic increase in, and prevalence of, ethnic segmentation in advertising signals the death of mass marketing. Universal communication in a multicultural society is impractical, if not impossible. Market segmentation works well in a multitude of media, including cable television. Targeted advertising messages, distinctive publications, and direct marketing are becoming more popular. Postmodern advertising has become a series of messages targeted at cultural, ethnic, and social segments of the marketplace.

6

Speed and Fragmentation: Toward Postmodern Consciousness

> In the contemporary world, messages about goods are all pervasive—advertising has increasingly filled up the spaces of our daily existence.
>
> —Sut Jhally

The advertising industry eclipses our mass media. Advertising more and more is consuming our public spaces. Most of our sporting and cultural events now have corporate sponsors. "As we head toward the twenty-first century, advertising is ubiquitous—it is the air that we breathe as we live our daily lives" (Jhally 1990, 79).

Postmodern advertising seems to be characterized by (1) *visual images* (of products, services, or the satisfaction or happiness the consumer will receive from using these products or services); and (2) the *speed* of those images.

> The visual images that dominate public space . . . are . . . not static. They do not stand still for us to examine and linger over. They are here for a couple of seconds and then they are gone. . . . As commercial time slots declined from sixty . . . to thirty seconds (and recently to fifteen seconds and even shorter), advertisers responded by creating a new type of advertising . . . the "vignette approach" . . . a rapid succession of lifestyle images, meticulously timed with music, that directly sell feeling and emotion rather than products. (Jhally 1990, 84)

This sped-up approach, combined with highly creative visual and sound editing, pulls the consumer directly to the commercial message. We cannot view these images casually. If we are not focused on them, it is too easy to miss part of an image or all of an extremely brief image. "Intensely pleasurable images, often sexual, are integrated into a flow of images" (Jhally 1990, 84). We have to pay attention in order to distinguish the brief images of visual pleasure from the fillers, such as information and logos.

Prior to this relatively new technique in advertising, narrative ads used information to elicit rational responses from viewers. Now sped-up advertising uses visual images to appeal to viewers' emotions. Postmodern advertising presents a highly visual, quickly paced set of images, often sexual, to consumers. It is typically successful in competing for our attention with visual imagery that is fresh, extraordinary, and even shocking. In order to outshock the competition, creative staff in the advertising indus-

try increase the visual seductiveness and the pace and noise level of television commercials in an ever-increasing spiral (Jhally 1990). This frantic style of quick editing cuts
and visual excess has crossed over from advertising into other media forms such as
MTV, dramatic programming, and even news broadcasting.

The institutional structure of consumer society slants culture toward the realm of
commodities and services. It's really no surprise that advertising is one of the most
dominant aspects of culture in the United States. The marketplace is the primary structuring institution of postmodern consumer society. Advertising not only tells us about
products, but it also tells us how they are linked to significant spheres in our lives and
relationships. Advertisers tell us that if we buy their products and use their services, we
will be content, successful, and happy. The conditions to which we most aspire are personal autonomy and control of our lives; self-esteem; a happy family life; loving relations; plenty of relaxed, tension-free leisure time; and good friendships (Jhally 1990).
Since none of these is intrinsically related to products or services, the burden is placed
on advertisers to convince us that by purchasing their commodities, we can attain such
sources of satisfaction.

We are misled by the notion that happiness can be obtained through the marketplace. Through its institutions and structures, advertising is the magnet that draws us
toward commodities. Since products themselves are not the focal point of perceived
satisfaction, they are then plugged in, albeit superficially, to those conditions that are
(see, e.g., the Cutty Sark ad in figure 2.1). Consequently, commercial messages present
images of the "American dream" or the "good life." In a way, advertising is postmodern cultural junk food, with unbelievable impertinence and without depth. For example, the long-running Virginia Slims campaign, "You've come a long way, baby," tried
to equate cigarette addiction with progress for women.

The Social Role of Advertising in Consumer Culture

> The average person is exposed to 3600 commercial impressions every day, making
> advertising the most pervasive message system in the consumer culture.
>
> —Sut Jhally

Advertising is so dominant that we are usually unaware of its presence. Two- to five-
year-olds average more than twenty-eight hours of television a week. Today's teens
probably have spent the equivalent of a decade of their lives being exposed to advertising. The average adult today sees some three thousand ads every day. However, we
notice only eighty and react to only twelve (Twitchell 1996: 3).

The work ethic has been replaced by the consumption ethic. We do not crave advertised products and services as much as we crave the shared meaning that they evoke.
Successful advertising does not manipulate naive and gullible dolts. Rather, it studies
and then reacts to the way the public thinks, acts, and lives. In short, it is advertising,
not the consumer, that is manipulated. Advertising does not force people to buy what
they do not need. Rather, it intersects and interrupts consumers' established patterns of
thought and behavior. Advertising is not so concerned with what we want, what we
claim to want, or what scientists claim we want; rather, it is concerned with what and
how we buy.

Advertising cannot change our desires or create new ones; it discovers our desires and helps us to achieve them by providing a product or service. Advertising is not a giant hypodermic needle that callously injects defenseless consumers with artificial and costly desires. Missing from such analyses is the fact that consumers are cognitive beings who actively interpret ads based on their particular belief systems, social experiences, worldview, and ideologies. Meaning, in this scenario, is the consequence of an ongoing interaction between the viewer and the ad.

Postmodern advertising is not so much characterized by new products as by new forms of media reaching the masses of new potential patrons. Mass culture derives from popular culture through technology. It is the dominant culture of the new millenium and has crossed all lines of taste, media, nationality, and genre. The term high culture is synonymous with art culture or the fine arts. For example, a classic painting is exclusively part of high culture until it is used in advertising (which is part of mass culture). Classic works of art in postmodernity are more sustainable as extensions of commercial interests than as aesthetic culture.

Advertising on Television

Television is . . . the business of delivering audiences to advertisers.
—Les Brown, *Television: The Business behind the Box*

Although television is composed of various categories of media messages, including commercials, sports, news, situation comedies, drama, talk shows, and game shows, all these categories share fundamental semblances of ideology, topic, significance, and desirability. Even the most widely accepted distinctions (e.g., commercials versus drama) are easily obscured. Judgments about which happenings constitute the news and about how to portray them are strongly driven by considerations of dramatic form and content (e.g., conflict and resolution) that is copied from fictional archetypes. The refined minidramas of some commercials indicate a complex mastery of fictional conventions (Gross 1991), just as dramatic programs encourage a style of conspicuous consumption and posh living that reverberates with commercial messages. In addition, the synthesis of stylistic practices permits greater force and shared support in marketing and dispersing common values.

Television has become almost an extension of the human mind, body, and soul; television is in our blood. "More than 95 percent of American households have at least one television set, and it is on more than six hours a day" (Twitchell 1996, 92). We spend the equivalent of one day per week watching it. Television exhibits most of our epistemology—what we know and what we believe.

Television is the principal medium of advertising. Television programs are, in essence, no more than scheduled interruptions sandwiched between marketing bulletins (i.e., commercials). "Commercial television is primarily a marketing medium and secondarily an entertainment medium" (Andrews 1980, 64). Advertising agencies are the television networks' real censors or gatekeepers. They have their own watchdogs that work to protect, not the viewer, but the program's sponsors (Twitchell 1996). Program content is never permitted to clash with advertised products.

The A. C. Nielsen Company collects and markets television audience profiles. Its research measures how long an audience watches particular programs. Through self-administered surveys and viewing journals, the company is able to link the demographic characteristics of viewers to the types of programs they watch. This is particularly valuable since broadcasters are in the business of selling the attention of an audience to advertisers.

There are two types of figures with which advertisers are most concerned, ratings and shares. "A rating is the percentage of the total television households in an area that are tuned in . . . the share indicates the percentage of viewers already watching who are tuned to a particular program" (Twitchell 1996, 94). There are five age categories in television-viewing demographic analysis: one to eleven years of age, twelve to seventeen, eighteen to thirty-four, thirty-five to fifty-five, and older than fifty-five. The youngest and the oldest viewers watch the most television. However, these same categories shop the least of all. The thirty-five- to fifty-five-year-olds have the most disposable income, while the eighteen- to thirty-four-year-olds spend the most liberally.

Although cable television allows advertisers to reach a demographic target and a predicted audience, the multitude of channels and the remote control have made it much easier, if not more desirable, to avoid watching commercials. The average male in the United States changes channels with the remote control every forty-seven seconds (Twitchell 1996). Advances in technology have now made it possible to activate the remote by voice. This means that a mere groan will render millions of dollars of imaginative advertising meaningless. This is not the only problem for advertising on television: there are simply too many ads, including short (fifteen-second) ads. "The networks are broadcasting about six thousand commercials a week, and more than a third of them are these shorties" (Twitchell 1996, 97). With this oversaturation of ads and the common practice of channel surfing, any particular ad is less likely to be seen by members of the target audience.

The new genre of postmodern advertising on television is the *infomercial*, which is nothing more than a half-hour commercial trying to disguise itself as a regular program. "Consumers are motivated to acquire products, services, and experiences that provide satisfaction and give shape, substance, and character to their identities" (Twitchell 1996, 126). Infomercials, like all ads, are successful if they are able to point out a deficiency in the viewer or something the viewer does and then provide a solution to that problem or weakness:

> [In] the Soloflex ad . . . godlike youngsters worked themselves into an almost sexual lather as the voice-over suggested reverently that such bodies are possible for us couch potatoes at home. We potatoes . . . can now also learn how to inhibit baldness, become rich in real estate, cut rocks with ginzu knives, cook in woks, become thin with body cream, quit smoking without using willpower, wax our cars so that they can resist a flame thrower, and learn to dance so that we'll never be dateless again. (Twitchell 1996, 105)

Significantly, television stations are not legally responsible for any deceptive ads that they may transmit. Perhaps that is why there are so many infomercials. In 1992 and 1993, the Lifetime channel used nearly 25 percent of its viewing schedule on infomercials (Twitchell 1996). Other stations that heavily transmit infomercials include the USA Network, the Family Channel, and the Nashville Network. Since stations get paid in advance for infomercials, we will, no doubt, continue to have:

> Cher answer the question "Did you ever look at your hair and want to cry?"; Barbi Benton assure you that you can "Play the piano overnight"; Dick Clark answer the question "Is there love after marriage?"; Morgan Fairchild tell "How to raise drug-free kids"; Fran Tarkenton help with "Personal power, thirty days to unlimited success" and, of course, Brenda Vacarro tell us how to "Light his fire." (Twitchell 1996, 105–6)

Note the pattern of celebrity endorsements in infomercials. Endorsement advertising uses celebrities to sanction products, thereby increasing their desirability; this, in turn, increases the marketability of the star. There are also shop-at-home networks, ATV (Advertising Television), and the National Advertising Channel.

The Latent Consequences of Advertising

> Learning about the world is increasingly a by-product of mass marketing. Most of the stories about life and values are told not by parents, grandparents, teachers, clergy and others with stories to tell, but by a handful of distant conglomerates with something to sell.
>
> —George Gerbner, *Television Violence*

It is difficult, if not altogether impossible, to measure the relationship between advertising and sales. If this were not true, manufacturers and service providers would be paying advertising agencies by the percentage of sales expansion instead of by how much media time or space they have bought.

Capitalism and advertising go hand in hand, just like work and spending. Similarly, the success of popular culture is based on profit and loss. The Frankfurt school espoused the position that popular culture is the manipulation of many for the profit of the few. In postmodern society, advertising has attracted a multitude of sharp critics:

> Advertising has been blamed for the rise of eating disorders, the eruption of violence in the streets, our epidemic of depression, the despoiling of cultural icons, the corruption of politics, the carnivalization of holy times like Christmas, and the gnatlike attention span of our youth. (Twitchell 1996, 100)

Advertising is more a reflection of society than vice versa. Clearly, advertising has some definite deleterious effects. Nevertheless, it should neither be demonized nor offered as the convenient scapegoat for contemporary urban problems. Consumers, typically, are not defenseless and innocent casualties of the "overbearing" and "unrestrained force" of advertising.

Advertising co-opts whatever is current in popular culture (e.g., vernacular dialect, the environment). This has the effect of "hooking" or familiarizing the consumer and legitimizing the product or service. Products that appear to be environmentally friendly, for example, have an edge over similar products that do not. This is an extension of political correctness. Later, parodies of this political correctness may become popular, and this, again, will be co-opted by advertising.

Advertisers ostensibly tell us that we are unique individuals who continuously exercise our free will. Yet they treat us just the opposite. "To ad agencies we are tribes of consumers wandering through aisles of objects, hopelessly confused and eternally willing—nay, eager—to be instructed, even intimidated" (Twitchell 1996, 124). Mass production translates into mass marketing, which in turn translates into the construction of mass stereotypes for categories of individuals. Mass production in the United States has transformed the modern world into a postmodern quagmire of dehumanizing archetypes. These stereotypes are nothing more than over-generalized population-segment demographics. Just like products in brightly colored packages on supermarket shelves, stacked neatly in columns and rows, we consumers also

cluster together, constructing shared meaning and value. The goal of advertising is to
satisfy as many needs of as many segments of the population as possible. Different
products have different meanings for different audiences, making research that pin-
points various target audiences extremely important for advertising agencies and
their ability to sell.

Target audiences are typically designated by four key interval variables: variations
and derivations of socioeconomic status (which includes occupation, level of education,
and income), age, gender, and ethnicity. Minority-oriented advertising is also increasing in volume and importance, making ethnicity and race substantial demographic
characteristics.

As I mentioned at the outset of this volume, advertising is more a reactor to, than a
creator of, culture. Accordingly:

> advertising is one of the most conservative forces in culture . . . Although individual ads
> do indeed claim the outer edge of acceptability, and their memorability often depends on
> this outrageousness, the accumulated force of commercial selling is more like a slow and
> continuous drumming of social norms. (Twitchell 1996, 159)

Advertising transmits rich, intimate, and astute cultural and subcultural messages and
images as well as universal, biological desires. It is this dynamic that gives advertising
its resilient character that refuses to displace old patterns but rather continuously
adapts to and accommodates changing hopes, urges, tastes, and seasons.

Segmentation in Cigarette Marketing

Second-hand smoke kills 53,000 nonsmokers a year nationwide.
—California Lavender Smokefree Project

The National Civil Suit

The tobacco industry is an estimated $40 billion per year business in the United
States (Woods 1995). Competition is fierce between cigarette producers. One share
point represents $250 million (Dagnoli 1989a). On January 14, 1998, previously private
tobacco industry documents were released to the public by Representative Henry Waxman, a Democrat from California and longtime foe of the industry. The papers document decades of deliberate cigarette sales to children.

Congress rejected a proposed national litigation settlement that would have severely
restricted cigarette advertising and provided a $368.5 billion package to individual
states. The settlement was designed to end forty-one state Medicaid lawsuits attempting to recover some of the massive costs incurred as a result of the advertising and marketing practices of the tobacco industry. In exchange, tobacco firms sought immunity
from any future class-action lawsuits and punitive damages, plus an annual cap on
payment to individuals who win suits against tobacco firms.

The reduction of teen smoking is a major issue in current settlement attempts. Attorneys general from several states and representatives of the tobacco industry are currently examining a twenty-five-year payout of roughly $200 billion to compensate up
to thirty-eight states for their costs of treating sick smokers. The settlement would also
restrict billboard ads and end tobacco sponsorship of musical events. This last "conces-

sion," while aimed at teen smoking, is irrelevant, since the industry has already discontinued concert sponsorship in lieu of other events. The new proposal, unlike the previous proposed settlement, makes no mention of fining tobacco companies if youth smoking is not reduced.

Age Segmentation

> Tobacco companies need to recruit 5,000 new smokers each day to replace the ones who quit or die.
> —California Lavender Smokefree Project

> Ninety percent . . . of all new smokers start smoking before the age of eighteen.
> —Patrick J. Coughlin, attorney who filed the California state antitobacco lawsuit

> We don't advertise to children. . . . We don't want children to smoke.
> —Philip Morris Company, to public

> Today's youth is tomorrow's potential regular customer.
> —Philip Morris Company, internal memorandum, March 31, 1981

> The industry is dominated by companies who most effectively meet the needs of younger smokers. Our efforts remain on these younger groups.
> —R. J. Reynolds Tobacco Company, internal memorandum

Internal documents indicate that the R. J. Reynolds Tobacco Company marketed cigarettes to children as young as thirteen. The documents included presentations to the board of directors and memos to its CEOs. One 1988 memo to top marketing officials stated: "Imagine a five-year-old child, who will be a future customer of your cigarettes in the next few years. How can your company begin to attract/tap into this next generation? . . . Children love cartoons." Reynolds officials tried to counter by insisting that the mention of thirteen-year-old customers was a typographical error. But if this were true, why did the error occur throughout the document?

The protest poster Kids Club (figure 6.1) was created to draw attention to the tobacco industry's use of cartoons to sell cigarettes to children. Evidently, Budweiser also got the message that children love cartoons. The Budweiser ad shown in figure 6.2 features Bud Man, a cartoon character whose major appeal is clearly to people under the age of twenty-one. This ad is in direct violation of the Beer Institute code that states that beer advertising should not "employ any symbol or cartoon character intended to appeal primarily to persons below the legal purchase age" (Consumers for Socially Responsible Advertising 1994). With increased consumer awareness and public advocacy, alcohol producers can perhaps be pushed to comply with the marketing standards set by their own industry.

Older smokers die at the rate of about four hundred thousand per year. Teenagers are virtually the only available replacements. Tobacco firms have survived and prospered by marketing to minors even though it is illegal. Philip Morris, the number one cigarette-producing firm, mentioned twelve-year-olds as a target audience in an internal memo. Another internal memo acknowledged: "The phenomenal growth rate in Marlboro cigarette sales has been attributable to young smokers" (defined as

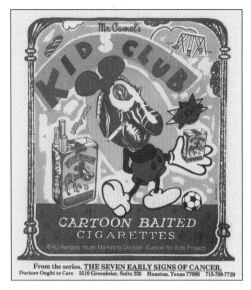

Fig. 6.1   Fig. 6.2

ages fifteen to nineteen). These "young starters" are seen as constituting the most important of all population segments in the long run (Pollay, Lee, and Carter-Whitney 1992) because of its size and, consequently, potential massive profit. Yet tobacco companies denied any such illegal promotions to children.

Antismoking activists and public health groups insist that perhaps the only way to challenge companies' huge incentive to sell to children is through severe marketing restrictions coupled with the "teeth" (i.e., large fines for policy violations) to back it up. This supports a process of collectively defining the marketing of cigarettes to children as a social problem that must be alleviated. The implication is that there should be an immediate global ban on marketing cigarettes to youth. Moreover, this should occur without granting tobacco firms immunity from any future class-action lawsuits.

Ethnic Segmentation

Advertising agencies use the dynamics of metonymy (the use of the name of one thing for that of another with which it is associated) to connect cigarettes with a natural, healthy, trendy lifestyle, as well as with horses, cowboys, and elements of nature (trees, sunshine, mountains, rivers, and sky). This hides the fact that cigarettes are an artificial, synthetic product, full of dangerous pesticides, preservatives, and other chemicals (Keller 1994). The tobacco industry spends a lot of money on certain population segments such as urban blacks and Latinos. Black magazines earn more of their revenue from cigarette ads than do similar mainstream publications (Ramirez 1991). Ethnic communities are disproportionately heavier users of alcohol and cigarettes. Consequently, they have high rates of cigarette- and alcohol-related illness. Cigarette billboards appear in black communities four to five times as often as in white communities (Woods 1995). However, Florida's precedent-setting ban on billboards advertising tobacco products is likely to spread.

Tobacco firms justify ethnic segmentation as niche marketing. Tobacco companies sponsor concerts (the Kool Jazz Festival, for instance), promotions, contests, and programs for ethnic communities. They often use the expertise of ethnic minority media, advertising agencies, and distributors to reach minority audiences. Tobacco firms provide lucrative economic incentives for liquor stores, bar owners, and distributors.

In 1989, at a time of falling sales, R. J. Reynolds developed a cigarette targeted to black consumers. Though smoking was declining at a rate of around 2 percent per year, blacks' smoking rates continued to increase, making blacks an ideal target market for a product searching for new users. With nearly four hundred brands of cigarettes on the market, black smokers had plenty of choices, but no brand was targeted only at the black smoker. Three out of every four black smokers smoke menthol brands (Centers for Disease Control 1990a). R. J. Reynolds's menthol cigarette, Salem, was losing ground to Lorillard's Newport. So Reynolds decided to chase the black smoker who wanted a menthol brand but found Salem too heavy.

When Reynolds planned to introduce Uptown, information about black smoking behavior and the related health risks was widely available. Nearly 40 percent of blacks smoked, compared to 29 percent for the rest of the population (Marcus and Crane 1984; Schoenborn 1987). In 1989, of the 50 million smokers in the country, 6 million were black (Alcohol, Drug Abuse, and Mental Health Administration 1989). The lung cancer rate for black males was 55 percent higher than for white males. Black males were the group most likely to be affected by cigarette-related illness. Thetruth.com sometimes targets young black smokers in antismoking campaigns (figure 6.3). Reynolds ignored research findings that 48,000 blacks died from smoking-related illnesses in 1988 (Centers for Disease Control 1990b). An uproar followed the announcement of the product, inducing Reynolds to pull Uptown from production before it was distributed to retail stores.

Smoking has also become very prevalent among Latinos (Woods 1995). Their smoking rate increased from 28 to 30 percent from 1983 to 1987 (Marcus and Crane 1984). Rio and Dorado target Latinos; Philip Morris is the single largest advertiser in Latino media (Levin 1988; Maxwell and Jacobson 1989). Reynolds runs a close second. Black, Latino, and youth-targeted magazines have been publishing more and more cigarette ads since at least 1965 (Schooler and Basil 1990).

Ethnic markets for cigarettes are currently approached principally with outdoor street advertising (billboards, bus shelters, taxi tops, buses). Black neighborhoods, in comparison with white areas, have especially high concentrations of billboards, the majority touting alcohol and tobacco ads (Schooler and Basil 1990). Civil rights activists and consumer advocates have sometimes responded by sabotaging or whitewashing these billboards. It is amusing but not altogether surprising that Philip Morris, in response to criticism and protest, now instructs its staff by having a professional actress role-play an intruder disrupting ethnic promotional events screaming, "You are killing my people" (STAT 1991).

Fig. 6.3

Sexual Orientation Segmentation

> Each year [tobacco companies] spend more money in our community getting more
> of us to smoke. Think about it. . . .
>
> —California Lavender Smokefree Project

Gay and lesbian adults smoke more than heterosexual adults. HIV-positive smokers are more likely to get AIDS dementia complex than nonsmokers. Lesbians may get certain cancers at a higher rate than straight women, according to the copy of an antismoking ad in a magazine targeted to gays. The illustration in the center of the ad is a color photograph of an opened pack of cigarettes with a red "X" over it. The ad represents another type of postmodern subvertising (see chapter 1).

Another example of postmodern subvertising is the sabotage of the Marlboro man. The California Department of Heath Services, funded by the Tobacco Tax Initiative, sponsored the ad shown in figure 6.4, which appeared in gay magazines and on billboards in notably gay West Hollywood. The ad has the graphic design and distinctive look of a Marlboro ad: two young, handsome yet rugged cowboys on horseback, out-of-focus rolling hills in the background. The cowboy on the left has just told the other one, Bob, something. Bob casts a startled look at the first cowboy. The brief bold-type copy covers the models in the center of the illustration: "Bob, I've got emphysema."

Gender Segmentation

Women have been the target for "slim" brands such as Style, Superslims, Capri, More, Eve, Virginia Slims, and the scented Chelsea (Dagnoli 1989a; Waldman 1989). Marketing cigarettes for weight management is nothing new. A cigarette advertisement in the 1930s urged the reader to "Reach for a Lucky instead of a sweet!" in order to avoid overindulgence in fattening foods and to maintain "a modern, graceful form." The ad ends by calling Lucky Strike cigarettes "your throat protection—against irritation, against cough."

The Texas Settlement

Texas's nearly $15 billion tobacco settlement in January 1998 produced a record $2.2 billion payday for the state's outside lawyers. Texas is the third state (after Mississippi, $3 billion, and Florida, $11 billion) to settle with the industry. The industry has also agreed to pay $250 million for an antismoking advertising campaign aimed at Texas teenagers.

Although $2.2 billion in legal fees for a settled case is uncommonly high, cigarette firms had never lost a smoking suit, never settled one, and never paid out a cent in damages in March of 1996 when the five trial lawyers

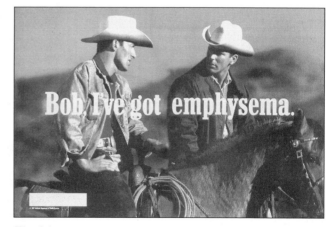

Fig. 6.4

agreed to represent Texas. Some tobacco firm attorneys earn as much as $500 an hour; analysts estimate that the industry spent more than a billion dollars in legal fees in 1997. How do you put a price on losing your voice box to laryngeal cancer or being imprisoned by dependency on an oxygen machine?

Nicotine inhaled by pregnant women kills 100,000 fetuses annually and causes sudden infant death syndrome (*U.S. News and World Report* 1998). Antitobacco activists cite similar studies to argue that nicotine is a drug that should be regulated by the Food and Drug Administration.

In the face of pressure to reduce the number of underage smokers, the tobacco industry has retired the likes of Joe Camel and the Marlboro man and has torn down billboards advertising cigarettes near schools and playgrounds. However, such concessions have no impact on teens and preteens outside the United States. The tobacco industry may be cooperative with a voluntary code of conduct in marketing to smokers at home, but when it comes to selling cigarettes around the world, it subscribes to an altogether different set of standards. The bottom line is that international sales are booming even as the U.S. market shrinks. While cigarette consumption in the United States declined by 4.5 percent between 1990 and 1995, it rose 5.6 percent in Eastern Europe and 8 percent in Asia (Headden 1998). According to the U.S. Department of Agriculture, exports of U.S. cigarettes have increased more than 1,100 percent since 1960. Philip Morris, the world's largest tobacco company, now sells three times as many cigarettes abroad as it does at home, producing overseas profits in 1998 of $4.5 billion (Headden 1998). Surging international sales are the major reason tobacco firms have maintained profits since U.S. residents now account for only 4 percent of smokers worldwide (Headden 1998).

Free Speech

> Congress shall make no law abridging the freedom of speech, or of the press, or the right of people peaceable to assemble, and to petition the government for a redress of grievances.
>
> —Bill of Rights, U.S. Constitution, First Amendment

The First Amendment was designed to protect free speech. In 1942, however, the Supreme Court ruled that the First Amendment did not protect commercial advertising (interpreted as speech that promotes a commercial transaction) (Woods 1995). The Court ruled that advertising did not serve the First Amendment interest of protecting free dialogue that enhances the democratic political process.

Despite this ruling, few products have been severely restricted from advertising. In 1970, however, Congress banned cigarette advertising on radio and television (Woods 1995). In spite of this restriction, cigarette advertising still thrived. The cigarette market was estimated to be worth $43 billion in 1988 (Dagnoli 1989b).

Advertisers attempt to quell the controversy over targeting ethnic minorities and youth by claiming that the issue is simply a matter of free speech. Should speech about dangerous products be muted? The First Amendment does not distinguish between political, commercial, and personal speech. It is clear that tobacco- and alcohol-producing companies are at the center of the target for consumer advocates. But one could just as easily toss in the lottery and other forms of gambling with the usual suspects. "In each case the ad budgets are huge, and most of that advertising is directed at those least able to afford addiction" (Twitchell 1996, 250). Cigarettes and alcohol are the top advertising-producing industries in this country. Together they control 65 percent of newspaper advertising space; beer commercials account for 22 percent of all television commercial time.

Popular Culture, Art, and Advertising

Art is always on the take.

—James B. Twitchell, *Adcult USA*

If life imitates art, advertising imitates both.

—James B. Twitchell, *Adcult USA*

I don't understand those who are professionally cultured. I like pop culture, the culture that doesn't need to be camouflaged, and it has a lightness that remains unchanged even when at its most profound.

—Gianni Versace, *Men without Ties*

Advertising often uses works of art, which are considered representations of high culture, to increase the value of the product that it is trying to sell. This is value by association, or value leakage. Advertising is well known for taking famous pieces of art (e.g., da Vinci's *Mona Lisa*, Michelangelo's *David*, and Wood's *American Gothic*—the most imitated of all) and sneaking them in the back door of popular culture. In a sense, this has broken down aesthetic taste differences that the elite has historically used as a social barrier between high culture and the "crude" tastes of the masses.

Class distinctions, certainly, are still paramount, but these distinctions are sometimes blurred as art is used as advertising. In the past, it was necessary to learn and follow subtle cultural cues to acquire a taste for high culture and thus become accomplished and cultured. Now all that is needed is to buy and use the product to become automatically linked to its aesthetic value through simple association. Advertising is the great equalizer—at least in terms of images.

The difference between high culture and mass culture is now capricious. Advertisers have used sources of everyday mass culture such as comics, caricature, and graffiti to target specialized audiences like youth and ethnic minorities. Marketers use these types of nonaesthetic images that tend to attract the attention of a particular subcultural category. This type of advertising has crossed over because of appeal to more affluent consumers. Popular art makes no pretense about distinctions. Advertising fuses art into the mass media; in this way art becomes mass produced and mass consumed. This eliminates the "middleman," the art critic. It removes the gatekeepers for high culture.

Marketers who depend heavily on advertising, not surprisingly, often sponsor the visual arts. Philip Morris, for example, "has occupied a special niche in corporate philanthropy . . . good graphic design is critical to the success of Marlboro cigarettes, Miller beer, and the rest of the company's products. 'It takes art to make a company great' is the company's advertising refrain" (Twitchell 1996, 217–18). Philip Morris instituted a Thurgood Marshall Scholarship for $200,000. This sounds generous until you discover that they spend $500,000 just to publicize it. Similarly, Philip Morris sponsors art museums and then firmly implores them to lobby against antismoking legislation, even using thinly veiled threats to withdraw financial support.

Decline in Advertising

Advertising seems to prosper only when the economy is in relatively good shape. This may explain the enormous amount of economic waste in advertising. (It has been estimated that it costs nearly $250 to get a consumer to switch brands of toothpaste [Twitchell 1996].) Advertising, however, is so resilient that it adapts to economic conditions of surplus and deprivation. As economic forces exert their muscle over the buying power and decision of consumers as individuals, groups, and businesses, advertising alternates between hard and soft sell. During affluent times, advertisers tend to use a softer sell; during economically tough times, they tend to use a hard sell.

Consumers use less advertising now than twenty years ago in making choices about their purchases. Bernstein's (1992) longitudinal study sampled a cross section of U.S. residents between 1982 and 1992. He found that 17 percent fewer consumers depended on advertising in clothing purchases, 15 percent fewer in appliance purchases, 10 percent fewer in furniture purchases, 9 percent fewer in automotive supply purchases, and 7 percent fewer in banking decisions at the end of the period than at the beginning (Bernstein 1992, 25). If advertising really works, then why isn't the payment for advertising linked to the growth in sales attributable to ads?

Why do we pay less attention to advertising now than a generation ago? First, consumers have become so oversaturated with advertising that it has created a numbing rather than stimulating effect. Second, as baby boomers reach middle age, security in retirement takes precedence over unbridled consumption for display. Finally, women are simply shopping less (Twitchell 1996). Demographic trends indicate that the majority of women in the United States work outside the home. As female baby boomers age, it is increasingly difficult for advertising to tempt them with new products; most have already developed nearly irrevocable loyalties to their favorite brands.

Generation X: Selling to Those Who Have Been Sold Out

Advertising uses a "vignette" or "speed-up" approach with a rapid succession of lifestyle images, meticulously timed with music, that directly sell feeling and emotion rather than products (Jhally 1990). It is important to recognize that the speed-up technique emerged in response to two sociohistorical developments. First is the escalating clutter of the commercial environment. Second is the coming of age, in terms of disposable income, of a generation that grew up on television and commercials (Jhally 1990). The necessity for an ad to stand out to a visually sophisticated audience drove the advertising industry to a greater passion for short, undiluted shots. Sexuality, to be sure, is a core characteristic of this.

What about Generation X, those born in the late '60s to late '70s? The mass media created and, through multinational advertising, promoted a shared identity for members of this generation around the globe. This shared identity was merely a reflection of attitudes, characteristics, and behavior as garnered from advertising research. And it has not painted a pretty picture. Teens (as well as younger children) are not developing ethical values, according to a survey and focus groups cosponsored by the Advertising Council (Farcus 1997). Both parents and teachers maintained that their authority had been undercut—sometimes by the other group—and that the threat of judicial or legal action had greatly diminished their capability to discipline children.

Adults perceive teens to be lacking honesty, self-discipline, and a work ethic. This does not sound like shocking news. After all, the older generation has always given credence to the notion that the young are useless, rotten, and insubordinate. What gives this message its particular sense of urgency is the fact that adults now think that the repercussions for youth and society are much more dreadful. Respondents also believed that government programs could not supply the solution. These postmodern attitudes certainly fly in the face of modernistic ideologies promoting progress, control over society, and an illusion of rational order.

More than four out of five adults believed that being a parent (81 percent) or a child (83 percent) today was harder than ever. They tended to view ethical values as a vaccine. If you inoculate teens with them, they will have the capacity to resist the temptations of alcohol, drugs, sex, and crime. Adult responses were consistent across ethnicity/ race, socioeconomic status, gender, age, and parental status. Teens were viewed as unrestrained, irresponsible, and impolite and as having too much leisure time; only a few teens are seen as bright or considerate.

Teens reported that they were typically happy and had good relationships with the adults in their lives. Nearly two-thirds (65 percent) stated that they received an encouraging comment or compliment from adults every day or almost every day. On the other hand, four out of ten (41 percent) indicated they see people using alcohol or drugs every day or almost every day. One-third of the teens said that there were no adults at home when they returned from school, and 60 percent responded that other teens pay too much attention to their appearance.

Young Generation X'ers seemed to have more in common with their counterparts halfway around the world than with members of their own families. The same may be true for younger adolescent boys. Three samples from South Africa, Sri Lanka, and the United States of boys aged eleven through fourteen, matched for age and social class, drew self-portraits and wrote self-descriptions (Stiles et al. 1998). In all three countries, more than three out of every four of the self-portraits depicted sporting activities (especially soccer and basketball) or sports clothing. This supports the notion of a shared leisure-activity culture and universal brand recognition by youth for athletic wear. Most of the boys came from high-income backgrounds, which may have given them an individualistic perspective, free time for sports, and the ability to purchase sports gear.

Generation X'ers were "so polluted by desire unmet, so overwhelmed by promises unkept that they override any claims" (Twitchell 1996, 240). Although Generation X'ers were cynical and apparently immune to the hard sell of modern advertising, it is clear that they, too, worshipped the brand names that represented their generation and wore their products religiously like a uniform. Their litany of designer labels included, but was not limited to, Guess, Tommy Hilfiger, Adidas, Banana Republic, Calvin Klein, Fila, Benetton, Donna Karan, Beverly Hills Polo Club, Perry Ellis, Diesel, Armani, Ralph Lauren (grunge line only), Reebok, Liz Claiborne (grunge line only), Nike, Mossimo,

Starter, Esprit, Umbro, Bugle Boy, Doc Marten, Gap, L.A. Gear, Pony, Etonic, Lotto, Stussy, and No Fear.

Of course, just parading around in designer labels advertises their brands. Designers became so concerned with displaying their labels that they (e.g., Tommy Hilfiger, Nike) began placing logos on shoe tips, the only exposed part of the shoe when the wearer is clad in oversized, baggy jeans that sag in the seat and cover the foot. Thus advertising reacts to what was originally subcultural (Latino and black) fashion and eventually became a mainstream trend. Clearly, youth are targeted because members are in the prime time of their lives for brand selection.

Selling and Advertising

> There is no simple correspondence between advertising and higher sales.
> —*Information Resources*

> With greater misgivings than ever, manufacturers are questioning whether advertising works.
> —James B. Twitchell, *Adcult USA*

Does advertising really work? "Although advertising is a reliable way to increase short-term sales, it does not do much to boost market share and profits" (Twitchell 1996, 242). Rather than advertising resulting in greater sales, the converse appears to be more true. Advertising budgets are typically a specified proportion of sales (or projected sales). Consequently, commerce seems to result in advertising, and not the other way around.

Recall does not necessarily result in greater sales (Lipman 1991, B1). It is no wonder that there has been a recent shift away from conventional television, radio, and magazine advertising toward special promotions, in-store displays, discounting, direct mail, and coupons.

With the increasing interactive capacities of television, viewers may soon be able to screen out commercials or have different ones inserted. Viewers may also be able to target the commercials they see rather than having the advertising agency target its audience (Twitchell 1996).

The amount of money spent on advertising indicates a sentiment of decreasing trust. In 1991, advertising costs decreased for the first time in thirty years. Even though an economic slump results in advertising cuts, the slices of budgets set aside for advertising do not project a recovery to the levels of the 1980s. In 1980, advertising consumed two-thirds of marketing expenses; in 1990, one-third (Twitchell 1996). There are fifteen hundred new products introduced to supermarkets each month (Twitchell 1996). Competition between manufacturers to introduce such new items to often-unpredictable consumers is fierce. The en vogue spaces for ads are now the ATM, the checkout line, and the shopping cart.

Advertising agencies must sell their ads to two very different audiences: the consumer and the client. Producing and placing an ad in the mass media in order to target a particular audience is not exceedingly difficult. What is hard is persuading the client to spend millions of dollars on space in magazines or newspapers or on television, radio, or billboards. For an advertising agency to create profit for itself, it must sell its product (the ad) to the client. The relationship between the advertising agency and its client, the manufacturer, has become increasingly strained and uneasy. At another level, so has the relationship between the consumer and the advertiser. For example, community activists in the inner city have worked successfully to remove tobacco and alcohol ads that focus on ethnic minorities and underage groups (e.g., Dakota and Uptown cigarettes, PowerMaster beer). That racial segmentation of cigarette and alcohol advertising is overtly exploitative has recently become a significant political issue (Pollay, Lee, and Carter-Whitney 1992).

Aggressive telemarketing techniques are backfiring. For example, some telemarketers are trained to push their products or services until the prospective customer says no three times. Consumers have tired of this hard-sell approach and hang up on telemarketers before they have a chance to pitch their product. Consumers with caller ID do not even have to respond to sales calls. Even when the consumer calls the manufacturer or service provider, callers hang up if advertising is played while they are on hold. Similarly, "many patients have rebelled when forced to read and view special programming at the doctor's office" (Twitchell 1996, 247). And, finally, "exercisers at health clubs have boycotted treadmills placed so that the exerciser can see only the monitor of an advertising network" (Twitchell 1996, 247).

Conclusion

> Values always decay over time. Societies that keep their values alive do so not by escaping the processes of decay but by powerful processes of regeneration.
> —John Garner

Advertising has become the predominant shared meaning system of postmodern society. Advertising not only tells us what to consume but how to consume it. Despite all claims to the contrary, advertising does not create artificial desires in consumers. Rather, culture has created these desires. If we have food to eat, clothes to wear, and a roof over our heads, our natural needs have been taken care of. All other needs are socially constructed and internalized.

Why is our culture so concerned with the visible signs of racial differences? Why are individuals so caught up, psychologically speaking, in physical appearance and ethnic distinctions? Differences in appearance are mistakenly interpreted as natural or biological characteristics of human beings.

The ads in this volume cannot be taken as representative behavior or scenarios in real life. Unfortunately, however, the images that we see in advertising are not perceived as unnatural or artificial; they are seen as real social life—something to be copied or emulated. People do not recognize the injustice and discriminatory nature of the way people are expected to act according to their gender, ethnicity, or race. Ads are very limiting in the types of images that portray women and minorities.

The postmodern woman in advertising is a superwoman. She is a successful, upper-middle-class professional mother and wife who also does volunteer work and raises Arabian horses in her spare time. No wonder she has so much self-esteem and independence. Advertisers pretend that it is their products that make her so successful, happy, and liberated. These postmodern images display a myth of social and economic progress for women. The stark reality of aggregate data clashes with this fantasy. In short, postmodern advertising is a delusion that trivializes complex social problems as everyday individual ones that can be solved by purchasing the appropriate product. This inauthenticity of advertising representations adds to a culture that is becoming increasingly chaotic, counterfeit, corrupt, and fictitious.

Advertising merely reflects social values and trends; it does not cause these problems. However, it clearly contributes to gender and ethnic inequality by developing and maintaining an atmosphere in which the marketing of ethnic stereotypes, women's bodies or parts thereof, sex as pornography (children as sex objects), and distorted body-image ideals are viewed as valid and acceptable. Perhaps most damaging is the omission of legitimate and more realistic ethnic and gender representations.

We play many roles during the course of our lives. Perhaps our gender and ethnic roles are the most consequential of all for our identity and behavior. We must avoid the trap of accepting advertising images as natural. We must critically reject the mythical, degrading, and stereotypical images that advertising portrays. We should strive for critical media literacy—the development of competencies in reading images critically (Kellner 1988). We have to be able to draw the line between social reality and media fantasy. We must not let ads tell us who we should be.

With the creation of new technologies and their application in mass media, the social foundations for the construction of gender, ethnicity, and race are being essentially altered. While the world's population is predominantly rural, ethnic minorities are disproportionately urbanized and impoverished. New information technology, the increased hegemony of market structures, and the resulting socioeconomic instability have changed the material circumstances of these and other poor and working-class urban dwellers.

If we consider that the overwhelming majority of the cost of a product is due to marketing and advertising costs and not product ingredients, we realize that consumer capitalism creates an enormous waste of money. This forces consumers to pay high prices for products that they are led to believe they need for self-realization, happiness, success, sex appeal, popularity, self-esteem, and so on. This endless process of waste and deception is particularly alarming considering the growing scarcity of resources. It also raises the issue of what can be done to counter the excesses of consumer capitalism.

Advertising has become a key public policy question (Kellner 1988). For example, should all cigarette advertising be banned, as cigarette television and radio commercials were discontinued in the 1970s? Cigarette smoking is clearly a threat to public health, considering its addictive and dangerous characteristics, including secondhand smoke. The younger one is at the time one starts smoking, the more likely he or she will continue smoking and the less likely he or she will stop smoking. We cannot depend on voluntary activity by cigarette manufacturers. One possible tactic is to base health insurance rates on health risks and quality of life, including smoking, drinking, recreational drug use, overeating, and exercise.

Considering the social effects of advertising also raises the question of whether advertising should be subject to taxation. Currently, it is written off by corporations as a business expense, thus passing on advertising expenses to the taxpayer as well as the consumer. Perhaps we should disallow tax write-offs for advertising and also tax advertising expenditures and advertising agencies at a higher rate, given the impact of advertising on our society and the huge waste of resources, talent, and human energy (*Advertising Age* 1988). Minimally, advertising, both print and television, for cigarettes, alcohol, and other socially undesirable and harmful products could be taxed.

What are the implications of an advertising industry whose visual images promise the good life through the purchase of commodities? We know that satisfaction cannot be provided by the consumption of products. At best, we can purchase the image of that happiness or satisfaction. Satisfaction and well-being are viewed as elusive in postmodern society. Advertising propels us toward commodities as a means to satisfaction.

The speed and fragmentation that characterize postmodern advertising images may have the same effect on the development of consciousness. The increasing widespread use of techniques that speed up and fragment images has crossed over into cultural consciousness and is taking hold as we begin the twenty-first century. This is perhaps the clearest example of advertising's effects on society. The question then becomes, How do we view this condition, as an acceptable situation or as a problem clamoring for amelioration?

We should be attentive to the gravity of the prevalent power, the repetitive message, and the latent consequences of advertising. Whether we like it or not, advertising is always "educating" us. Advertising affects our self-esteem and trains us in the cultural rules and rituals of social interaction. This volume contributes to the development of critical media literacy. Such cognitive capacity can counter the way that advertising works to obscure our awareness, impeding our movement toward liberating social change. Critical reflection on mass media images empowers consumers to become more independent people, able to free themselves from patterns of domination and become more dynamic constituents, eager to undertake positive social transformation, and capable of doing so.

If we are to understand how advertising affects us, we must pay attention not only to individual advertisements but also to the way that advertising functions as a cultural system. Commercial imagery, most of which goes completely unnoticed by most individuals, plays an important role in the social order.

Advertising tells us that material objects will make us happy and satisfied. Responses to marketing surveys tell us that consumers highly value family, love, and friendships. In other words, we desire meaningful human relationships rather than commodities. Advertisers know this, of course. (That is why they do marketing research.) Consequently, they have stopped pushing commodities alone. Instead, advertisers have linked the representations of a highly efficacious social life, the "dream life" of society, to the world of goods and services, seductively offering us a quality of lifestyle that objects alone cannot provide.

A culture may be characterized by the dialogue and discourse of its members (what they talk and write about). A capitalistic market system talks about commodities and services that can be bought and sold by individuals or groups. Discourse about key social issues such as inequality, justice, the environment, racism, sexism, health care, education, and poverty is often kept on the back burners of society. The dominant culture of commercialism makes it boorish even to discuss more urgent social issues.

If industrial production maintains its current record-breaking pace, an environmental crisis will follow within the next fifty years. Only by taking preventive measures today can such a catastrophe be averted. Yet the culture of consumerism compels us to search for immediate remedies to commonplace problems with no consideration of obligations, responsibilities, and future costs. There is a lack of long-range thought about environmental preservation. The so-called new world order of postmodernity will be noted for its international struggle over increasingly sparse assets. Postmodernism could benefit all societies through the development of a collective yet humane vision of the future. Through critical analyses of popular media, such as advertising, we are able to discern that a largely white, capitalist patriarchy is an interconnecting system of domination that fixes the limits of our reality.

We can acknowledge the influence of mass media without denying our own power to act autonomously. We should not try to deceive ourselves by denying the impact of advertising and other forms of popular media on ourselves. Rather we should engage those images in popular culture with discernment, caution, knowledge, and attentiveness.

Policy Implications for Advertising

Advertising is more reactive to cultural ideologies and structural dynamics than a dominant social force itself. Following are implications for public policy and advertising. Clearly, some of the responsibility for institutionalized racism and sexism lies in the hands of advertisers. Aggressive and violent behavior and related gender and ethnic stereotyping are strongly correlated with exposure to advertising at an early age. Advertisers sustain cultural myths, gender roles, and patterns of intergroup behavior that underlie social justification for stereotyping, discrimination, and violence against women and ethnic minorities. They also are extremely creative in structuring new representations of long-standing cultural ideologies of intergroup hegemony.

One implication of this volume for policy analysis is the need for an immediate global ban on marketing cigarettes to youth. This is a health issue and not one of free speech.

A second implication involves the regulation of television viewing for children. Empirical evidence such as that collected by the Institute for Social Research at the University of Michigan clearly demonstrates that long-term exposure to television violence makes children behave more aggressively. The research does not, however, show the same effect on adults. The regulation of tobacco and alcohol provides precedent for regulating children's exposure to television violence. This is not to deny that psychological, physiological, and large-scale social factors such as institutional discrimination also contribute to violent or aggressive behavior.

Third, advertising should not reinforce or trivialize the problem of violence against women. This includes disassociation from adversarial, abusive, or violent relationships or situations.

Fourth, advertising should not degrade, demean, or objectify the form, representation, or status of women or any ethnic minority group (Consumers for Socially Responsible Advertising 1994).

A final implication is the need to continue to increase ethnically diverse representations in advertising and other forms of mass media. More important than numbers is the removal of dehumanizing and stereotypical images. Advertisers and their firms should cultivate realistic representations of diverse segments of the target population.

Postcolonialism, Postmodernism, and Chaos

Marketing policy and practices in modern societies have evolved from mass marketing to increasingly narrow subcultural segments in postmodern societies. It is highly ironic that this seemingly orderly, rational, and step-by-step extension of advertising has such serious implications for social chaos. Postmodernity is characterized by the tensions between postmodern consciousness and postconventional morality (Cortese 1990).

What are the implications for chaos via ethnic advertising? Advertisers have targeted, and will continue to target, ethnic minority population segments to sell products and services. This will promote further balkanization, ethnic tensions, social fissures, and fragmentation in postmodern societies.

The preface to the first edition discussed postmodern and postcommunist ethnic turmoil around the globe. In the new millennium, ethnic cleansing will undoubtedly continue. These ongoing, low-intensity wars have no real winners or losers, no major defeats or victories, no defined battlefields or boundaries (Ahmed 1997). In a May 30, 1998, commencement address at the U.S. military academy at West Point, the secretary of defense stressed the ever-changing, and often turbulent, global environment in which military personnel work. The Israeli-Palestine conflict exemplifies yet another regional ethnic tension in a postmodern period seemingly increasingly characterized by uncertainty and disorder. Ethnic cleansing is a sign of our overrationalized times. We need to understand that before we can suppress and repel it.

The majority of the earth's population, from Asia to Africa and beyond, lives in the aftermath of colonialism (McClintock, Mufti, and Shohat, 1997). Their everyday existence is shaped by their history as colonized peoples in ways that are sometimes subtle or difficult to define. America's relationship with its ethnic minorities, and perhaps even women, is similar to postcolonialism. For example, African Americans, as a group, have never recovered from the economic, social, and political disadvantages of slavery. Moreover, America's relationship with Mexican Americans and Native Americans can be characterized as *internal colonialism*. Group dynamics are characterized by postcolonial interracial relations.

Postmodernism raises the key issue of the postcolonial condition, forcing us to reassess the notions of gender, ethnicity, and identity. What are the limitations of gender and ethnicity in an ever-changing world? How have women and ethnic minorities been kept away from political power? What has been the historical aftermath of different forms of postcolonialism? What is the possibility of postconventional morality emerging as a leader in postmodern consciousness?

Combating Symbolic Racism at the Individual Level: A Litany to Live By

You can take any of the following actions to challenge symbolic racism:

1. Be alert to the prevailing power of advertising, especially its inauthenticity, omission of real diversity, repetitive message, and latent consequences.

2. Work to develop critical media literacy in order to offset the way that advertising, through its false images, tries to dim our awareness of social reality.

3. Boycott products and services that use demeaning or stereotypical images in their advertising.

4. Boycott establishments whose policies or actual treatment of people is discriminatory or otherwise unjust.

5. Respect the cultural diversity of others. (This necessitates more open-mindedness in interacting with people.)

6. When traveling, adapt to local custom, culture, and cuisine.

7. Respect the law, and especially the principles and rights it is meant to protect.

8. Challenge unjust laws and rules.

9. Learn about and celebrate your own ethnic background.

10. Learn about and celebrate someone else's ethnic background.

11. Teach others, especially those within your own ethnic group, about your culture.

12. Learn to recognize and accept multiethnic identities.

13. Speak out when you witness ethnic intolerance or racist stereotyping.

14. Donate your time and resources to fight hunger, disease, poverty, racism, or abuse.

15. Work to develop a balance between tradition and modernity in your life (Ritzer 1996).

Just do it! to resist a culture that embraces profit over ethics; quantity over quality; inflexible policy and standardized scripts over openness, diversity, discernment, and creativity; and technology over its people. It is ultimately the responsibility of all citizens in a democratic process.

Appendix: Advertising Evaluation

Select a print ad or series of ads on a particular theme and analyze using the following outline.

1. DECONSTRUCTION OF NONVERBAL BEHAVIOR
   A. Facial expression
   B. Body posture, body language, touch
   C. Gestures
   D. Provocateur
      1. Youth
      2. Sexual allure
      3. Flawless
      4. Good looking/beautiful
2. DECONSTRUCTION OF COPY
   A. Analyze headline, subheads, written description
   B. What is the message communicated to the consumer?
   C. Is there a double meaning? Contrast literal meaning with implied, actual, or assumed meaning.
3. MARKETING ANALYSIS
   A. Magazine title and date (month, year, and, if possible, day)
   B. Target audience of magazine and ad
      1. Race/ethnicity
      2. Age range
      3. Gender
      4. Socioeconomic class (upper, upper-middle, middle, lower-middle, all socioeconomic classes)
      5. Special interest group (e.g., cigar smokers, hip hop music fans, horseback riders)
   C. Seasonal ad (e.g., Father's Day, Valentine's Day, Back to School, etc.)
   D. Why did the advertiser place this ad in *this* magazine/newspaper? (compare magazine/newspaper to product/service)
   E. Where is the ad placed in the magazine? (back cover, inside front cover, opposite a black-and-white ad, etc.)
4. ARTISTIC COMPOSITION ANALYSIS
   A. What is the visual message or meaning?
   B. Colors
      1. What color combination is used and why?
      2. What color is dominant and why?

    3. Composition (arrangement of objects in ad)

    4. What type of font or cursive is used and why?

5. NARRATIVE ("tell the story")

  A. Past

  B. Present (frame frozen in ad)

  C. Future

Write a three-part story that narrates what happens before the frame frozen in the ad, what is happening in the ad, and what is likely to happen in the immediate future. The story should be consistent with, yet expand, what is displayed in the ad.

6. Apply one of the models to the ad(s) or provide alternative model

  A. Equal presentation

  B. Social reality

  C. Cultural attitudes

Glossary

advertisement: a message that is called to the attention of a public audience, especially by paid announcement

advertising: "a paid, mass-mediated attempt to persuade" (O'Guinn, Allen, and Semenik 1998, 577)

advocacy advertising: advertising that attempts to influence public opinion on important social, political, or environmental issues of concern to the sponsoring organization (O'Guinn, Allen, and Semenik 1998)

art: "any graphics, photography, film, or video that offers visual information to a receiver" (O'Guinn, Allen, and Semenik 1998, 275)

body-chopping: dismemberment or hacking apart of human bodies in ads

body-clowning: portrayal of individuals or groups as playful clowns (e.g., silly arm, leg, and head gestures), supporting the attitude that they are childish and cannot be taken seriously (Goffman 1976)

brand extension: a way of introducing goods by adding the familiarity of a proven brand

branding: the process of differentiating similar products or services

copy: "the verbal or written part of a message" (O'Guinn, Allen, and Semenik 1998, 275)

copycat: the concurrent production of two nearly identical ads except for the ethnic background of the models

cultural attitudes model: the view that cultural attitudes toward ethnic minorities affect how minorities are portrayed in advertising (see also *cultural transmission*)

cultural transmission: the "process by which one generation passes culture to the next" (Macionis 1996, 34)

culture industry: the collection of entertainment industries dedicated to amusing the populace in their leisure time: music, film, television, radio, and magazines (Horkheimer and Adorno 1972)

equal presentation model: the view that whites and minorities should be shown in exactly the same way in ads, regardless of any cultural, economic, or physical differences

function ranking: an ad display in which an individual performs the important role or takes an active position

gay-image advertising: advertising that attempts to use a dual-market approach that will attract gays and lesbians in a subtle way that heterosexual consumers will not notice

hybritising: combining two types of advertising

ideology: images, concepts, and premises that provide the frameworks through which we represent, interpret, understand, and try to understand some point of view of social life (Hall 1981)

institutional advertising: advertising that attempts to persuade a public audience to adopt a certain attitude about a particular firm or institution (Henshel 1990)

licensed withdrawal: psychological removal from the situation, disorientation, or defenselessness

mock assault: playful treatment of an individual as prey under attack by a predator

objectification: culture conditioning using observer's perspective that sexualizes the human body, especially females, through gaze or "checking out"

predator: stereotypical image of ethnic minorities or males as powerful beings who injure or exploit others for their own gain or sexually prey, plunder, destroy, or devour

provocateur: media gender image characterized by youth, flawlessness, attractiveness, and sexual allure

racial assimilation: commodified image of ethnic minorities conforming to white standards of beauty: light skin, straight or wavy hair, blue or green eyes, or Euro-American features

relative size: a visual indication of comparative power and authority, often a height advantage

self-objectification: culture conditioning using observer's perspective that sexualizes the human body, especially females, through gaze or "checking out," leading people to internalize this perspective. Characterized by habitual self-monitoring of one's physical appearance. Consciousness of one's body as an object has three components: body surveillance, internalization of cultural body standards, and beliefs about the controllability of appearance.

servant: stereotypical image of ethnic minorities as objects that perform menial chores for a white person who has authority or political power over them. Servants wear uniforms and always seem to be smiling.

sexism: any attitude, behavior, institutional arrangement, or policy that favors one gender over the other

social reality model: the view that since minorities are more likely to be poor or in lower-status occupations than whites, ads should reflect any differences that may currently exist in society, drawing the public's attention to ethnic inequalities

subvertising: use of brand recognition and brand hegemony either against itself or to promote an unrelated value or idea

symbolic racism: subtle ethnic stereotyping, trivialization of minority empowerment or racial equality, or the absence of ethnic representations

References

Advertising Age. 1986. "Show More Minorities in Ads: *Post.*" 11 August, 3.
———. 1988. "What's Ahead? Read My Lips: Taxes." 7 November, 1.
———. 1997. "Tire Maker's Racist TV Ad Causes International Blowout." 22 December, 14.
Ahmed, Akbar S. 1997. "Ethnic Cleansing: A Metaphor for Our Time." In *The Conceit of Innocence: Losing the Conscience of the West in the War against Bosnia,* ed. Stjepan G. Mestrovic. College Station: Texas A&M University Press.
Alcohol, Drug Abuse, and Mental Health Administration. 1989. *National Institute on Drug Abuse, National Household Survey on Drug Abuse: Population Estimates 1988.* Washington, D.C.: U.S. Department of Health and Human Services, Alcohol, Drug Abuse, and Mental Health Administration.
American Psychological Association. 1993. *Violence and Youth: Psychology's Response.* Washington, D.C.: American Psychological Association.
Andelin, Helen B. 1963. *Fascinating Womanhood.* Santa Barbara, Calif.: Pacific Press.
Andrews, Peter. 1980. "Peddling Prime Time." *Saturday Review,* 7 June, 64–65.
Association of National Advertisers. 1988. *The Role of Advertising in America.* New York: Association of National Advertisers.
Astroff, R. 1989. "Commodifying Cultures: Latino Ad Specialists as Cultural Brokers." Paper presented at the Seventh International Conference on Culture and Communication, Philadelphia.
Bakhtin, M. 1984. *Rabelais and His World.* Cambridge: MIT Press.
Balkan, Carlos D. 1988. "The Hispanic Market's Leading Indicators." *Hispanic Business,* December, 26–28.
Baudrillard, Jean. 1988. *America.* Trans. Chris Turner. New York: Verso.
———. 1990. *Seduction.* Trans. Brian Singer. London: Macmillan.
Bauman, Zygmunt. 1993. *Postmodern Ethics.* Oxford: Blackwell.
Benson, Dennis, Catherine Charlton, and Fern Goodhart. 1992. "Acquaintance Rape on Campus: A Literature Review." *Journal of American College Health* 40: 157–65.
Berkman, Harold W., and Christopher C. Gilson. 1978. *Consumer Behavior: Concepts and Strategies.* Encino, Calif.: Dickinson.
Berkowitz, Alan. 1992. "College Men as Perpetrators of Acquaintance Rape and Sexual Assault: A Review of Recent Research." *Journal of American College Health* 40: 175–81.
Bernstein, Sid. 1992. "Are Ads Less Important?" *Advertising Age,* 21 September, 25.
Berry, Jon. 1990. "Help Wanted." *Ad Week,* 9 July, 28–31.
Bonacich, Edna. 1973. "A Theory of Middleman Minorities." *American Sociological Review* 38: 583–94.
Bordo, Susan. 1993. *Unbearable Weight: Feminism, Western Culture, and the Body.* Berkeley and Los Angeles: University of California Press.
Bovee, Courtland L., and William F. Arens. 1989. *Contemporary Advertising.* Homewood, Ill.: Richard D. Irwin.

Brod, Harry. 1987. *The Making of Masculinities: New Men's Studies.* Boston: Allen & Unwin.

Brown, Les. 1971. *Television: The Business behind the Box.* New York: Harcourt Brace Jovanovich.

Brownski, M. 1984. *Culture Clash: The Making of Gay Sensibility.* Boston: South End Press.

Burrell, Tom. 1992. Interview by Gail Baker Woods. Burrell Building, Chicago, 12 March.

Bush, Ronald F., Paul Solomon, and Joseph Hair. 1974. "There Are More Blacks in Television Commercials." *Journal of Advertising Research* 17 (February): 21–25.

Buss, David M. 1994. *The Evolution of Desire: Strategies of Human Mating.* New York: Basic Books.

Carby, H. 1987. *Reconstructing Womanhood: The Emergence of the Afro-American Woman Novelist.* New York: Oxford University Press.

Cassidy, Marsha, and Richard Katula. 1990. "The Black Experience in Advertising: An Interview with Thomas J. Burrell." *Journal of Communication Inquiry* 14 (1): 93–104.

Center for Science in the Public Interest. 1990. *Marketing Booze to Blacks.* Washington, D.C.: Public Interest Video Network. Video.

Centers for Disease Control. 1990a. "Cigarette Brand Use among Adult Smokers—United States, 1986." *Morbidity and Mortality Weekly Report* 39: 671–73.

———. 1990b. "Smoking-Attributable Mortality and Years of Potential Life Lost: United States, 1988." *Morbidity and Mortality Weekly Report* 36: 693–97.

Children's Literature Review Board. 1977. "Starting Out Right: Choosing Books about Black People for Young Children." Pp. 107–45 in *Cultural Conformity in Books for Children: Further Readings in Racism,* ed. D. MacCann and G. Woodard. Metuchen, N.J.: Scarecrow Press.

Clark, Dana. 1996. "Commodity Lesbianism." *Camera Obscura* 25.

Colfax, J. David, and Susan Frankel Sternberg. 1972. "The Perpetuation of Racial Stereotypes: Blacks in Mass Circulation Magazine Advertisements." *Public Opinion Quarterly* 36 (Spring): 8–18.

Conill Advertising. 1993. *A Closer Look at Conill.* New York: Conill Advertising.

Consumers for Socially Responsible Advertising. 1994. Dangerous Promises Campaign: Alcohol Advertising and Violence against Women. Berkeley, Calif. Scripted slide presentation.

Cortese, Anthony J. 1990. *Ethnic Ethics: The Restructuring of Moral Theory.* Albany: State University of New York Press.

———. 1995. "The Rise, Hegemony, and Decline of the Chicago School of Sociology, 1892–1945." *Social Science Journal* 32 (3): 235–54.

———. 1999. "Ethical Issues in a Subculturally Diverse Society." Pp. 52–123 in *Handbook on Ethical Issues and Aging,* ed. Tonya Johnson. Westport, Conn.: Greenwood.

Cox, Keith K. 1970. "Social Effects of Integrated Advertising." *Journal of Advertising Research* 10 (April): 41–44.

Curran, Daniel J., and Claire M. Renzetti. 1996. *Social Problems: Society in Crisis.* 4th ed. Boston: Allyn & Bacon.

Dagnoli, Judann. 1989a. "RJR's Chelsea." *Advertising Age,* 6 February, 3ff.

———. 1989b. "RJR's Uptown Targets Blacks." *Advertising Age,* 18 December, 4.

Dates, Jannette L. 1990. "Advertising." Pp. 421–54 in *Split Image: African Americans in the Mass Media,* ed. Jannette L. Dates and William Barlow. Washington, D.C.: Howard University Press.

Davis, Riccardo A. 1994. "Competition Ignites Outdoor Spending." *Advertising Age,* 11 April.

DeAnda, Roberto M., ed. 1996. *Chicanas and Chicanos in Contemporary Society.* Boston: Allyn & Bacon.

Delener, Nejdet, and James P. Neelankavil. 1990. "Informational Sources and Media Usage: A Comparison between Asian and Hispanic Subcultures." *Journal of Advertising Research,* June–July, 45–58.

Deloitte & Touche Trade Retail and Distribution Services Group. 1991. *Market Opportunities in Retail: Insight into Black American Consumers' Buying Habits.* January. New York: Deloitte & Touche.

D'Emilio, J. 1983. "Capitalism and Gay Identity." In *Powers of Desire: The Politics of Sexuality,* ed. A. Snitow, C. Stansell, and S. Thompson. New York: Monthly Review Press.

Diamond, Jared. 1997. *Why Is Sex Fun? The Evolution of Human Sexuality.* New York: Basic Books.

Dines, Gail, and Jean M. Humez, eds. 1995. *Gender, Race, and Class in Media.* Thousand Oaks, Calif.: Sage.

Dubin, Steven. 1987. "Black Representations in Popular Culture." *Social Problems* 34: 122–40.

Durkheim, Emile. 1961. *Moral Education*. Trans. E. K. Wilson and H. Schnurer. 1925. Reprint. Glencoe, Ill.: Free Press.

Dyer, R. 1988. "White." *Screen* 29 (4): 44–65.

Eigen, Lewis D. 1992. "Sex, Alcohol, Drugs, and College Students." *Prevention File*, fall.

Elliott, J., and A. J. Wootton. 1997. "Some Ritual Idioms of Gender in British Television Advertising." *Sociological Review*, 437–52.

Ellsworth, E. 1986. "Illicit Pleasures: Feminist Spectators and *Personal Best*." *Wide Angle* 8 (2).

Ellwood, D. 1988. *Poor Support: Poverty in the American Family*. New York: Basic Books.

Erikson, Kai. 1976. *Everything in Its Path*. New York: Simon & Schuster.

Espiritu, Yen Le. 1997. *Asian American Women and Men: Labor, Laws, and Love*. New York: Sage.

Farcus, Steve. 1997. "Youth Values Survey." Advertising Council and Ronald McDonald House Charities. *Public Agenda*.

Federal Bureau of Investigation. 1992. *Federal Crime Reports*. Washington, D.C.: U.S. Government Printing Office.

Fiske, J. 1988. "Critical Response Meaningful Moments." *Critical Studies in Mass Communications* 5.

Foote, Jennifer. 1988. "The Ad World's New Bimbos." *Newsweek*, 25 January, 44–45.

Fredrickson, B. L., and T-A. Roberts. 1997. "Objectification Theory: Toward Understanding Women's Lived Experiences and Mental Health Risks." *Psychology of Women Quarterly* 21: 173–206.

Fredrickson, B. L., T-A. Roberts, S.M. Noll, D.M. Quinn, and J.M. Twenge. 1998. "That Swimsuit Becomes You: Sex Differences in Self-Objectification, Restrained Eating, and Math Performance." *Journal of Personality and Social Psychology* 75: 269–284.

Fregoso, Rosa Linda. 1993. *The Bronze Screen: Chicana and Chicano Film Culture*. Minneapolis: University of Minnesota Press.

Frieze, I. H., and J. Noble. 1980. "The Effects of Alcohol on Marital Violence." Paper presented at the American Psychological Association convention. Cited in D. Murdoch et al., "Alcohol and Crimes of Violence: Present Issues," *International Journal of the Addictions* 25 (9) (1990): 1065–81.

Fry, Susan L. 1991. "Reaching Hispanic Publics with Special Events." *Public Relations Journal* 47 (2): 12.

Gamson, William A., David Croteau, William Hoynes, and Theodore Sasson. 1992. "Media Images and the Social Construction of Reality." *Annual Review of Sociology* 18: 373–93.

Gans, Herbert. 1979. *Deciding What's News*. New York: Random House.

Gardner, Robert W., Bryant Robey, and Peter C. Smith. 1985. "Asian Americans: Growth, Change, and Diversity." *Population Bulletin* 40 (4).

Gerbner, George, and Larry Gross. 1976. "Living with Television." *Journal of Communication* 26 (2): 172–99.

Gilbert, M. Jean, and Richard Cervantes. 1986. "Alcohol Services for Mexican Americans: A Review of Utilization Patterns, Treatment Considerations, and Preventive Activities." *Hispanic Journal of Behavioral Sciences* 8 (3): 191–223.

Goffman, Erving. 1976. *Gender Advertisements*. Cambridge: Harvard University Press.

Goldman, R. 1987. "Marketing Fragrances: Advertising and the Production of Commodity Signs." *Theory, Culture, and Society* 4: 691–725.

Goodman, Ellen. 1991. "Danger Signs for Women." *San Francisco Chronicle*, 1 August.

Gordon, Milton. 1978. *Human Nature, Class, and Ethnicity*. New York: Oxford University Press.

Gould, John W., Norman B. Sigband, and Cyril E. Zoerner Jr. 1970. "Black Consumer Reactions to 'Integrated' Advertising." *Journal of Marketing* 34 (July): 20–26.

Greeley, Andrew. 1974. *Ethnicity in the United States*. New York: John Wiley.

Greenberg, B. S. 1972. "Children's Reaction to TV Blacks." *Journalism Quarterly* 49: 5–14.

Greenburg, Eric Rolfe, et al. 1987. *Successful Marketing to U.S. Hispanics and Asians*. New York: American Management Association, 81.

Griswold, Wendy. 1981. "American Character and the American Novel: An Expansion of Reflection Theory in the Sociology of Literature." *American Journal of Sociology* 86: 740–65.

Gross, Larry. 1991. "Out of the Mainstream: Sexual Minorities and the Mass Media." In *Gay*

People, Sex, and the Media, ed. Michelle A. Wolf and Alfred P. Kielwassen. Binghamton, N.Y.: Haworth Press.

Guy, Pat. 1991. "Study Says Ads Overlook Minorities." *USA Today,* 24 July, 2B.

Hall, Stuart. 1981. "The Whites of Their Eyes: Racist Ideologies and the Media." In *Silver Linings: Some Strategies for the Eighties,* ed. G. Bridges and R. Brunt. London: Lawrence & Wishart.

Headden, Susan. 1998. "The Marlboro Man Lives!" *U.S. News and World Report,* 24 September, 58–59.

Henshel, Richard L. 1990. *Thinking about Social Problems.* New York: Harcourt Brace Jovanovich.

Herman, E. 1990. "Media in the U.S. Political Economy." Pp. 75–87 in *Questioning the Media: A Critical Introduction,* ed. J. Downing, A. Mohammadi, and A. Sreberny-Mohammadi. Newbury Park, Calif.: Sage.

Herrnstein, Richard J., and Charles Murray. 1994. *The Bell Curve: Intelligence and Class Structure in American Life.* New York: Free Press.

Hirsch, Paul M. 1972. "Processing Fads and Fashions: An Organization-Set Analysis of Cultural Industry Systems." *American Journal of Sociology* 77: 639–59.

Horkheimer, Max, and Theodore Adorno. 1972. *The Dialectic of Enlightenment.* Trans. J. Cumming. New York: Herder & Herder.

Hume, Scott. 1991. "Barriers to Data Remain High." *Advertising Age,* July, 20.

Humphrey, Ronald, and Howard Schuman. 1984. "The Portrayal of Blacks in Magazine Advertisements: 1950–1982." *Public Opinion Quarterly* 48: 551–63.

Humphreys, Jeffrey M. 1997. "Black Buying Power by Place of Residence: 1990–1997." At www.selig.uga.edu/forecast/totalbuy/afr-amer/bbptext.htm.

Hunter and Associates. 1991. *Report on Black Buying Behavior.* Chicago: Hunter and Associates.

Jackman, Mary. 1994. *The Velvet Glove: Paternalism and Conflict in Gender, Class, and Race Relations.* Berkeley and Los Angeles: University of California Press.

Jacobs, Karrie, and Steven Heller. 1992. *Angry Graphics: Protest Posters of the Reagan-Bush Era.* Layton, Utah: Gibbs Smith.

Jaffe, Alfred J. 1986. "New Immigration Act: What's Its Impact on Population Size?" *Television and Radio Age,* November, A3–A14.

Jameson, F. 1991. *Postmodernism, or the Cultural Logic of Late Capitalism.* London: Verso.

Jaramillo, Adrian. 1997 "The Trouble with Time Warner." *Hispanic,* June.

Jhally, Sut. 1988. *Advertising and the End of the World.* Northampton, Mass.: Media Education Foundation. Video.

———. 1990. "Image-Based Culture: Advertising and Popular Culture." *The World and I,* July.

Karins, Marvin, Thomas L. Coffman, and Gary Walters. 1969. "On the Fading of Social Stereotypes: Studies in Three Generations of College Students." *Journal of Personality and Social Psychology* 13: 1–16.

Kassarjian, Harold H. 1969. "The Negro and American Advertising, 1946–1965." *Journal of Marketing Research* 6 (February): 29–39.

Katz, Jackson. 1995. "Advertising and the Construction of Violent White Masculinity." Pp. 133–41 in *Gender, Race, and Class in Media,* ed. Gail Dines and Jean M. Humez. Thousand Oaks, Calif.: Sage.

Keller, Gary D. 1994. *Hispanics and United States Film: An Overview and Handbook.* Tempe, Ariz.: Bilingual Press, Hispanic Research Center, Arizona State University.

Kellner, Douglas. 1988. "Reading Images Critically: Toward a Postmodern Pedagogy." *Journal of Education* 170 (3).

Kern, Richard. 1989. "The Asian Market: Too Good to Be True?" *Sales and Marketing Management,* May, 39.

Kilbourne, Jean. 1989. "Beauty and the Beast of Advertising." *Media and Values,* winter.

Kitano, Harry H. L. 1976. *Japanese American: The Evolution of a Subculture.* 2d ed. Englewood Cliffs, N.J.: Prentice-Hall.

Klein, A. 1993. *Little Big Men: Bodybuilding Subculture and Gender Construction.* Albany: State University of New York Press.

Klein, Gillian. 1985. *Reading into Racism: Bias in Children's Literature and Learning Materials.* London: Routledge & Kegan Paul.

Koss, Mary P., Christine A. Gidycz, and Nadine Wisniewski. 1987. "The Scope of Rape: Incidence and Prevalence of Sexual Aggression and Victimization in a National Sample of Higher Education Students." *Journal of Consulting and Clinical Psychology* 55 (2): 162–70.

Kovach, Jeffrey L. 1985. "Minority Sell: Ads Target Blacks, Hispanics, but . . ." *Industry Week*, 11 November, 29.

Kuhn, A. 1989. "The Body and Cinema: Some Problems for Feminism." *Wide Angle* 11 (4).

Landler, Mark, Walecia Konrad, Zachary Schiller, and Lois Therrien. 1991. "What Happened to Advertising?" *Business Week*, 23 September, 66–72.

Langer, Judith. Quoted in Jennifer Foote,"The Ad World's New Bimbos," *Newsweek*, 25 January 1988, 44–45.

Larrick, Nancy. 1965. "The All-White World of Children's Books." *Saturday Review*, 11 September.

Lefcourt, H. M. 1991. "Locus of Control." Pp. 413–500 in *Measures of Personality and Social Psychological Attitudes*, ed. J. P. Robinson, P. R. Shaver, and L. S. Wrightsman. San Diego, Calif.: Academic Press.

Levin, M. 1988. "The Tobacco Industry's Strange Bedfellows." *Business and Society Review* 65 (Spring): 11–17.

Levinger, George, and J. D. Snoek. 1972. *Attraction in Relationships: A New Look at Interpersonal Attraction*. Morristown, N.J.: General Learning Press.

Lewis, Bryon. 1992. Interview by Gail Baker Woods. Unimar Headquarters, Chicago, 12 August.

Lipman, Joanne. 1991. "Ads on TV: Out of Sight, out of Mind?" *Wall Street Journal*, 14 May, B1.

Lockhart, Keith. 1992. Interview by Gail Baker Woods. Lockhart and Pettus, New York, 30 July.

Logan, Rayford W., and Michael R. Winston, eds. 1982. *Dictionary of American Negro Biography*. New York: W. W. Norton.

Lyman, Stanford M. 1990. *Civilization: Contents, Discontents, Malcontents, and Other Essays in Social Theory*. Little Rock: University of Arkansas Press.

Macionis, John J. 1996. *Society: The Basics*. Englewood Cliffs, N.J.: Prentice-Hall.

———. 2002. *Social Problems*. Englewood Cliffs, N.J.: Prentice-Hall.

Marcus, Alfred, and Lori Crane. 1984. "Smoking Behavior among U.S. Latinos: A Preliminary Report." In *Advances in Cancer Control: Epidemiology and Research*. New York: Alan R. Liss.

Marcuse, Herbert. 1964. *One-Dimensional Man: Studies in the Ideology of Advanced Industrial Society*. London: Routledge & Kegan Paul.

Marx, Karl. 1967. *Capital: A Critique of Political Economy*. 3 vols. 1867–1895. Reprint. New York: International Publishers.

Maxwell, B., and M. Jacobson. 1989. *Marketing Disease to Hispanics*. Washington, D.C.: Center for Science in the Public Interest.

McAdam, Doug. 1982. *Political Process and the Development of Black Insurgency, 1930–1970*. Chicago: University of Chicago Press.

McAdoo, Hariette Piper. 1979. "Black Kinship." *Psychology Today*, May.

McCarroll, Thomas. 1993. "It's a Mass Market No More." *Time*, special issue: *The New Face of America*, 142 (121): 80–81.

McClintock, Anne, Aamir Mufti, and Ella Shohat, eds. 1997. *Dangerous Liaisons: Gender, Nation, and Postcolonial Perspectives*. Minneapolis: University of Minnesota Press.

McKinley, N. M. 1999. "Women and Objectified Body Consciousness: Mothers' and Daughters' Body Experience in Cultural, Developmental, and Familial Context." *Developmental Psychology* 35: 760–769.

McKinley, N. M., and J. S. Hyde. 1996. "The Objectified Body Consciousness Scale: Development and Validation." *Psychology of Women Quarterly* 20: 181–215.

McLemore, Dale S., and Harriet D. Romo. 1998. *Racial and Ethnic Relations in America*. 5th ed. Boston: Allyn & Bacon.

Mellott, Douglas W. 1983. *Fundamentals of Consumer Behavior*. Tulsa, Okla.: Pennwell.

Menard, Valerie. 1997. "Luscious Latinos: The Pros and Cons of an Evolving Stereotype." *Hispanic*, May, 21–26.

Merelman, Richard M. 1992. "Cultural Imagery and Racial Conflict in the United States: The Case of African-Americans." *British Journal of Political Science* 22: 315–42.

Mills, C. Wright. 1959. *The Sociological Imagination.* New York: Oxford University Press.

Moody's Handbook of Common Stocks. 1993. "RJR Nabisco Holdings Corporation." New York: Moody's Investors Service.

Moreno, Armando. 1997. "Profit Motives," *Hispanic,* June, 56–57.

Morin, Richard. 1993. "Polls Uncover Much Common Ground on L.A. Verdict." Pp. 114–17 in *Society in Crisis,* by the Washington Post Writers Group. Washington, D.C.: Washington Post.

Morris, Desmond. 1956. "The Feather Postures of Birds and the Problem of the Origin of Social Signals." *Behaviour* 9: 75–113.

———. 1977. *Manwatching: A Field Guide to Human Behavior.* New York: Harry N. Abrams.

———. 1986. *The Illustrated Naked Ape.* 1967. Reprint. London: Jonathan Cape.

———. 1996. *The Human Zoo.* 1969. Reprint. New York: Kodansha.

Morris, Desmond, Peter Collett, Peter Marsh, and Marie O'Shaughnessy. 1979. *Gestures.* New York: Stein & Day.

Muehlenhard, Charlene, and Melaney Linton. 1987. "Date Rape and Sexual Aggression in Dating Situations: Incidence and Risk Factors." *Journal of Counseling Psychology* 34 (2): 186–96.

Myrdal, Gunnar. 1944. *An American Dilemma.* New York: Harper & Row.

NBC Evening News. 1996. 6 February.

New York Times Magazine. 1984. Four-page Christian Dior ad, 27 May.

Noll, S. M., and Fredrickson, B. L. 1998. "A Medicational Model Linking Self-Objectification, Body Shame, and Disordered Eating." *Psychology of Women Quarterly* 22: 623–636.

Norris, Jeanette, and Lisa Cubbins. 1992. "Dating, Drinking, and Rape: Effects of Victim's and Assailant's Alcohol Consumption on Judgments of Their Behavior and Traits." *Psychology of Women Quarterly,* June.

O'Guinn, Thomas C., Chris T. Allen, and Richard J. Semenik. 1998. *Advertising.* Cincinnati, Ohio: South-Western College Publishing.

O'Hare, William P. 1992. "America's Minorities: The Demographics of Diversity." *Population Bulletin* 47: 1–46.

Olzak, Susan. 1992. *The Dynamics of Ethnic Competition and Conflict.* Stanford, Calif.: Stanford University Press.

Parsons, Elizabeth M., and Nancy E. Betz. 2001. "The Relationship of Participation in Sports and Physical Activity to Body Objectification, Instrumentality, and Locus of Control among Young Women." *Psychology of Women Quarterly* 25: 209–222.

Perkins, H. W. 1992. "Gender Patterns in Consequences of Collegiate Alcohol Abuse: A Ten-Year Study of Trends in an Undergraduate Population." *Journal of Studies of Alcohol* 53 (5) (September): 458–62.

Perkins, Tessa E. 1979. "Rethinking Stereotypes." Pp. 135–59 in *Ideology and Cultural Production,* ed. Michèle Barrett, Philip Corrigan, Annette Kuhn, and Janet Wolf. New York: St. Martin's.

Perlez, J. 1991. "Kenyans Do Some Soul-Searching after Rape of Seventy-One Schoolgirls." *New York Times,* 29 July, A1.

Pescosolido, Bernice A., Elizabeth Grauerholz, and Melissa A. Milkie. 1997. "Culture and Conflict: The Portrayal of Blacks in U.S. Children's Picture Books through the Mid- and Late-Twentieth Century." *American Sociological Review* 62: 443–64.

Peterson, Richard. 1976. *The Production of Culture.* Beverly Hills, Calif.: Sage.

Pettigrew, Thomas F. 1985. "New Black-White Patterns: How Best to Conceptualize Them?" *Annual Review of Sociology* 11: 329–46.

Pollay, Richard W., Jung S. Lee, and David Carter-Whitney. 1992. "Separate, but Not Equal: Racial Segmentation in Cigarette Advertising." *Journal of Advertising* 21: 1.

Portes, Alexandro. 1996. *The New Second Generation.* New York: Russell Sage Foundation.

Ramirez, A. 1991. "A Cigarette Campaign under Fire." *New York Times,* 12 January, D1.

Reid, Leonard N., and Bruce G. Vanden Bergh. 1980. "Blacks in Introductory Ads." *Journalism Quarterly* 57 (Autumn): 485–88.

Ridley, Matt. 1994. *The Red Queen: Sex and the Evolution of Human Nature.* New York: Penguin.

Ritzer, George. 1996. *The McDonaldization of Society.* Rev. ed. Thousand Oaks, Calif.: Pine Forge Press.

Rojek, Chris. 1995. *Decentring Leisure: Rethinking Leisure Theory.* London: Sage.

Rose, Peter. 1968. *The Subject Is Race.* New York: Oxford University Press.

Rossi, Carlos. 1993. Interview by Nileeni Meeawa. Conill Advertising, New York, 20 March.

Rubinstein, S., and B. Caballero. 2000. "Is Miss America an Undernourished Role Model?" *Journal of the American Medical Association* 283: 1569.

Sadker, Myra P., and David M. Sadker. 1977. *Now upon a Time: A Contemporary View of Children's Literature*. New York: Harper & Row.

Saegert, Joel, Robert J. Hoover, and Mayre Tharp Hilger. 1985. "Characteristics of Mexican American Consumers." *Journal of Consumer Research* 12 (1): 104–9.

Saenz, Rogelio, and Clyde S. Greenlees. 1996. "The Demography of Chicanos." Pp. 9–23 in *Chicanas and Chicanos in Contemporary Society*, ed. Roberto M. DeAnda. Boston: Allyn & Bacon.

Said, Edward W. 1978. *Orientalism*. London: Routledge & Kegan Paul.

Schlaad, Richard G., and Peter T. Shannon. 1994. *Drugs, Misuse and Abuse*. Englewood Cliffs, N.J.: Prentice-Hall.

Schoenborn, Boyd. 1987. *Smoking and Other Tobacco Use: United States, 1987*. Washington, D.C.: U.S. Department of Health and Human Services, Public Health Service, National Center for Health Statistics.

Schooler, C., and M. D. Basil. 1990. "Alcohol and Cigarette Advertising on Billboards: Targeting with Social Cues." Paper presented at the International Communication Association Conference, Dublin, Ireland, June.

Schudson, M. 1984. *Advertising: The Uneasy Persuasion; Its Dubious Impact on American Society*. New York: Basic Books.

Schulze, L. 1990. "On the Muscle." In *Fabrications: Costume and the Female Body*, ed. J. Gaines and C. Herzog. New York: Routledge.

Scott, Sophfronia. 1989. "It's a Small World after All." *Time*, 25 September, 56.

Seiter, Ellen. 1995. "Different Children, Different Dreams: Racial Representation in Advertising." Pp. 99–108 in *Gender, Race, and Class in Media*, ed. Gail Dines and Jean M. Humez. Thousand Oaks, Calif.: Sage.

Smikle, Ken. 1992. *The Buying Power of Black America*. Chicago: Target Market News Group.

Stabiner, K. 1982. "Tapping the Homosexual Market." *New York Times Magazine*, 2 May.

Standard Directory of Advertising Agencies. 1993. No. 229, July. New Providence, N.J.: National Register Publishing.

STAT (Stop Teenage Addiction to Tobacco). 1991. "The New Money Changers at Philip Morris." *STAT News*, 4 May.

Stein, A. 1989. "All Dressed Up, but No Place to Go? Style Wars and the New Lesbianism." *Outlook* 1 (4).

Steinem, Gloria. 1990. "Sex, Lies, and Advertising." *Ms*, July–August.

Stiles, Deborah A., Judith L. Gibbons, Suneetha S. da Silva, and Daniel J. Sebben. 1998. "Self-Portraits and Self-Descriptions of Young Adolescent Boys from South Africa, Sri Lanka, and the United States." Paper presented at annual meetings of the Society for Cross-Cultural Research and the Association for the Study of Play, St. Petersburg, Florida, April.

Straus, Murray A., R. J. Gelles, and S. K. Steinmetz. 1990. *Physical Violence in American Families: Risk Factors and Adaptations to Violence in 8,145 Families*. New Brunswick, N.J.: Transaction Publishers.

Strnad, Patricia. 1993. "Nothing Tops the Woman's Touch." *Advertising Age*, 4 October, S6.

Swidler, Ann. 1986. "Culture in Action: Symbols and Strategies." *American Sociological Review* 51: 272–86.

Target Market News. 2003. "The Buying Power of Black America." *www.targetmarketnews.com/Buying%20Power%20report%202003.htm*

Thibodeau, Ruth. 1989. "From Racism to Tokenism: The Changing Face of Blacks in *New Yorker* Cartoons." *Public Opinion Quarterly* 53: 482–94.

Tiggemann, Marika, and Amy Slater. 2001. "A Test of Objectification Theory in Former Dancers and Non-Dancers." *Psychology of Women Quarterly* 25: 57–64.

Tiryakian, Edward. 1979. "The Significance of Schools in the Development of Sociology." Pp. 211–33 in *Contemporary Issues in Theory and Research: A Metasociological Perspective*, ed. W. E. Snizek, E. R. Furman, and M. K. Miller. Westport, Conn.: Greenwood.

Tuchman, Gaye. 1978. "Introduction: The Symbolic Annihilation of Women by the Mass Media." Pp. 3–38 in *Hearth and Home: Images of Women in the Mass Media*, ed. G. Tuchman, A. K. Daniels, and J. Benet. New York: Oxford University Press.

Twitchell, James B. 1996. *Adcult USA: The Triumph of Advertising in American Culture*. New York: Columbia University Press.

U.S. Census Bureau. 1990. *Current Population Reports*. April. Washington, D.C.: Government Printing Office. P-23–1095.

———. 1993. *Current Population Reports, Population Projections of the United States by Age, Sex, Race and Hispanic Origin: 1993–2005*. November. Washington, D.C.: Government Printing Office. P-25-1104.

———. 2000a. *Educational Attainment in the United States—March 2000 (Update)*. Current Population Reports, P20–536. Washington D.C.: U.S. Government Printing Office.

———. 2000b. Table F-7. "Type of Family (All Races) by Median and Mean Income: 1947 to 1999." At *www.census.gov/hhes/income/histinc/f07.html*.

———. 2000c. *Poverty in the United States, 1999*. Current Population Reports, P60–210. Washington, D.C.: U.S. Government Printing Office.

———. 2001. "Resident Population Estimates of the United States by Sex, Race, and Hispanic Origin: April 1, 1999, to July 1, 1999, with Short-Term Projections to November 4, 2000." At *www.census.gov/population/estimates/nation/intfile3–1.txt*.

U.S. Department of Commerce. 1990. *Statistical Abstract of the United States*. Washington, D.C.: Government Printing Office.

U.S. Hispanic Market Survey. 1991. Miami: Strategy Research Corp.

———. 1994. Miami: Strategy Research Corp.

U.S. News and World Report. 1998. 14 September, 7.

Van Deburg, William L. 1984. *Slavery and Race in American Popular Culture*. Madison: University of Wisconsin Press.

Van den Berghe, Pierre L. 1967. *Race and Racism*. New York: Wiley.

Versace, Gianni, ed. 1994. *Men without Ties*. New York: Abbeville Press.

Vinikas, Vincent. 1992. *Soft Soap, Hard Sell: American Hygiene in an Age of Advertisement*. Ames: Iowa State University Press.

Vranica, S., and O'Connell, V. 2003. "PR Firms Try to Generate News about Super Bowl Ads." *Wall Street Journal*, 22 January.

Waldman, P. 1989. "Tobacco Firms Try Soft, Feminine Sell." *Wall Street Journal*, 19 December, B1.

Weber, Max. 1946. *Essays in Sociology*. Ed. and trans. Hans H. Gerth and C. Wright Mills. New York: Oxford University Press.

———. 1951. *The Religion of China: Confucianism and Taoism*. New York: Free Press.

Wilkes, Robert E., and Humberto Valencia. 1989. "Hispanics and Blacks in Television Commercials." *Journal of Advertising* 18: 19–25.

Williams, Raymond. 1981. "The Analysis of Culture." Pp. 43–52 in *Culture, Ideology, and Social Process*, ed. T. Bennett, G. Martin, C. Mercer, and J. Wollacott. London: Open University Press.

Williams, Robin M., Jr. 1970. *American Society: A Sociological Interpretation*. 3d ed. New York: Knopf.

Williamson, Judith. 1986. "Woman Is an Island: Femininity and Colonization." In *Studies in Entertainment: Critical Approaches to Mass Culture*, ed. T. Modleski. Bloomington: Indiana University Press.

Wilson, William Julius. 1996. *When Work Disappears: The World of the New Urban Poor*. New York: Knopf.

Winski, Joseph M. 1992. "The Ad Industry's Dirty Little Secret." *Advertising Age*, 15 June, 18.

Wolf, Naomi. 1991. *The Beauty Myth: How Images of Beauty Are Used against Women*. New York: Doubleday.

Woll, Allen L. 1980. *The Latin Image in American Film*. Los Angeles: UCLA Latin American Center Publications.

Woods, Gail Baker. 1995. *Advertising and Marketing to the New Majority*. Belmont, Calif.: Wadsworth Publishing.

Woods, Milton. 1993. "American Indians Discover Money Is Power." *Fortune*, 19 April, 138.

Wright, John W., ed. 1989. "The American People Today." Pp. 236–37 in *The Universal Almanac*. New York: Andrews & McMeel.

Wuthnow, Robert, and Marsha Witten. 1988. "New Directions in the Study of Culture." *Annual Review of Sociology* 14: 49–67.

Wynter, Leon E. 1998. "Global Marketers Learn to Say No to Bad Ads." *Wall Street Journal,* 5 June, B8.

Zinkhan, George M., Keith Cox, and Jae Hong. 1986. "Changes in Stereotypes: Blacks and Whites in Magazine Advertisements." *Journalism Quarterly* 63: 568–72.

Zinkhan, George M., William Qualls, and Abhijit Biswas. 1990. "The Use of Blacks in Magazine and Television Advertising." *Journalism Quarterly* 67: 547.

Index

A. C. Nielsen Company, 139
Abercrombie and Fitch, 44
abuse. *See* sexual abuse; violence: against
     women
ACT-UP, 18
Adidas, 150
advertising: analysis and evaluation of, outline
     for, 159–60; cultural dominance of, 137–39,
     152; as culture industry, 6–8; culture inter-
     preted through, 2, 3; daily exposure of con-
     sumers to, 4, 12, 138; deceptive, 140; decline
     in, 149, 151; definition of, 3; dramaturgical
     interpretation of, 13; effectiveness of, xi–xii,
     151; latent function of, 22, 141–42, 154; as mir-
     ror of consumers, 13, 141–42, 153; modern,
     8–9; opinions of, 3; persuasiveness of, 67–68,
     154; postmodern, 8–9; social role of, 12–13,
     138–39, 152; spending on, 4–5; study of, 3 (*see
     also* consumer research); visual analysis of,
     25–42. *See also* brand names; direct marketing;
     ethnic advertising; target advertising
advertising agencies: clients as customers of,
     151–52; ethnic, 133–34
Advertising Council, 150
advocacy advertising, 16–18
African Americans. *See* blacks
Afro-Sheen hair products, 125
aggression in media, 70–71
aging, 25
AIDS: in Benetton ads, 10–11; cigarette smoking
     and, 146; safe sex advertising, 18, 19
alcohol: blacks and, 125–26, 132; Chicanos and,
     128–29; Native Americans and, 103, 130–31;
     and sex in ads, 101–2; and violence against
     women, 71–73
Alhazmi, Nawaf, ix–x
Ali, Muhammad, xv
Allen, Fred, 32
Allstate Insurance, 21
Almidhar, Khalid, ix–x
American Civil Liberties Union (ACLU), 16

American Express, 127
American Gothic (Wood), 148
American Nazi Party, xv
American Red Cross, x
Amrine, Joseph, 9
analysis and evaluation of ads, outline for,
     159–60
Anheuser-Busch, 42–43
animal rights, 18
anorexia, 55–61, 63–64
antiwar advertising, 18
Armani, 150
art: definition of, for advertising, 2; use in ads
     of, 148
Asian Americans: African Americans' tensions
     with, xiv; demographic data on, 121–22; tar-
     get marketing of, 129–30. *See also* Asians
Asian-language media/ads, 130
Asians: sociohistorical background and ad
     response of, 87
stereotypes of, 103–4. *See also* Asian Americans
assimilation: primary, 95; racial, in ads, 90–91;
     secondary, 94
AT&T, xi
ATV (Advertising Television), 141
Aunt Jemima, 85
AutoZone, x

Bacardi, 73
Baker, C. Edwin, 35
Bakhtin, Mikhail, 6
Banana Republic, 150
Bansnan, Osama, ix
Barbie doll, 61–62
Baudrillard, Jean, xv–xvi, 62, 64
al-Bayoumi, Omar, ix
beauty: cultural standards of, 30; and eating
     disorders, 55–61; industries promoting, 54;
     lesbians and standards of, 46–47; minorities
     and white standards of, 90, 102; perfect
     provocateur and, 53–55

beauty pageants: for children, 70; physique
    standards for, 56
beer advertisements, 19–20. *See also individual
    companies*
Beer Institute, 143
Benetton, 9–12, 106, 114, 150
Benton, Barbi, 18, 140
Berger, John, 67
Berman, Gary, 123
Beverly Hills Polo Club, 150
Bijan, 53
Bill of Rights, 147
billboards, 132–33, 144
black mammy character, 84–85, 104
Black Media Association, 84
Black Panthers, xv
blacks: Asian Americans' tensions with, xiv;
    athletes in ads, 119; children in ads, 105–8;
    in children's book illustrations, 108–13; cig-
    arette marketing to, 144–45; copycat ads
    and, 89; cultural effect on mainstream of,
    118–20; general marketing and, 118–20; his-
    torical representations of, 104; and inequal-
    ity with whites, 122–23; predator stereo-
    type, 97; presence in ads of, 85–86, 94, 104;
    presence in media of, 84; and riots, xiv; ser-
    vant stereotype, 101; slavery's effects on,
    156; sociohistorical background and ad
    response of, 87–89; stereotypes of, 84–85, 97,
    101, 104, 110, 126; target marketing of,
    124–26
blue-collar model of appearance, 63
body: in advertising, sexual stimulation and,
    26–30; body weight, 53, 55–61; cultural vari-
    ance in presentation of, 30; defects of, ad
    messages about, 67–68; dismemberment of,
    38; images of ideal, 56; muscularity as mas-
    culinity, 62–66; objectification of, 55; of per-
    fect provocateur, 53–55, 62
body-clowning, 41
body language, 23
Body Mass Index (BMI), 56
body shame, 55–56
bodybuilding, 48–49, 63–64
Braga, Sonia, 102
brand names: and brand extension, 4; and
    brand loyalty, 118, 127, 129; and branding, 4;
    designer labels, 150–51; subverting and,
    19–20
Braniff Airlines, 131
Bravo Group, 131, 134
Brown Berets, xv
Brown, Les, 139
Bryant, Kobe, 119
Budweiser, 102, 143
Buffalo Bill's Wild West shows, 97
Bugle Boy, 151
bulimia, 55–61
Burrell, Tom, 117
Bush, George W., x, 18

Caballero, B., 55
Caldecott Award–winning books, 110–13
California Department of Health Services, 146
California Lavender Smokefree Project, 142, 143
Calvin Klein, 20, 44, 45, 150
Campbell Soup, 127
Canadian Mist, 87, 89
capitalism: advertising as promotion of, 12–13;
    cultural effects of, 154; economic waste of,
    153; and family life, 48
catalytic effect, learned violence and, 74
Cease Fire, 17
chaos, ethnic advertising and, 155–56
Chapman, Stephan, 75
Charo, 102
Chen Yu, 34
Cher, 140
Chesebrough-Ponds, 133
Chicago school of sociology, xv
Chicano/as, 121
children: black, in ads, 105–8; cigarette market-
    ing to, 142–44, 155; and function ranking in
    ads, 39–40; as sex objects, 68–70; standard of
    appearance for, 106
children's books: blacks represented in, 108–13;
    gender roles illustrated in, 52
Christianity: advertising compared to, 3, 9; and
    Calvin Klein logo, 20
cigarette marketing, 142–48
Citibank, 131
civil rights movement, 16, 84, 110, 112
Clark, Dick, 140
class: distinctions of, blurred by advertising,
    148; working class male as model of appear-
    ance, 62–63; working class powerlessness
    and violence, 75
Coca-Cola, 120, 127
cognac, 126, 130
Cole, Nat King, 85
Columbine High School, Littleton, Colorado, x
competition, and sexual selection in advertising,
    25
Consumer Reports (magazine), 129
consumer research, 3
consumers: activist, versus advertisers, 152;
    advertising as mirror of, 13, 141–42, 153; atti-
    tudes toward advertising of, 9; daily expo-
    sure to advertising of, 4, 12, 138; memory of
    advertising, xii, 5; reliance on ads by, 149
Coors, 131
copy, definition of, for advertising, 2
copycat ads, 22, 87–90
Cornwell, Dean, x
cosmetic surgery, 56
cosmetics, 54, 56
Coughlin, Patrick J., 143
Council on Racial Equality, xv
counteradvertising, 16, 19
courtship, 30–32
Courvoisier, 130

Crazy Horse, 103, 130–31
cultural attitudes model of minorities in ads, 92
cultural insensitivity, 103, 128, 131–33, 135
culture: advertising as dominant in, 137–39, 152;
    black influence on mainstream, 118–20; and
    gender attitudes, 78–79; Latino/a influence
    on mainstream, 127; popular, 139, 148; of
    poverty, xvi; variable beauty standards in, 30
culture industry, 6–8
culture jamming, 19
Cutty Sark, 24–25

Dallas Child (magazine), 70
Dallas Morning News, ix
dancers, self-perception of, 56
Dangerous Promises Coalition, 19–20
date rape, 72–73
David (Michelangelo), 148
De La Hoya, Oscar, 128
death row inmates in Benetton ads, 9–10
deceptive advertising, 140
deconstruction, definition of, 1
defects, products as compensation for, 67
Del Rio, Delores, 102
democracy, global rise of, xiii
demographic data, 120–23
Desert Storm, 18
designer labels, 150–51
Diallo, Amadou, 16
Diesel, 150
diet industry, 56
Dines, Gail, 51
direct marketing, 8
discount retail outlets, 4
dismemberment of women in ads, 38
Doc Marten, 151
domestic abuse, 71–72
Domino's Pizza, 127
Donna Karan, 150
Doom (video game), x
dramaturgy, advertising as, 13
Dress for Success, 17
drunk driving, 21
dual-marketing advertising strategy, 44–47
Durkheim, Emile, xv
Dyer, Richard, 6

eating disorders, 55–61
economic issues: muscular masculinity as reac-
    tion to, 64; violence as male reaction to, 75
education, advertising versus, 4
Elle (magazine), 114
Energizer Bunny, 9
environmental crisis, industrial production and,
    154
Equal Employment Commission, 97
equal presentation model of minorities in ads,
    86–90
Eskimo tattooing, 30
Esprit, 114, 151

Esquire (magazine), 85
Essence Communications, 128
Estefan, Gloria, 127
ethnic advertising, 117–35; ethnic marketing,
    123–31; and fragmentation of social fabric,
    155–56; mistakes in, 131–33 (*see also* cultural
    insensitivity); studies of, 117–18
ethnic cleansing, xiii–xiv, 156
ethnic groups: copycat ads and, 22, 87–90; and
    ethnic cleansing, xiii–xiv, 156; and ethnic
    conflict, xiv–xv; U.S. conflicts involving, xv.
    See also ethnic advertising; minorities; race;
    racism; *specific groups*
Etonic, 151
evolution, 24–25
EXP (magazine), 42

F. Scott's Nightclub, 73
Fairchild, Morgan, 140
Al-Faisal, Princess Haifa, ix
false consciousness, 80
Falwell, Jerry, 42–43
Family Channel, 140
Fannie Mae, 94
fashion: lesbians and standards of, 46–47; for
    men, 62–63
fashion models. *See* modeling industry
female-headed households, 17, 122
feminism: and advertisers' exploitation of
    women's lib, 35, 56; advertising critique by,
    64–65, 79–80; versus Barbie, 62; beauty myth
    challenged by, 54; and heterosexist interpre-
    tations, 47–48; and postmodernism, 6;
    women portrayed as victims by, 56
feminization of poverty, 17
Ferraro, Geraldine, 36
Fila, 150
film industry, role of stereotyping in, 102. *See
    also* movies
First Amendment, 147–48
Fitzgerald, F. Scott, 3
Foote, Cone and Belding, 131, 133, 134
Ford Motor Company, 128
Frankfurt School, 141
free speech, advertising as, 147–48
Frito Bandito, 131
Frito-Lay, 131
function ranking in ads, 39–40

Gap, 151
Garner, John, 152
Garnett, Kevin, 119
gatekeepers, cultural: characteristics of, 15; and
    children's book illustrations, 108, 109, 112;
    and social change, 15, 85
gay window advertising, 46
gays: cigarette marketing to, 146; and coming
    out, 49; gay-image advertising, 42–49; and
    politics, 49; and postmodernism, 6
gender: aging and, 25; cultural attitudes on,

78–79; emphasis in ads of, 75–76; gay- and lesbian-image advertising and, 42–49; genetic conflict based in, 26; and inequality, 14–16, 35–37, 39–40; and relative size in ads, 34; and sexual display, 24; and social roles, 13–14, 51–53; violence and social roles, 70–71. *See also* men; sexism; women
General Motors, 131
Generation X, 149–51
Gerbner, George, 74–75, 141
G.I. Joe (toy), 62
Givenchy, 78–80, 114
glass ceiling, 37
global-village look in ads, 114
Goffman, Erving, 1, 2, 13, 14, 23, 34, 39, 41
Gone with the Wind (film), 85
Goodis, Jerry, 5
Goodyear Tire & Rubber Co., 133
Gornick, Vivian, 83
Gossage, Howard, 9
GQ (magazine), 85
Grauerholz, Elizabeth, 108–12
Greeley, Andrew, xv
Green, Nancy, 85
Grey Advertising, 134
Guess, 150
gun safety, 17

Hall, Stuart, 1
Hallejulah (film), 97
hands, in ads, 42
hard sell, 9, 152
Harris, Eric, x
Hayek, Salma, 102
Hayworth, Rita, 102
HBO, 128
Henshel, Richard L., 21
Hickory Creek, Texas, xi
Hill, Grant, 119
Hispanic (magazine), 128
HIV: in Benetton ads, 10–11; cigarette smoking and, 146
homelessness, 18
homosexuality. *See* gays; lesbians
hooks, bell, 90
Hope, Edgar Ace, 9
Hormel & Company, 130
Hornell Brewing Company, 130
Huesmann, L. Rowell, 70
Humez, Jean M., 51
humor, and double meanings in ads, 35–37
hybritising, 16, 21

ideology, definition of, 2
Imitation of Life (film), 85
immigration, xiv, 121
inequality: black-white, 122–23; function ranking and, 39–40; gender, 14–16, 35–37, 39–40; structures of, 14–16
infomercials, 140

Information Resources, 151
Institute for Social Research, University of Michigan, 155
institutional advertising: definition of, 16; purpose of, 20–21; by Saudi Arabia, ix; by U.S. government, x
international advertising, culturally insensitive, 133
interracial relationships, 95, 111, 112
Iraq, 18
Iverson, Allen, 119

J. C. Penney, 127
Jaguar, 91–92
Japan, ads in, 114
Jeep Cherokee, 103
Jhally, Sut, 137, 138
Jodi (eating disorder case study), 61
Johnson Products, 125
Jordan, Michael, 4
Juan Valdez, 127

Kansas City Chiefs, 132
Kellner, Douglas, 12
KFC, 125
Kilbourne, Jean, 14, 55, 56–57
King, Martin Luther, Jr., xv, 9
King, Rodney, xiv
Kithia, Joyce, 73
Klebold, Dylan, x
Kraft Foods, 127, 128
Ku Klux Klan (KKK), xv

L.A. Gear, 151
La Opinion (newspaper), 127
Ladies' Home Journal (magazine), 94, 104
Land O'Lakes, 103
latent function of advertising, 22, 141–42, 154
Latina (magazine), 128
Latino/as; cigarette marketing to, 145; copycat ads and, 89–90; cultural effect on mainstream of, 127; demographic data on, 120–21; as largest minority group, x, 120; luscious Latina stereotype, 101–3; predator stereotype, 97; presence in ads of, 101–3; real estate ads and, 94; servant stereotype, 101; sociohistorical background and ad response of, 87–90; stereotypes of, x–xi, 97, 101–3; target marketing of, 126–29; undocumented immigrants, 120
laughter, 31
lawsuits against tobacco industry, 142–43, 146–47
Lawyers Committee for Civil Rights under Law, 94
Leakey, Richard, 30
Leo Burnett (advertising firm), 134
Leonardo da Vinci, 148
lesbians: bodybuilding and, 48–49; cigarette marketing to, 146; lesbian-image advertising,

42–49; and postmodernism, 6; and social standards of beauty and fashion, 46–47; sociopolitical issues among, 46–47, 49
Lewis, Sinclair, 3
licensed withdrawal in ads, 40–41
Life (magazine), 104
Lifetime, 140
Listerine, 118
literacy, media, 153, 154
Little Golden Books, 111, 112
Little House on the Prairie (television show), 52
Liz Claiborne, 150
locum (Swedish company), 37
Look (magazine), 104
Lopez, Jennifer, 102
Lori (eating disorder case study), 59–61
Los Angeles riots (1992), xiv
Los Angeles Times, 19
Lotto, 151
Loveland (Colo.) Reporter-Herald, 36–37
Lucky Strike, 146
Lyman, Stanford, xv

Machiavelli, Niccolo, xiii
Maddox, Lester, 14
Malcolm X, xv
mammy, black, 84–85, 104
Manson, Charles, 18
marketing. *See* ethnic advertising: ethnic marketing; mass marketing; target advertising
Marlboro Man, 19, 39, 146
Marx, Karl, xv, 80
masculinity, muscularity as, 62–66. *See also* men
mass culture. *See* popular culture
mass marketing, 135, 141
mass media. *See* media
Mattel, 61–62, 106
McDonald's, 91, 120, 125, 127
McKinney, Nina Mae, 97
media: advertiser control of, 5, 52; advertising revenue of, 5; aggression in, 70–71; predator stereotype in, 95, 97; social connection through, 14–15; violence in, 70–71, 74–75. *See also* television
media literacy, 153, 154
Megan (eating disorder case study), 57–59
men: bodybuilding as obsessive-compulsive behavior, 63–64; and function ranking in ads, 39–40; genetics of, 26; and hand grasp, 42; muscularity as masculinity, 62–66; perfect provocateur standard of appearance, 62; sexual arousal in, 32; and violence, 70–71, 74–75; and violence in ads, 75–78. *See also* gender
Men's Health (magazine), 128
men's rights and ad portrayals of men, 65
Merchant, Larry, 128
Mexican American Anti-Defamation Committee, 131
Mexican Americans, 121, 156
Miami riots (1980s), xiv

Michelangelo, 148
Michelob, 67
Milkie, Melissa, 108–12
Miller, J. Howard, 20
Mills, C. Wright, xvi
minorities: absence from ads of, 85; cigarette marketing to, 144–45; consumer research and, 3; and demographic changes, 120–23; largest groups of, x; multicultural ads, 114–15; presence in ads of, 113–15, 155; presence in advertising industry of, 133–34; presence in media of, 155; social position of, 84–86; as target of advertising, 2, 118, 119–20, 123–24; typology of, in ads, 22, 86–92; white standards of beauty and, 90, 102. *See also* ethnic groups; race; racism
Miranda, Carmen, 102
Miss America Pageant, 56
Mitchell, Martha, 83
modeling effect, learned violence and, 74
modeling industry: minority fashion models, 113, 114; physique standards for female models, 56; physique standards for male models, 64; role of stereotyping in, 102; training of models in, 13
modernism: in advertising, 8–9; characteristics of, 5
Moffitt, Willliman B., 10
Mona Lisa (da Vinci), 148
Mondale, Walter, 36
Moral Majority, 42
More cigarettes, 33
Moreno, Rita, 102
Morris, Desmond, 2, 23
Moss, Kate, 61
Mossimo, 150
Mothers Against Drunk Driving (MADD), 21
movies, violence in, 74–75
"Mr. Microphone" ad, 85
Muhammad, Elijah, xv
multicultural ads, 114–15
multiple meanings in advertisements, 35–37
muscle dysmorphia, 64
muscularity as masculinity, 62–66
Museum of Questionable Medical Devices, 32
music: black, 119; Latino, 128
Myrdal, Gunnar, xv

NAACP (National Association for the Advancement of Colored People), 133
Nabisco, 133
Nashville Network, 140
Nation of Islam, xv
National Advertising Channel, 141
Native Americans: demographic data on, 122; internal colonialism and, 156; stereotypes of, 97, 103, 132; target marketing of, 130–31
Nazis, 16
neo-Nazis, xv
New York Life Insurance Company, 131

Newsweek (magazine), 128
Nike, 150
No Fear, 151
nonprofit organizations, advocacy advertising and, 16
nonverbal communication, 23, 44
nostalgia, 7–8

obsessive-compulsive behavior, 63–64
O'Neal, Shaquille, 119

paparazzi, 14
parody in postmodern advertising, 8
People en Español (magazine), 128
People (magazine), 128
Pepsi, 127, 133
Perdue, 131
perfect provocateur: female, 53–55; male, 62–66
Perry Ellis, 150
Pescosolido, Bernice A., 108–12
phallic symbols, 33–34
Philip Morris, 120, 128, 143–47, 148–49
pictures, private versus public, 14
Pillsbury, 127
Playboy (magazine), 128
police, and advertising, xi
politics, and homosexuality, 49
Pony, 151
popular culture, 139, 141, 148
pornography, advertising and, 29, 50, 102
positive realism in black advertising, 126
postage stamp, commemorative, x
postcolonialism, 155–56
postmodern advertising, 8–9, 137
postmodernism, 137–57; cultural consciousness in, 154; elements of, 5–6; rules questioned in, 10–11
poverty: blacks and, 122, 123; culture of, xvi; feminization of, 17; Native Americans and, 130
predator stereotype, 95, 97
Premier Operating Services, 97
primary assimilation of minorities, 95
Procter & Gamble, 20, 127, 133
provocateur: female, 53–55; male, 62–66
psychological distance in black advertising, 126
public policy and advertising, 153, 155

al-Qaida, x
Quaker Oats, 120, 133

R. J. Reynolds, 143, 145
race: in Benetton ads, 10–11; copycat ads and, 22, 87–90; and function ranking in ads, 39–40; significance in advertising of, 15; and supremacy movements, xv. *See also* ethnic groups; minorities; racism; *specific racial or ethnic groups*
race relations: and advertising, 84–86; and assimilation, 94–95; and children's book illustrations, 108–13; cultural attitudes on, 92
racial assimilation in ads, 90–91

racism, 83–115; historical background of, 15; as public policy issue, 155; responses to, 156–57; symbolic, 15, 83–115, 156–57; Timberland ad against, 21
Ralph Lauren, 150
Ramsey, JonBenet, 70
rape, date, 72–73
Reader's Digest (magazine), 104
Reagan, Ronald, 18
Reebok, 150
Remy Martin, 130
Revlon, 132
Rice, Anne, 53
Rice, Speedy, 10
Ridley, Matt, 24–25
Robinson, Amy, 70
Robinson, Jackie, 119
Rockwell, Norman, 7–8
Rojek, Chris, 6, 7
Roman Catholic Church, 3, 12
Ronco, 85
Rose, Peter, xv
Rosie the Riveter, 20
Rubinstein, S., 55

Sambo image, 85, 104
Saudi Arabia, ix–x
secondary assimilation of minorities, 94
self-image in advertising, 13
self-objectification, xi, 55–56
September 11, 2001 terrorist attacks, ix–x
servant stereotype, 101
sex: evolution and, 24; safe, 18, 19; television advertising effectiveness and, xi–xii; and violence in ads, 75–78
sex objects: children as, 68–70; Latinas as, 101–3; women as, 38
sexism, 51–81, 155
sexual abuse, 71–72
sexual attraction, 26–30; and courtship, 30–32; cultural variance in, 30; subliminal advertising and, 32–33
sexual selection, 24–25
shampoo, 4
Simpson, O. J., 119
size, significance in ads of, 34
skinheads, xv
Slim Hopes (video), 56–57
Smith, Emmit, 119
social issues: advocacy advertising and, 16; Benetton ads and, 9–12; capitalism's ignoring of, 154; children's book illustrations and, 108–13; global, xiii–xiv; muscular masculinity as reaction to, 64; postmodern advertising and, 152–53; social reality ads and, 91–92; violence as male reaction to, 75
social reality model of minorities in ads, 91–92
socialization through advertising, 12–13
sociology of advertising, 2
Socrates, 105

soft sell, 9
Southern Christian Leadership Conference, xv
Spam, 130
Spanish-language media/ads, 120, 126–27, 128
speed, postmodernism and, 137–38, 149, 154
sports: black athletes in ads, 119; role of adver-
    tising in, 4–5; and women's body image,
    55–56
Sports Illustrated (magazine), 85, 128
Starbucks, x
Starter, 151
stereotypes, 95–104; in children's book illustra-
    tions, 110; civil rights movement effect on,
    84; luscious Latina, 101–3; mass production
    and consumer, 141; predator, 95, 97; role in
    film industry of, 102; role in modeling indus-
    try of, 102; servant, 101. *See also under indi-
    vidual ethnic and minority groups*
Student Nonviolent Coordinating Committee,
    xv
Stussy, 151
subconscious, advertising appeal to, 32–33
subcultures, definition of, 117
subliminal messages, 32–33
subordination, rituals of, 42
subvertising, 16, 19–20, 146
Super Bowl, xi, 5
symbolic racism, 15, 83–115, 156–57

Taco Bell, 127
target advertising: and copycat ads, 89–90; crite-
    ria for, 43–44; ethnic issues in, 132; and
    minorities, 2, 118, 119–20, 123–24; vehicles
    for, 134–35. *See also* ethnic advertising
Tarkenton, Fran, 140
tattooing, 30
taxation of advertising, 153
telemarketing, 152
Telemundo, 127
television: advertiser control of, 52, 139; adver-
    tising on, 139–41; regulation of children's
    viewing of, 155; time spent watching, 74,
    125, 138, 139; violence in, 74–75
Texas, tobacco lawsuit settlement in, 146–47
Thomas, Derrick, 132
Timberland, 21
Time (magazine), 94
Time Warner Communications, 128
Tobacco Tax Initiative, 146
Tommy Hilfiger, 20, 150
tourism, 6
Toyota, 128
Twitchell, James B., 3, 8, 23, 25, 79, 148, 151

Umbro, 151
Uptown cigarettes, 145
urban coon image, 104
USA Network, 140
USA Today (newspaper), 125

V-chip, 74
Vacarro, Brenda, 140
Valenzuela, Fernando, 127
Van den Berghe, Pierre, xv
Velez, Lupe, 102
Versace, 44, 101
Versace, Gianni, 63, 148
violence: as learned through media, 70–71, 74;
    as public policy issue, 155; and sex in ads,
    75–78; television and movie, 74–75; against
    women, 71–74
Virginia Slims, 35, 36, 137
visual analysis of ads, 25–42
Vogue (magazine), 85

waif look, 56, 61, 63
Wal-Mart, 114
Walker, Madam C. J., 123
Washington Post (newspaper), 94
Waxman, Henry, 142
Weber, Max, xv
weight, body, 53, 55–61
Welch, Raquel, 102
Whitaker, Pernell, 128
White Aryan Resistance, xv
White, Barbi, 71
White Rose, 16
whiteness: as norm in ads, 106; and nostalgia,
    7–8
Williams, Doug, 119
Williams, Reggie, 119
Williams, Serena, 119
Williams, Venus, 119
Wilson, William Julius, xv
Wine Institute, 19
Wolf, Naomi, 79
women: and body dismemberment, 38; cigarette
    marketing to, 146; demeaned in ads, 35–37;
    eating disorders in, 55–61; female-headed
    households, 17, 122; and function ranking in
    ads, 39–40; genetics of, 26; objectification of,
    55; perfect provocateur standard of appear-
    ance, 53–55; postmodern, in ads, 152; preda-
    tor stereotype, 97; and touching, 42; violence
    against, 71–74, 155; as withdrawn, 40–41. *See
    also* gender; sexism
Wood, Grant, 148
Woods, Gail Baker, 20, 117
Woods, Tiger, 4, 119
World Health Organization, 56
World War II posters, x, 20
Wouk, Herman, 3

Young and Rubicam, 131, 134
yuppies as target market, 47
Yves Saint Laurent, 78

zip coon, 104
zoot suiters, 97

About the Author

Anthony J. Cortese is professor of sociology at Southern Methodist University. His major areas of research and teaching are ethnic and race relations, social problems, social policy, and social theory. He is the author of over thirty-five scholarly articles and essays and of *Ethnic Ethics: The Restructuring of Moral Theory* (1990), *Walls and Bridges: Social Justice and Public Policy* (2004), and *Opposing Hate Speech* (forthcoming). He is currently working on a book on cyber trust and privacy. He received his Ph.D. from the University of Notre Dame. As a Fulbright fellow in Japan in 1990 and 1991 he taught courses on ethnic diversity in the United States. He has also taught maximum-security inmates at Illinois's Pontiac Correctional Center. He has served as director of ethnic studies and director of Mexican American studies at Southern Methodist University and served on the American Sociological Association's Committee on Professional Ethics.